Beyond al-Qaeda

PART 2

The Outer Rings of the Terrorist Universe

Angel Rabasa • Peter Chalk • Kim Cragin • Sara A. Daly • Heather S. Gregg
Theodore W. Karasik • Kevin A. O'Brien • William Rosenau

Prepared for the United States Air Force

Approved for public release, distribution unlimited

PROJECT AIR FORCE

The research described in this report was sponsored by the United States Air Force under Contract F49642-01-C-0003. Further information may be obtained from the Strategic Planning Division, Directorate of Plans, Hq USAF.

Library of Congress Cataloging-in-Publication Data

Beyond al-Qaeda. Part 2. The outer rings of the terrorist universe / Angel Rabasa
... [et al.].
   p. cm.
   "MG-430."
   Includes bibliographical references.
   ISBN-13: 978-0-8330-3932-3 (pbk. : alk. paper)
   1. Qaida (Organization) 2. Terrorists. 3. Terrorism—Government policy—United
States. 4. Terrorism—United States—Prevention. 5. War on Terrorism, 2001–
I. Rabasa, Angel.

HV6432.B4932 2006
363.325 42—dc22

                                        2006025206

The RAND Corporation is a nonprofit research organization providing objective analysis and effective solutions that address the challenges facing the public and private sectors around the world. RAND's publications do not necessarily reflect the opinions of its research clients and sponsors.

RAND® is a registered trademark.

Published 2006 by the RAND Corporation
1776 Main Street, P.O. Box 2138, Santa Monica, CA 90407-2138
1200 South Hayes Street, Arlington, VA 22202-5050
4570 Fifth Avenue, Suite 600, Pittsburgh, PA 15213-2665
RAND URL: http://www.rand.org/
To order RAND documents or to obtain additional information, contact
Distribution Services: Telephone: (310) 451-7002;
Fax: (310) 451-6915; Email: order@rand.org

Preface

The September 11, 2001, terrorist attacks and the U.S. response—the global war on terrorism—have changed the world, and the terrorist enterprise that we know as al-Qaeda has changed with it. The current status of al-Qaeda's network remains unclear, but it is certain that it and other terrorist groups continue to threaten the lives and well-being of Americans, at home and abroad, and the security of our friends and allies. This continuing danger leads to ongoing U.S. and international efforts to monitor, disrupt, and dismantle terrorist groups before they can cause large-scale destruction to our people or our interests.

The objective of this RAND Corporation study, undertaken as part of a project entitled "Beyond al-Qaeda: Countering Future Terrorist and Other Nontraditional Threats to U.S. Security," is to understand the shape of future threats to the United States and U.S. security interests from terrorist and other extremist organizations. We do this through analyses that draw together the various threat strands that are informing current U.S. thinking in the war on terror. The study looks specifically at four sources of threats:

1. *Al-Qaeda.* We examine how al-Qaeda has changed since September 11, the loss of its operating base in Afghanistan, and the death or capture of key operatives; and we assess what forms the al-Qaeda threat to the United States and U.S. interests take now and might take in the future.

2. *Terrorist groups that may not be formally part of al-Qaeda but that have assimilated al-Qaeda's worldview and concept of mass-casualty terrorist attacks.* This, we believe, is where the center of gravity of the current global terrorist threat lies.

3. *Violent Islamist and non-Islamist terrorist and insurgent groups without known links to al-Qaeda.* These groups threaten U.S. regional interests, friends, and allies, as well as other nontraditional threats.

4. *The nexus between terrorism and organized crime.* In each case, we examine how the presence of these threats affects U.S. security interests, and we identify distinct strategies that the United States and the U.S. Air Force may take to neutralize or mitigate each of these threats.

The results of the study are reported in two volumes. This book is the seccond of the two; the first, by Angel Rabasa, Peter Chalk, Kim Cragin, Sara A. Daly, Heather S. Gregg, Theodore W. Karasik, Kevin A. O'Brien, and William Rosenau, is entitled *Beyond al-Qaeda: Part 1, The Global Jihadist Movement.*

This research builds on previous RAND Project AIR FORCE work on counterterrorism, notably the following:

- Angel Rabasa, Cheryl Benard, Peter Chalk, Christine Fair, Theodore Karasik, Rollie Lal, Ian Lesser, and David Thaler, *The Muslim World After 9/11*, MG-246-AF, 2004
- Nora Bensahel, *The Counterterror Coalitions: Cooperation with Europe, NATO, and the European Union*, MR-1746-AF, 2003
- Kim Cragin and Sara Daly, *The Dynamic Terrorist Threat: An Assessment of Group Motivations and Capabilities in a Changing World*, MR-1782-AF, 2004
- Lynn Davis, Steven Hosmer, Sara Daly, and Karl Mueller, *The U.S. Counterterrorism Strategy: A Planning Framework to Facilitate Timely Policy Adjustments*, DB-426-AF, 2004
- David Ochmanek, *Military Operations Against Terrorist Groups Abroad: Implications for the United States Air Force*, MR-1738-AF, 2003.

This research was sponsored by the Deputy Chief of Staff for Air and Space Operations, U.S. Air Force (A3/5), and conducted in the Strategy and Doctrine Program of RAND Project AIR FORCE. Research for this project was completed in September 2004. This book should be of value to the national security community and to interested members of the general public, especially those with an interest in combating the blight of international terrorism.

RAND Project AIR FORCE

RAND Project AIR FORCE, a division of the RAND Corporation, is the U.S. Air Force's federally funded research and development center for studies and analyses. PAF provides the Air Force with independent analyses of policy alternatives affecting the development, employment, combat readiness, and support of current and future aerospace forces. Research is performed in four programs: Aerospace Force Development; Manpower, Personnel, and Training; Resource Management; and Strategy and Doctrine.

Additional information about PAF is available on our Web site at http://www.rand.org/paf.

Contents

Figure and Tables

Figure

Tables

Summary

The "al-Qaeda universe" does not incorporate the entirety of the terrorist or extremist threat facing the United States. Clearly, Osama bin Laden and other al-Qaeda leaders hope that their efforts will persuade other Islamic militant groups to join the global jihad. But what about the terrorist or extremist groups that are not part of the al-Qaeda network and do not adhere to its agenda? The temptation for policymakers is to set aside groups that have not chosen to join al-Qaeda as less dangerous. Yet these Islamist groups, non-Islamist terrorists, and criminal organizations still pose a threat to the United States, its interests, and its allies. This volume, therefore, addresses the threats outside the al-Qaeda universe.

Islamist Groups

The first category of groups examined in this part of the study consists of terrorist groups that articulate an Islamist agenda for their own country but are not part of the global jihadist movement. Two considerations guide the analysis of these groups: the threat that they pose to U.S. friends and allies and U.S. regional interests, and the conditions under which they could rise to the level of global threat.

Of the groups in this category, Lebanese Hezbollah is perhaps the best known and the most capable. This group was responsible for the 1983 suicide attack against the U.S. Marine barracks in Beirut, which inaugurated the era of mass-casualty terrorism, and for two terrorist attacks in the Western hemisphere, both in Buenos Aires: the 1992 bombing of the Israeli embassy and the 1994 bombing of the Jewish Community Center. In addition, since the early 1980s, Hezbollah has established a far-flung financial network, stretching from the tri-border area of South America (where the borders of Brazil, Argentina, and Paraguay intersect), to North America, to West Africa, and Southeast Asia. So Hezbollah has the potential to inflict damage on U.S. interests and allies across the globe. Yet this group remains relatively detached from the al-Qaeda network and has not directly threatened the United States since the 1983 attack. Today, Hezbollah projects an image of political legitimacy in Lebanon. At the same time, the group maintains its terrorist network of 20,000–25,000 members, conducting some limited attacks on Israeli forces and supplying military aid to Palestinian groups.

Although Hezbollah is predominantly a Shi'ite group, its leaders articulate a universalistic view of the Muslim community, the *umma,* that incorporates Shi'ites, Sunnis, and even secularists. Hezbollah's universalism is tempered by pragmatism. The ideological foundations of Hezbollah, therefore, explain at least part of the group's reluctance to join the al-Qaeda network. Its leadership might feel some spontaneous sympathy with wider pan-Islamist, Sunni agendas, but these movements do not necessarily align with Hezbollah ideologically. However, just because Hezbollah does not align with other Islamist groups ideologically, it may still coordinate with them. Despite the ideological disparities between Hezbollah and the al-Qaeda network, some parallel interests exist. In particular, Hezbollah historically has opposed "Western domination" of the Muslim world and the United States specifically. So although the ideological background of Hezbollah might explain its lack of affiliation with the al-Qaeda network, Hezbollah's strategic objectives pave the way for possible cooperation in the future. (See pp. 5–15.)

After Hezbollah, the most capable of the groups in this category is the Islamic Resistance Movement, known by its acronym, Hamas. Hamas's fundamental objective is to establish a Palestinian Islamic state in Israel proper, the West Bank, and Gaza. To achieve its strategic objectives, Hamas has followed a two-pronged strategy: One part of the strategy, designed to secure a Palestinian state, involves a terror campaign against the Israeli government and citizens. A key tactic in this campaign is suicide bombings. Although Hamas was not the first Palestinian terrorist group to adopt the tactic of suicide bombings, it has made the most extensive use of this tactic—even though at times the wider Palestinian community has been highly critical of it. The second part of the Hamas strategy requires the group to pursue its Islamic agenda vis-à-vis al-Fatah and the Palestinian Authority.

Like many Islamic movements in the Arab world, Hamas's ideology is firmly grounded in the teachings of Egypt's Muslim Brotherhood. One key ideological difference between the Brotherhood and Hamas is that Hamas believes in the use of violence in addition to religious proselytizing and political activity. In addition, Hamas's ideology is strongly nationalistic, in contrast to the Brotherhood's pan-Islamism.

Hamas presents an interesting contradiction in strategic and operational objectives, especially when it comes to potential shifts. On the one hand, an assessment that the U.S.-Israeli relationship is the center of gravity of its opponent might encourage Hamas to take on a more global agenda, attacking the United States and U.S. targets overseas. On the other hand, Hamas's leadership appears to be pragmatic enough to realize that widening the conflict may alienate its own support base, bring in a strong U.S. response, and jeopardize its political advances. After the the January 2006 Palestinian elections in which Hamas won an outright majority in the Palestinian Legislative Council, the group was warned by al-Qaeda's deputy leader, Ayman al-Zawahiri, to continue the struggle against Israel, and was criticized in jihadi forums for participating in elections and not pursuing an Islamist agenda. The jihadist criticism lays bare the rift between the global jihadist movement, with its supra-national goals, and local groups and organizations that have more limited objectives and are open to tactical use of the political process. (See pp. 15–24.)

Other Islamist groups examined include Algeria's Armed Islamic Group, known by its French acronym, GIA; Egypt's al-Gama'a al-Islamiyya and al-Wa'ad; South Africa's People Against Gangsterism and Drugs (PAGAD); and the Eritrean Islamic Jihad–Islamic Reform Movement. The GIA saw the establishment of an Islamic government in Algeria as its primary goal; to that end, the group employed methods so extreme and brutal that they went beyond those employed by some of the most virulent terrorist organizations operating today. As a result, the GIA alienated its potential support base. Unlike its splinter faction, the Salafist Group for Preaching and Combat (GSPC), the GIA never established a solid relationship with al-Qaeda outside the few members who were veterans of the Afghan war and who knew or had met bin Laden in that context. The GIA has not conducted any attacks outside Algeria since 1996. (See pp. 25–30.)

Egypt's al-Gama'a al-Islamiyya, like other Islamist terrorist groups, began as an offshoot of the Muslim Brotherhood. Al-Gama'a gained a renewed sense of purpose after the return of its members from the Afghan jihad. Al-Gama'a leaders were energized by what they believed was a moral victory of Islamism in Afghanistan and were convinced that they could accomplish in Egypt what the mujahidin achieved in Afghanistan by ousting the "illegitimate" governing power. As a result, al-Gama'a put its theories into practice in Egypt by attacking a wide variety of targets—including Coptic Christians, banks, police, politicians, tourists, and the media—with the goal of undermining Egyptian state power, secular institutions, and the economy. Al-Gama'a's operational leader, Rifa'i Taha Musa, signed bin Laden's 1998 declaration of war against "Jews and Crusaders." However, Taha Musa was unable to recruit many of his cadre to support bin Laden and join the global jihad. Al-Gama'a witnessed how the Egyptian Islamic Jihad had suffered significant setbacks because of its decision to join al-Qaeda. In 1999, the group's historic leadership declared a unilateral ceasefire and in 2002 issued a statement renouncing the use of violence.

Al-Wa'ad ("the Promise") is a shadowy Islamic extremist organization based in Egypt about which not much is known. According to press reports of the recent trials of al-Wa'ad members in Egypt, the group is rather small and made up largely of Egyptian citizens with dual nationality, including Russians (Chechens), Dutch, Germans, Canadians, and reportedly even Americans. The group was accused in a 2001 indictment of raising money for international jihadist causes, including Palestinian and Chechen groups. Although the arrests may have eliminated or reduced the potential al-Wa'ad threat, some press reports indicate at least two new terrorist groups have formed in Egypt as of this writing—the Jihad Group for the Victory of Muslims at Home and Abroad and Jundullah, a faction of the Egyptian Islamic Jihad. The Egyptian investigation of Jundullah's activities found that it had ties to al-Zawahiri and was in contact with leaders in other extremist organizations in Europe, Pakistan, and Afghanistan. (See pp. 30–37.)

People Against Gangsterism and Drugs (PAGAD) was formed in 1996 as a community anticrime group to fight drugs and violence in South Africa. By early 1998, PAGAD had also become violently antigovernment and anti-Western. It is closely associated, if not intertwined, with a South African Iranian-inspired Islamic group, Qibla. In addition to the few hundred estimated criminal victims of PAGAD's targeted violence, PAGAD's bombing targets have included South African authorities, moderate Muslims, synagogues, gay nightclubs, tourist attractions, and Western-associated restaurants. There are indications that South Africa could become a haven for jihadists from other parts of the world and a source for radicalizing Muslim youth to mobilize against Western interests globally. (See pp. 37–44.)

The last group examined in this category is the Eritrean Islamic Reform Movement (EIRM), also known as the Islamic Salvation Movement, a Sunni Islamist group. The group has been active in the Horn of Africa in various guises since the mid-1970s and seeks the violent overthrow of Eritrea's secular government and its replacement with an Islamic government. The leadership of the ERIM and of the umbrella organization to which it belongs, the Eritrean National Alliance (ENA), has indicated that it sees its struggle against Eritrea's government within the wider context of a push for a new Islamic caliphate, but the focus of the group remains firmly fixed on overthrowing the government. There is a possibility that the EIRM could become involved with other like-minded Islamic organizations throughout the Horn of Africa to promote common interests and perhaps seek to establish an Islamic federation in the Horn. (See pp. 44–49.)

The Iraqi Insurgency

The nonaffiliated part of the Iraqi insurgency—that is, the component that is outside of the al-Qaeda and al-Zarqawi networks—is diverse and widespread, and composed of groups of both nationalist and religious provenance. In response to the insurgents, both the Shi'ite and Kurdish communities have continued to rally around their new national leaders and have apparently refused to engage in sectarian revenge. (However, Shi'ite revenge killings against Sunnis have been on the rise since the bombing of the al-Askari mosque in Samarra on February 22, 2006.)

This section focuses on the Sunni insurgents. We do not place the Shi'ite militiamen associated with Muqtada al-Sadr in the same category, because—even though al-Sadr's militiamen, organized in the so-called "Mahdi's Army," share the Sunnis' hostility toward the United States and have certainly engaged in violent activities—these activities generally do not rise to the level of Sunni terrorism. Moreover, al-Sadr must operate within the broader framework of Shi'ite politics in Iraq. (Other Shi'ite and Kurdish militias are in fact the military arms of political organizations that are part of Iraq's legitimate political spectrum. Nevertheless, we discuss them here because they are outside of the Iraqi government's control and could become engines of sectarian conflict.) (See pp. 51–60.)

At least 28 different insurgent groups have formed from 2003 through 2005. Some—but not all—are based in the Sunni triangle north and west of Baghdad. The danger of bloodshed is intensified because some of these groups increasingly embrace tactics imported by foreign fighters, such as the car bombings of civilian targets. It goes without saying that the universe of insurgent groups in Iraq is both dynamic and fluid. Groups appear, change, merge, divide, and disappear, operate under different names and sometimes under no name at all.

This insurgency, certainly one of the most complex and challenging ever faced by the United States, presents no single coherent enemy against which the United States can mass its superior military strength. The insurgency's various components, generally characterized more by their heterogeneity than by their homogeneity, fight for their own unique reasons and have little in common other than a desire to remove the U.S. and coalition presence from the country. In general, they seek to create a crisis between the Iraqi government and the Iraqi people in the hopes that outside support for the government will wane, forcing the withdrawal of foreign forces.

The strategic and operational objectives of these groups vary widely. The jihadists, as discussed in the first volume of this study, are seeking to foment a religious war between Sunnis and Shi'ites, who—until the February 2006 bombing of the al-Askari mosque in Samarra—largely refrained from engaging in sectarian revenge. Former regime loyalists believe that they have no option but to continue fighting and are also convinced that the United States and its coalition partners will tire long before they do. These groups are trying to apply the experiences of other guerrilla and terrorist organizations to their operations. Their objective is to restore the former Ba'ath party establishment to power. Nationalists do not necessarily support the return of the Ba'ath—some actively oppose it—but they resent what they consider to be the occupation of Iraq and are angered by the coalition's failure to restore order and security. Iraqi Islamists have emerged after decades of suppression by the Ba'thist regime but have the experiences of Islamist organizations in other countries to help them. Their objective is the establishment of an Islamic state in Iraq. (See pp. 54–56.)

As of the time of this writing, the Iraqi insurgency is in a transitional stage. It is evolving in response to transcendent political events in Iraq—the January 2005 elections, the approval of a new Iraqi constitution, and the January 2006 elections for a permanent Iraqi government—which center, of course, on the rise of the Shi'ites and the Kurds to a dominant position in the state. (See pp. 58–60.) In the end, terror alone cannot guarantee success for the insurgents. The insurgency can continue to wreak havoc but will become an exercise in political futility. In these circumstances, three general scenarios are possible:

In the most benign case, significant elements of the Sunni community realize that a return of the status quo ante is no longer viable and accept a minority role within a democratic Iraq. The Sunnis might find a common interest with the Kurdish parties in balancing

Shi'ite predominance, and a rough balance of power could develop, allowing for what we called in another study "democracy with Iraqi characteristics."

In the second scenario, the representatives of the Sunni community are too alienated or terrorized to enter into a political arrangement with the Shi'ites and the Kurds. The insurgency could continue, perhaps at high levels of violence, but would be unable to transcend its narrow social base or to prevent the nascent government from gradually consolidating its control over the country.

In the third scenario, if the new government is unable to contain the insurgents and terrorists, or to win broad support among the diverse ethnic and religious communities in Iraq, it will be no match for local warlords and will have to contend with the growth of terrorist infrastructures. A failure of central authority could lead to a formal or de facto partition of the country.

The wild card in Iraq's political evolution is external interference. There is the potential for non-Iraqi state and nonstate actors—particularly Iran—to interfere more actively in Iraqi politics. The activities of Iranian operatives in Iraq suggest a long-term strategy by Tehran to create an Iranian sphere of influence in southern Iraq. Matters are complicated by the existence of Iraqi Shi'ite political parties that have varying degrees of loyalty to Iran. The key question is whether they will identify themselves as Shi'ites first, united with their Iranian brethren, or as Iraqis, threatened by Iranian encroachment. The answer may not become clear for years.

Non-Islamist Threats

U.S. friends and allies and regional interests are not threatened by Islamist extremist and terrorist groups alone, of course. There are several capable non-Islamist insurgent and terrorist groups seeking to overthrow governments friendly to the United States or to carve out separate ethnic-based states. (See pp. 61–84.) These groups include the following:

- *The Liberation Tigers of Tamil Eelam (LTTE) in Sri Lanka, one of the world's most innovative and successful terrorist-insurgent groups.* It is one of the few that has institutionalized a permanent, highly trained martyr wing—the Black Tigers—as a formal component of its overall organizational structure. Although the LTTE does not presently threaten the United States, it does provide a benchmark of the sophistication that a substate insurgency can achieve given the right combination of circumstances. (See pp. 68–78.)
- *Basque Fatherland and Liberty* (Euskadi ta Askatasuna, *or ETA*), *a Marxist group that uses terrorism in hopes of forming an independent* Basque state in parts of northern Spain and southwest France. Although the ETA has not targeted U.S. interests, an increasingly anti-American tenor within the ETA after Operation Iraqi Freedom and connections with Abu Musab al-Zarqawi's terror network could make U.S. citizens and interests an ETA target in Europe. (See pp. 78–80.)
- *The Revolutionary Armed Forces of Colombia (FARC) and the National Liberation Army (ELN), Marxist armed groups that have operated in Colombia since the 1960s.* The FARC, the most important of the two, has not deviated from its original strategy of "protracted people's war," a strategy based on Maoist and Vietnamese precepts that involves gradually extending the organization's presence and control in the countryside and eventually isolating the government forces in the major cities. This strategy of territorial control is linked to the FARC's involvement in the cocaine drug trade that generates much of the revenues that fund the organization's operations, together with extortion and kidnapping. (See pp. 61–65.)
- *Maoist insurgencies.* This rubric refers to the "People's Army" phenomena found in Peru (Shining Path), Nepal (Communist Party of Nepal), India (Naxalites), Bhutan (Ngolops), and the Philippines (Communist Party of the Philippines/New People's Army). These groups are Marxist-Leninist-Maoist entities that practice the "vanguard" philosophy, which holds that a small armed group (sometimes through the employment of extreme violence) will lead the proletariat in establishing a worker's utopia. Although not a direct

threat to the United States, these groups are terrorists inherently hostile to the international order and may find common interests with al-Qaeda and associates. They are also increasingly participating in drug trafficking to fund their activities. Factors that could move the Maoists to become a larger threat include U.S. support for governments under attack by Maoists, spillover effects from insurgency, and recruitment and indoctrination of native peoples against urban elites and governments. (See pp. 65–68.)

To complete the picture of the universe of terrorism, actual and potential, this study provides an overview and assessment of anarchist groups, the "New, New Left" and right-wing extremists in Europe and North America; movements in Latin America; and ecoterrorists and other niche extremists on the even farther fringe of the movement. In the context of this analysis, we examine the possibility of a tactical alliance between non-Islamic fringe extremist groups and Islamist extremists. Al-Qaeda, according to some accounts, has shown some interest in reaching out to non-Islamic militant groups, with anti-Semitism, anti-Americanism, and anti-Westernism serving as a common ground. The possibility of tactical alliances cannot be discounted and warrants carefully watching. However, although neo-Nazis, Islamists, and the New, New Left share an anti-Zionist stance (and a deep well of anti-Semitism), opposition to Israel remains a relatively minor component of the non-Islamic extremists' agenda, and so is unlikely to serve as the foundation for any real partnership. (See pp. 85–99.)

The Convergence of Terrorism and Crime

An analysis of the future of terrorism cannot be complete without a discussion of the convergence of terrorism and crime. Criminals generally seek economic gain through illicit means, while terrorists seek political or ideological goals and use criminal means to achieve those ends. Nevertheless, the important fact is that these two sets of actors are joining forces against the state and society. This phenomenon is growing because similar conditions give rise to both terrorism and transnational crime and because terrorists and organized criminals use the same strategies to promote their operations and sometimes engage in strategic alliances.

During the Cold War, many of the insurgent and terrorist organizations were largely dependent on great-power support. The end of the Cold War brought an effective end to external support for these groups. The Soviet Union disappeared, and the United States simply lost interest in the fate of many of its former clients. The post–Cold War survival strategies of these groups hinged on their ability to generate new sources of revenue to support their operations. Some groups were unable to make the transition and disbanded or made peace with the governments that they were seeking to overthrow, as in the case of the Salvadoran and Guatemalan rebels. Other groups, however, tapped into locally available sources of revenue and grew in strength. The most successful in making the transition were those that operated in countries that produced high-value commodities, legal or otherwise—for example, diamonds in West Africa, minerals in Central Africa, cocaine and heroin in Colombia, and opium and heroin in Southwest Asia and the "Golden Triangle" of Southeast Asia.

Other groups were able to fund themselves successfully from smuggling and arms trafficking, kidnapping and extortion, piracy, compact disc counterfeiting, and a variety of other criminal activities. These commodities provided easy targets of opportunity for terrorist or rebel movements. The groups had the firepower to deal themselves into the trade. They could trade the commodities themselves, as in the case of the Liberia-backed Revolutionary United Front of Sierra Leone and "conflict diamonds"; or protect and "tax" them, which is the preferred approach of the Revolutionary Armed Forces of Colombia (FARC); or set themselves up as middlemen in human and arms trafficking.

This transition from more conventional forms of financing to crime has also been a feature of the evolution of al-Qaeda. Al-Qaeda's effort to hide assets and capitalize on trade in West African conflict diamonds appears to date from September 1998, following international efforts to freeze al-Qaeda and Taliban accounts after the August 1998 bombings of the U.S. embassies in Tanzania and Kenya. As mentioned previously, Lebanese Hezbollah is known to maintain a global network to support fundraising and operational and logistical requirements for its operations abroad. Hezbollah has raised significant amounts of funds through drug trafficking and diamond sales from Sierra Leone, and through smuggling, black market activity, and money-laundering operations in the tri-border area of South America. We examine several other case studies of the convergence of insurgent and terrorist organizations and crime in this study.

The criminal activities of these groups tend to weaken and corrupt political and social institutions, particularly when trafficking in a lucrative and social destructive commodity such as cocaine is involved. To the extent that they are successful, these groups also displace state and government institutions, usually weak to begin with, in the areas where they establish a foothold. Unchecked, the groups will expand their resource base, increase their recruiting pool, and generate greater capacity at the expense of the state. Therefore, there is a high correlation between the development of these groups and failed or failing states. (See pp. 101–160.)

Conclusions and Recommendations

From a policy perspective, the first-order question is whether the trajectory of insurgent and terrorist groups outside the global jihadist movement will bring them closer to that movement. To answer this question, we examine what factors could affect this outcome and what the U.S. policy response should be. The second-order question is what level of threat these groups represent for U.S. regional interests, including the security of U.S. friends and allies, and what the U.S. policy response should be. (See pp. 161–166.)

With regard to convergence with al-Qaeda, the groups that generate the greatest concern are the Islamist groups that share aspects of al-Qaeda's worldview. Of the groups examined, only two—Egypt's al-Wa'ad and the Iraqi insurgents—have developed since bin Laden's notorious 1998 Khost fatwa against "Jews and Crusaders." The other groups were well established and active, and had articulated their own agendas prior to al-Qaeda's emergence in the international arena.

Therefore, they can be assumed to be less receptive to al-Qaeda's ideology of global jihad than the groups that have emerged since that time. Among these groups, the majority interpret their jihad much more narrowly than groups affiliated or associated with al-Qaeda. Hezbollah's interests center on Lebanon and its immediate vicinity; Hamas is focused on the Palestinian issue; and the GIA on overthrowing the Algerian government. In the groups for which association with al-Qaeda might be operationally attractive, external and internal factors have held such tendencies in check. For example, Hezbollah appears to be influenced by its ties to Syria and Iran, as well as by its involvement in Lebanese politics. Al-Gama'a al-Islamiyya appears to be concerned about carving out some political space to operate in Egypt.

Even some of the non-Islamist groups could also decide to cooperate with al-Qaeda or other Islamist groups for their own reasons. For example, many of these militant groups now maintain representatives in the criminal and black market world. This interconnectivity allows terrorists to acquire weapons as necessary, perhaps even to expand their capabilities. It is also important to stress that some terrorist groups could shift their worldview, thus adopting an agenda similar to al-Qaeda's. Alternatively, others could simply capitalize on a perceived anti-U.S. trend, shifting the focus of their attacks toward U.S. targets to increase their own potential through alliances with more capable al-Qaeda affiliated groups or simply to gain greater recognition.

A recent RAND study analyzed factors that caused terrorist groups to adjust their intentions (e.g., ideology or worldview) and their capabilities. Specifically, the study isolated the following three key factors that cause terrorist groups to shift from their chosen paths: (1) counterattacks by security forces; (2) external support from states or other militant organizations; and (3) gain or loss of popular support. To those, we add a fourth: general shifts in the international security environment—such as that brought about by the U.S.-led global war on terrorism. Some extremist organizations, such as the Moro Islamic Liberation Front (MILF), have tried to distance themselves from al-Qaeda to reduce their exposure to the global war on terrorism. Similarly, according to a well-informed Sri Lankan source, the global war on terrorism has reduced international tolerance of LTTE terrorism and influenced the LTTE's decision to enter into peace negotiations with the Sri Lankan government.

A potentially dangerous shift can be seen in the emerging Hamas-Hezbollah nexus, as seen in the March 14, 2004, attack in the Israeli port of Ashdod. The significance of this attack was not the number of casualties; indeed, Hamas has killed many more in single suicide bombing attacks. But rather, it demonstrated—especially to Israeli counterterrorism experts—Hamas's ability to hit more strategic targets.

Given the qualitative leap in Hamas's efforts, it might not be a surprise that Hezbollah financed and, indeed, allegedly planned this attack. Yet this degree of aid and coordination is greater than anything seen before in the Hamas-Hezbollah relationship. From an Israeli viewpoint, some security officials have stated that this attack motivated the government to assassinate Sheikh Ahmad Yasin. But the Ashdod attack also holds other, more global implications for the war on terrorism. First, it demonstrates that Sunni and Shi'ite militants *will* work together, given a mutual enemy. In this case, the enemy is Israel, but this does not preclude cooperation between Sunni and Shi'ite militants against the United States. Second, up to this point, Hamas was facing significant counterterrorism pressure from the Israeli government. Thus, it could have been more willing to take strategic guidance from Hezbollah: not just aid, but actual suggestions for types of attacks and targets. Parallel counterterrorism efforts by the United States and its allies in the war on terrorism could provoke other nonaffiliated terrorists to accept guidance from al-Qaeda in the future, as Hamas did from Hezbollah. Finally, in the case of Hezbollah, one potential explanation for the shift in its aid is that Hezbollah may be struggling to sustain attention and support now that Israel has pulled out of southern Lebanon. Greater involvement in the Palestinian resistance could help Hezbollah increase its momentum and support. It is therefore possible that Muslim anger at the U.S. presence in Iraq could similarly provoke shifts in the agenda of Hezbollah or other groups vis-à-vis the United States, as these groups continue to vie for local recruits and support.

The bottom line is that these groups have political aspirations as opposed to outright murder and mayhem. Because of their political agendas, they are more likely to accept political rules and social norms acceptable to a majority than are al-Qaeda and its affiliates.

Beyond the question of convergence, it is important to keep in mind that just because some of these groups have not joined the global jihadist movement, they should not be dismissed as unthreatening. Some represent deadly threats to the states that they seek to subvert; others, like Hezbollah, could suddenly emerge as global threats.

Implications for the U.S. Military and the U.S. Air Force

In Part 1, we discussed the use of air power as an option to attack terrorists in difficult or inhospitable terrain, as well as the use of air transport in counterterrorist or counterinsurgency operations in countries with widely dispersed populations and poor land transportation infrastructure. These considerations apply as well to many of the cases discussed in this volume, with the difference that, with the exception of the Iraqi insurgency, the United States is not—and as a general principle should not—be involved in direct military operations against these groups. (See pp. 164–166.)

Therefore, the emphasis should be on strengthening the capabilities of friendly governments to confront insurgents, terrorists, and other extremist groups. U.S. Air Force Special Operations Forces (active duty, Reserve and National Guard units)—at approximately 11,000 personnel, second only to Army SOF at 29,000—can be particularly pertinent for the counterinsurgency and counterterrorism training role required by the new environment.

The judgment in Part 1 of the study—that these local wars must be fought and won by the local governments and security forces with the United States in a supporting role—is even more valid in the case of local conflicts, some of which are driven by legitimate (or at least rational) grievances and in which the rebel movements enjoy significant support. By the same token, because some of these groups have limited political agendas, under the right circumstances they can become part of a negotiating process leading to a political solution of the conflict—a major difference from groups that are part of the global jihadist movement, which have to be destroyed or forced to leave the field.

To develop effective strategies against insurgent and terrorist groups, it is important to look at these groups in a broad context, even if they operate locally, because the migration of tactics, techniques, and procedures (TTPs) is creating a globalization of violence. They are learning what works and adopting best practices. Their tactical models contribute to the proliferation of effective styles of unconventional warfare throughout different zones of conflict. Innovations include the use of improvised explosive devices (IEDs) and their evolution into sophisticated weapons designed to interrupt supply lines by Hezbollah. Hamas has been known to use ambulances as a cover for bombs or logistical support. Man-portable air defense systems (MANPADS) and now suicide bombers with suicide vests, first used against Israeli targets in Israel and in the Palestinian territories, are now used as mass casualty weapons by Chechens against Russian military and civilian jets.

The first implication for the U.S. military and the Air Force is that they must understand clearly that the tactics, techniques, and procedures used by all groups, whether part of the global jihad or not, are beginning to mimic each other. This means that, from a tactical standpoint, U.S. military doctrine must anticipate the dissemination of these tactics across theaters in the war on terror.

The second implication is that, although the United States has a supporting role in opposing the groups in the "al-Qaeda universe," the potential role for the United States in countering those extremist groups beyond al-Qaeda is even more indirect. The challenge for the U.S. military is to be prepared either to provide increased levels of support to key allies should they require it or to engage these extremist groups should they shift their attention toward the United States, while at the same time avoiding direct involvement in these conflicts. This strategic challenge has particular relevance to the U.S. Air Force. Understanding the circumstances that might stimulate change in extremist groups, for example, may require the allocation of intelligence, surveillance, and reconnaissance resources. It may also necessitate broad global readiness, incorporating regions such as Southeast Asia and Latin America in addition to the Middle East, in the war on terrorism.

For the U.S. military and the U.S. Air Force in particular, there are tools for targeting terrorist groups that can also be used in cooperation and coordination with host state operations against terrorist, insurgent, and criminal groups. It is important to note that the criminal transport of narcotics, arms, illegal migrants, explosives, etc., occurs in hubs and spokes concurrent or collocated with terrorist groups. This argues for the "dual use" of U.S. security assistance for both counterterrorism and counternarcotics purposes. Older aircraft with high-tech intelligence-collection capabilities can be used to mitigate both terrorist havens and criminal nodes. In addition, air support for host country coast guard operations in and around waterways that harbor terrorists or criminal activity is a critical component of coastal and riverine surveillance and interdiction of smuggling routes.

Acknowledgments

The authors of this report wish to thank all those who made this study possible. First, we thank our sponsors in the U.S. Air Force and particularly Lt Col John Jerakis, our point of contact in the Office of Regional Plans and Issues (USAF HQ A5XX); Terrence M. Doyle, Office of Plans and Policies (USAF HQ A5XS); and the staff of the U.S. embassies and Defense Attaché Offices that facilitated our work overseas. In this regard, we thank Col James Tietjen, former U.S. Air Attaché in Singapore; Lt Col Benjamin Coffey, U.S. Assistant Air Attaché in London; and Maj Guermantes Lailari, U.S. Assistant Air Attaché in Tel Aviv and an astute analyst of Islamic extremist movements.

We owe a great debt to the reviewers of this manuscript, Brian M. Jenkins, Rohan Gunaratna, and Thomas A. Marks, and to Lieutenant Commander Youssef Aboul-Enein of the Office of the Secretary of Defense, whose comments greatly improved the manuscript. Any shortcomings are entirely the responsibility of the authors. We also express the appreciation for the collaboration that we received in our work on this study from the State Intelligence Agency of Indonesia (BIN), the National Intelligence Agency of Thailand, the Security and Intelligence Division of the Ministry of Defence of Singapore, the Intelligence Service of the Armed Forces of the Philippines, the Joint Terrorism Analysis Center of the United Kingdom, and other agencies.

We are also indebted for invaluable insights into terrorist networks to Zachary Abuza, Martin Kramer, Elie Karmon of the International Policy Institute for Counter-Terrorism (ICT), Herzliya, Israel; the staff of the International Center for Political Violence and Terrorism Studies of the Institute of Defence and Strategic Studies of Singapore; Carolina Hernandez and the Institute for Strategic and Development Studies of the Philippines; and Thailand analysts Paul Quaglia of PSA Asia and Anthony Davis.

Within RAND we cannot fail to acknowledge the important contributions to our understanding of al-Qaeda finances made by the RAND Air Force Fellow, Lt Col Steve Kiser, and the work on the charts illustrating the links between terrorism and crime by the RAND Navy Fellow LCDR Mark Edwards. We also thank Andrew Hoehn and Alan Vick, the Director and former Acting Director of the RAND Project AIR FORCE Strategy and Doctrine Program, under whose auspices this research was conducted; David Shlapak; and many other colleagues such as John Parachini, Brian Jackson, and John Baker, who—although not part of this project—contributed to the cross-fertilization of ideas. We thank our assistants Colleen O'Connor and Natalie Ziegler, and Ursula Davies and Thomas Young, RAND Cambridge summer interns, for their assistance with mapping jihadist networks in Europe and Africa and Douglas Farah and Alexandra Zavis for work on jihadist activities in West, Central, and Southern Africa.

Finally, we acknowledge the invaluable contributions of our editor, Miriam Polon; our production editor, Todd Duft; Project AIR FORCE editor Phyllis Gilmore, for her help with the summary; and our marketing director, John Warren.

Abbreviations

ANSWER	Act Now to Stop War and End Racism Coalition
ASG	Abu Sayyaf Group (Philippines)
AUC	United Self-Defense Forces of Colombia
BfV	*Bundesamt für Verfassungsschutz* [Office for the Protection of the Constitution] (Germany)
CBRN	Chemical, biological, radiological, and nuclear
CID	Criminal Investigation Department (Sri Lanka)
CPA	Coalition Provisional Authority (Iraq)
CPN(M)	The Communist Party of Nepal (Maoist)
CPP	Communist Party of the Philippines
CSIS	Canadian Security Intelligence Service
DEA	(U.S.) Drug Enforcement Agency
EIJ	Egyptian Islamic Jihad
EIJM	Eritrean Islamic Jihad Movement
EIRM	Eritrean Islamic Reform Movement
ELN	National Liberation Army (Colombia)
ENA	Eritrean National Alliance

ETA	Euskadi ta Askatasuna (Basque Fatherland and Liberty) (Spain)
EU	European Union
FARC	Revolutionary Armed Forces of Colombia
FIS	Islamic Salvation Front (Algeria)
FLN	Front de Libération Nationale (Algeria)
FMLN	Farabundo Marti National Liberation Front (El Salvador)
FTAA	Free Trade Area of the Americas
GIA	Armed Islamic Group (Algeria)
GSPC	Salafist Group for Preaching and Combat (Algeria)
Hamas	Islamic Resistance Movement
HIDTA	High Intensity Drug Trafficking Area (California)
IDF	Israel Defense Forces
IED	improvised explosive device
IIB	Internal Intelligence Bureau (Sri Lanka)
IID	Internal Intelligence Directorate (Sri Lanka)
INR	Bureau of Intelligence and Research, U.S. Department of State
JI	Jemaah Islamiyah (Southeast Asia)
KFR	kidnappings for ransom
LRPG	Long Range Patrol Group (Sri Lanka)
LTTE	Liberation Tigers of Tamil Elam (Sri Lanka)
MANPADS	man-portable air defense systems
MAS	Movement Toward Socialism (Bolivia)

MILF	Moro Islamic Liberation Front (Philippines)
MIP	Pachakuti Indian Movement (Andes)
MNLF	Moro National Liberation Front (Philippines)
NDFB	National Democratic Front of Bodoland (India)
NPA	New People's Army (Philippines)
PAGAD	People Against Gangsterism and Drugs (South Africa)
PFDJ	Popular Front for Democracy and Justice (Eritrea)
PIRA	Provisional Irish Republican Army
PLO	Palestine Liberation Organization
RCMP	Royal Canadian Mounted Police
RIM	Revolutionary Internationalist Movement
RPG	rocket-propelled grenade
RUF	Revolutionary United Front (Sierra Leone)
SCIRI	Supreme Council for the Islamic Revolution in Iraq
SL	Sendero Luminoso–Shining Path (Peru)
SLAF	Sri Lankan Armed Forces
SLNS	Sri Lankan naval ship
SOF	Special Operations Forces
TNT	Tamil New Tigers
TTPs	tactics, techniques, and procedures
UK	United Kingdom
ULFA	United Liberation Front of Asom (India)

UNITA   National Union for the Total Independence of
               Angola

ZDI   Zimbabwe Defense Industries

CHAPTER ONE

Introduction

Part 1 of this study describes and analyzes what has become of al-Qaeda after the removal of its safe haven in Afghanistan and the death or capture of a significant part of its leadership, as well as what we call the "al-Qaeda nebula." This concept includes affiliated or associated militant groups that have adopted al-Qaeda's worldview and vision of a global jihad and its methodology of mass-casualty terrorist attacks.[1]

Yet the "al-Qaeda universe" does not incorporate the entirety of the terrorist threat or potential threat. A number of other militant groups threaten U.S. regional interests or allies and pose a potential direct threat to the United States. We did not include these groups in Part 1 because they neither share al-Qaeda's view of a global jihad nor rise to the level of a global threat.

Clearly, Osama bin Laden and other leaders of al-Qaeda hope that their efforts will persuade other Islamic militant groups to join the

---

[1] As discussed in Part 1 of the study, the global jihad has a universal goal—the reconquest of Muslim lands usurped by infidels and the eventual global expansion of Islam—and incorporates groups and cells that no longer consider themselves bound to concrete territories and populations. Although jihadist ideology is full of atavistic elements, the global jihad is a modern phenomenon that reflects what Oliver Roy calls "globalized Islam," a "universal" Islam valid in any cultural context and detached from the cultures in which Islam has been historically embedded. This reformulation of an imaginary universal *umma* leads also to the reformulation of the jihad as a cataclysmic confrontation between the Islamic world and the West. Of course, in the view of jihadists, these two objectives—the global jihad and the toppling of "apostate" Muslim regimes—are closely interrelated. For al-Qaeda and the groups that share its ideology, governments in the Muslim world primarily exist because of U.S. support; their destruction thus is contingent on removing that support by expelling the United States from the region.

global jihad. Moreover, it would seem logical that terrorists with similar ideological beliefs would be inclined to enter into a cooperative relationship with al-Qaeda or other elements in the global jihadist movement, since such cooperation could enhance their own capabilities. But what about the terrorist group that is not part of the al-Qaeda network and does not adhere to its agenda? The temptation for policymakers is to set aside terrorist groups that have not chosen to join al-Qaeda as less dangerous. Yet these groups still pose a threat to the Unites States, its interests, and its allies.

This volume, Part 2 of the study, focuses on three categories in this "second circle" of terrorist groups: (1) terrorist groups that articulate an Islamist agenda for their own country but are not directly linked to the global jihadist movement; (2) Muslim terrorist groups whose agendas are primarily separatist or ethno-nationalist but that present a threat to the stability or territorial integrity of U.S. allies, although not to the United States directly; and (3) highly capable, non-Islamist terrorist groups. By examining these groups, we hope to establish a framework for evaluating the threat that these groups currently pose and assessing the likelihood and the conditions under which some of them could evolve into regional or global threats. We also examine antiglobalization threats. Some of these groups have risen to the level of terrorism; others have not, but could. Finally, we discuss the nexus between terrorism, insurgency, and crime.

Anaytical Framework

We begin with the assumption that terrorist groups move along the same path—sustaining their ideology, objectives, and tactics—until some outside force causes them to shift. Our analysis, therefore, requires that we first classify terrorist groups' current paths and then determine what factors might affect change. Four characteristics can be said to influence terrorists' strategic choices: ideology and leadership mindset, lack of internal restraint, opportunity, and technical capacity. This framework provides a starting point for the analysis in this section. Because we are interested in how these categories of terrorists might threaten the United States in the future, it is important to determine which characteristics are the most likely to indicate a change in behavior or strategic path. Part 1 of this study provides an overview of terrorist groups in the tier below the al-Qaeda "nebula," their ideological foundations, their strategic and operational objectives, and the key environmental factors that have shaped their evolution.

Because of the potential of some antiglobalism movements to pose a violent threat to the political, economic, and social order, we identify and analyze antiglobalization threats and their convergence with terrorist groups. Our evaluation takes into account the local context in which these groups develop and linkages among the groups and with other extremist and terrorist organizations and rogue states.

The last chapter of this volume addresses the connections between terrorism, insurgency, and crime. We examine a number of specific case studies in areas ranging from the tri-border region of South America to the southern Philippines to identify the characteristics of this nexus across regions and different types of terrorist and insurgent movements, the conditions that give rise to this phenomenon, and its implications for counterterrorism policy.

CHAPTER TWO

Hezbollah and Hamas

Hezbollah, Party of God

Hezbollah is perhaps the best known and the most capable of the Islamist militant organizations that employ terrorism yet are not affiliated with al-Qaeda. This group was responsible for the 1983 suicide attack against the U.S. Marine barracks in Beirut, which killed 241 U.S. and 58 French servicemen who were part of a multinational peacekeeping force in Lebanon at that time. In addition, since the early 1980s, Hezbollah has established a far-flung financial network, stretching from the tri-border area of Argentina, Paraguay, and Brazil to the United States and to Southeast Asia—Indonesia, Thailand, and the Philippines. Hezbollah thus has the potential to inflict damage on U.S. interests and allies across the globe. Yet this group remains relatively detached from the al-Qaeda network and has not directly threatened the United States since the 1983 attack. It therefore represents an interesting and important case study.[1]

From September 1970 to August 1982, the Palestinian Liberation Organization (PLO) used Lebanon as its political and military base of operations.[2] Around that same time, the minority Shi'ite population was engaged in a struggle for national power with the country's Maronite Christians. In this local struggle, the Israeli military

---

[1] For more information on Hezbollah's criminal activities, see Chapter Seven.

[2] See Black and Morris (1991); and Bickerton and Klausner (1995).

sometimes sponsored or provided support to the Maronites, while the PLO helped train and equip Shi'ite militias in southern Lebanon.[3] These militias were the precursor to Hezbollah.

After the Israeli invasion of Lebanon in 1982, the Shi'ite militias shifted their focus from internal rivalries to Israeli forces. Hezbollah was aided, in part, by Iran. Approximately 1,500 Iranian Revolutionary Guards helped to train and organize the Shi'ite militias, which allowed Hezbollah to expand its activities and its capabilities.[4] Despite frequent assassinations and attacks by Israeli forces, Hezbollah continued to expand its influence and presence in southern Lebanon throughout the 1980s and 1990s.[5] In May 2000, in part as a result of Hezbollah's continued guerrilla campaign, the Israeli military pulled out of southern Lebanon.[6] Many Islamist terrorist groups—especially the Palestinians—view the Hezbollah campaign as a model. In a 2001 interview, Marwan Barghouti, a key leader of the militant branch of the Palestinian Liberation Organization, al-Fatah, said,

> To be candid, I must say that Israel's withdrawal from Lebanon was indeed one contributing factor to the [al-Aqsa] Intifada. I won't say that it was the single reason, but the Palestinians looked on carefully as the army pulled out of Lebanon. They asked how could it be that Israel was able to withdraw from an entanglement of nearly 20 years—all in one night. Not one soldier remained behind. So I say that if that was accomplished literally overnight in Lebanon, the retreat from Ramallah to Tel-Aviv should require no more than three nights at most.[7]

---

[3]   Jaber (1997), p. 17.

[4]   For information on the impact of the Iranian Revolution on the Shi'ite militias, see Saad-Ghorayeb (2002), pp. 14–15. See also, "Baalbek Seen as Staging Area for Terrorism," *The Washington Post*, January 9, 1984; and Wege (1994), pp. 151–164.

[5]   Black and Morris (1991), pp. 394–399.

[6]   Some counterterrorism experts in Israel suggest that the Israeli reluctance simply to pull out of the Gaza Strip, without inflicting significant damage on Palestinian terrorist groups, is, in part, a result of their experience in southern Lebanon. Cragin interview, Israeli counterterrorism experts, April 2004.

[7]   Marwan Barghouti, quoted in "Hizballah Lends Its Services to the Palestinian Intifada" (2001).

Today, Hezbollah has obtained a degree of political legitimacy in Lebanon—its political party won eight seats in the 1992 parliamentary elections, and in 2000 it won nine affiliated and three nonaffiliated seats.[8] At the same time, the group maintains its armed wing, conducting some limited attacks on Israeli forces and supplying military aid to Palestinian groups.

With the advent of the second (al-Aqsa) intifada[9] (2000–2004), Hezbollah also appeared to take a greater—or at least more direct—role in the Palestinian conflict with Israel. Although Hezbollah had provided weapons and training in the past, some believe it was also beginning to provide some strategic direction to Palestinian groups as well as helping various factions match needs with skills. To illustrate this point, some Israeli counterterrorism experts point to the March 2004 Ashdod attack. Two Hamas suicide bombers hid in a commercial container, which allowed them to exit the tightly guarded Gaza Strip and travel to Ashdod. Upon arriving at the port, one of the suicide bombers managed to enter the guarded compound, detonating his explosives among a number of workers near a warehouse. The second bomber detonated outside the port's security fence. In total, the attack killed 10 Israelis and wounded an additional 18. The significance of this attack was not the number of casualties; indeed, Hamas has killed

---

[8] For an overview of Hezbollah and Lebanese elections, see Usher (1997).

[9] *Intifada* literally means "throwing off."

many more in single suicide bombing attacks. Rather, it demonstrated (1) Hezbollah's willingness to help Hamas pick its targets and plan its attacks, and (2) Hamas's ability to hit more strategic targets.[10]

Ideological Foundation

Hezbollah articulates a universalistic view of the Muslim community, the *umma*, which incorporates Shi'ite, Sunnis, and even secularists.[11] In 1995 the *Journal of Palestine Studies* published an interview with the spiritual leader of Hezbollah, Sheikh Muhammad Husayn Fadlallah. In the interview, Sheikh Fadlallah stated:

> The Muslims are having difficulty bringing forth the kind of Islamic resistance to which they aspire. . . . Speaking in general terms, you could say they are seeking what could be termed a concrete expression of Islamic reality—a movement, a way of life, a political position in particular. There is a visceral Muslim identity, even among secularists who may not be consciously aware of it. This involves a spontaneous identification with other Muslims—in Bosnia, Chechnya, Afghanistan, wherever—irrespective of the merits of the case.[12]

---

[10] Usher (1997) and Cragin interviews, Israeli counterterrorism experts, April 2004. The research for this book was conducted immediately following the March 2004 Ashdod attack. That attack spurred more counterterrorism analysts within Israel to focus on the nexus between Hezbollah and Palestinian militants. Since that time more information has come to light. What has been discovered is that Hamas has been reluctant to allow Hezbollah too much foothold in the Palestinian Territories. But the al-Aqsa Martyrs' Brigades has accepted more and more help from Hezbollah. For example, in March 2004, Israel's Ministry of Foreign Affairs issued a press release on the arrest of Shadi Abu Alhatzin, the leader of an al-Aqsa Martyrs' Brigades cell in Khan Yunis (Gaza Strip). The release stated that Alhatzin had revealed to Israeli security officials that a Hezbollah representative came to Khan Yunis in 2003 to provide training in communications security. "ISA arrests head of Gaza Strip Hezbollah cell," Israel Ministry of Foreign Affairs, http://www.mfa.gov.il (as of March 10, 2004). Similarly, subsequent interviews with Israeli security officials suggest that Qeis Ubeid, an Israeli Arab from Taibeh associated with Hezbollah, aided the al-Aqsa Martyrs' Brigades cell in Nablus. Interview with authors, Israeli security official, June 2005.

[11] For more on the ideology of Hezbollah, see Saad-Ghorayeb (2002), pp. 69–87.

[12] Soueid (1995), p. 61.

Some have argued that this universalism is somewhat paradoxical, given that Hezbollah is a Shi'ite group and that clear divisions exist between the minority Shi'ites and majority Sunnis in the Muslim world. To a degree, this argument holds true. Since its inception, Hezbollah has maintained its belief that the Ayatollah Khomeini was the divinely inspired ruler of the umma and that his successor, Ali Khameini is the true "Legal Guardian of the Muslims" today.[13] This concept, referred to as *Velayat al-Faqih,* places Iran's religious leader at the center of Hezbollah's religious and pan-Islamic worldview—a position that Sunnis oppose. Additionally, it is important to note that Hezbollah combines this Islamic outlook with strong Lebanese nationalistic rhetoric. In this sense, Hezbollah is not purely pan-Islamic in its outlook.

Hezbollah may publicly sympathize with Islamic revolutions in countries such as Algeria, but it has not adopted these movements into its lexicon of "our umma." Indeed, the only Muslim community that in Hezbollah's view requires a pan-Islamic jihad on its behalf is the Palestinians.[14] The universalism of Hezbollah's ideology, therefore, appears to have pragmatic overtones that allow the group to pick and choose the Islamic movements with which it publicly associates, such as the 1979 Iranian Revolution and the Palestinian national movement.

Hezbollah's adoption of the Palestinian movement is also fairly complex. Palestinians are predominantly Sunnis, not Shi'ites. Moreover, the PLO contributed to the chaos and civil war that afflicted Lebanon for much of the 1970s and 1980s. Hezbollah appears to justify its support for the Palestinian movement by rationalizing that the Israeli occupation of Jerusalem, rather than Palestinian nationalism per se, is the epitome of a pan-Islamic cause. Thus, Jerusalem is a symbol of the umma itself, and its liberation is a Muslim duty, not a Palestinian duty.[15] This justification allows Hezbollah to support the Palestinian jihad but not other Muslim struggles.

---

[13] Saad-Ghorayeb (2002), pp. 64–65.

[14] Saad-Ghorayeb (2002), pp. 75–76.

[15] Saad-Ghorayeb (2002), p. 73.

Not all the help that Hezbollah provides the Palestinians, however, can be tied directly to the status of Jerusalem. For example, in February 2004, Hezbollah successfully negotiated a prisoner swap with the Israeli government—the return of Israeli soldiers (or their remains) for the release of Hezbollah and Palestinian prisoners. By including Palestinian terrorists in its negotiations, Hezbollah gained legitimacy with the sympathetic Lebanese and Palestinian population. Similarly, Hezbollah has reportedly encouraged Hamas and the Palestinian Islamic Jihad to shift its attacks toward more strategic targets (such as the Israeli port in Ashdod).[16] So Hezbollah's ideological base for support clearly gives way to more pragmatic purposes at times.

The ideological foundations of Hezbollah, therefore, explain at least part of the group's reluctance to join the al-Qaeda network. Its leadership might feel some spontaneous sympathy with wider pan-Islamist, Sunni agendas, but these movements do not necessarily align with Hezbollah ideologically. Sheikh Fadlallah continues in the aforementioned interview to say:

> Despite this strong identity, the Islamic world is suffering from a lack of clear and objective understanding of the true situation of Islam and Islamic thought. This is evident from the proliferation of Islamic movements, some reactionary, wanting to live as if it were five hundred or six hundred years ago, some archaic, some resorting to violence in situations when peaceful means can be pursued, some with a sound grasp of reality and whose tactics, whether violent or peaceful, are guided by objective analyses.[17]

In this interview, Sheikh Fadlallah is strongly critical of many Islamic movements. Yet he does not name specific deviant groups. Part of the reason for this reluctance to criticize other movements may be strategic. Even though Hezbollah does not align with other Islamist groups ideologically, it may still coordinate with them. We will discuss the issue of pragmatic strategies in other chapters. Here, we emphasize merely that, despite the ideological disparities that appear evident

---

[16] Cragin interview, Israeli counterterrorism experts, April 2004.

[17] Soueid (1995), p. 62.

between Hezbollah and the al-Qaeda network, some parallel interests exist. In particular, Hezbollah has historically opposed "Western domination" of the Muslim world in general and U.S. influence specifically. According to Sheikh Nassan Nasrallah, Secretary-General of Hezbollah, "They are primarily responsible for all Israeli crimes."[18] So while the ideological background of Hezbollah might explain its lack of affiliation with the al-Qaeda network, Hezbollah's strategic objectives pave the way for cooperation.[19]

Strategic and Operational Objectives

Until May 2000, Hezbollah's primary objective was to remove the Israeli military presence from southern Lebanon. In addition, Hezbollah has gradually expanded its support base in Lebanon in order to gain political legitimacy and power. Yet unlike many of the Islamist militant groups, Hezbollah's terrorist and guerrilla campaigns are directed outward toward Israel, rather than at its political adversaries inside Lebanon. This pattern is likely due to Syria's strong influence both with Hezbollah and more generally in Lebanon.[20] Hezbollah's support for the Palestinian movement represents a final strategic objective. Indeed, in April 2001, Sheikh Nasrallah made this statement at a conference on the Palestinian intifada in Tehran:

---

[18] Quoted in "Lo, the Party of God Still Vows Victory," *Time*, August 9, 1993, p. 33.

[19] In August 2003, CNN reported that U.S. intelligence officials were concerned about a potential alliance between Imad Mugniyah and Mussab al-Zarqawi in Iraq. Mugniyah has been linked with Hezbollah since the early 1980s, while Zarqawi has been linked with al-Qaeda. At the time of writing, this link does not appear to be a strategic alliance, rather a practical arrangement between two individuals. "New Terrorism Alliance Suspected in Iraq," CNN, 13 August 2003, http://edition.cnn.com/2003/WORLD/meast/08/13/iraq.terror (as of Mach 10, 2006).

[20] In the late 1980s, Hezbollah and Amal (another Shi'ite insurgent group) fought for supremacy in Lebanon. Syria stepped in and forced a truce between the groups. See "Syria Troops Enforce South Beirut Truce; Inter-Shiite Fighting Ends," *World News Digest*, LexisNexis, June 3, 1988.

We should look at the Intifada as the spearhead of the nation that needs our support. The Palestinians are defending our nation as well as its dignity and holy shrines.[21]

Hezbollah's militant activities follow its strategic objectives closely. For example, Hezbollah conducted the bulk of its suicide bombings against U.S., French, and Israeli targets from the spring of 1983 to the summer of 1985. After the summer of 1985, Hezbollah began to move toward more guerrilla-like warfare against Israeli troops in southern Lebanon. This shift appears to be the result of Syria's intervention in the Lebanese civil war in 1988 and 1989. At this time, Hezbollah's main competitor, Amal,[22] was forced to give up its weapons, while Hezbollah negotiated to keep its weapons as long as they were used to dislodge the Israeli military presence in southern Lebanon. Yet even though Hezbollah radically decreased its use of suicide bombings in the summer of 1985, it did not lose its capabilities to conduct such attacks. Indeed, after Israeli forces assassinated the group's leader, Abbas Musawi, in February 1992, Hezbollah apparently retaliated with a suicide attack against the Israeli embassy in Buenos Aires. Two years later, Hezbollah apparently conducted a similar attack against the Jewish Cultural Center in that same city (see Chapter Seven).[23]

Israeli experts submit that Hezbollah conducted the attacks in Argentina only after it appeared to be losing ground in the fight against Israel.[24] For the most part, however, Hezbollah has remained focused on its regional agenda. Hezbollah is also known for launching Katyusha

---

[21] Taken from the Hezbollah Web site, http://www.hizballah.org (as of January 19, 2003).

[22] The Amal movement was established in 1975 by Imam Musa as Sadr, an Iranian-born Shi'ite cleric of Lebanese ancestry. It is a fierce competitor of Hezbollah for leadership of the Lebanese Shi'ite community.

[23] Hezbollah is generally accepted as responsible for these two attacks, but it has not claimed them. After a long investigation by officials in the Argentine Supreme Court, security authorities issued a warrant for the arrest of Imad Mugniyah in 1999, for ordering the 1992 attack in Buenos Aires. For more information, see "Argentina Issues Warrant in Israeli Embassy Bombing," *International Counterterrorism Center*, September 4, 1999, http://www.ict.org.il/spotlight/det.cfm?id=318 (as of March 10, 2006).

[24] Cragin interviews, Israeli counterterrorism experts, April 2004.

rockets across the border into northern Israel and for kidnapping Israeli soldiers along the border. Throughout most of its guerrilla campaign, Hezbollah was able to keep one step ahead of the Israeli military.[25] Some argue that this ability was due to the nature of the Israeli military position, which was predominantly defensive and static.

Environmental Factors

The degree of influence that Syria and Iran have over Hezbollah's behavior is still in question. Clearly, Syria has played a significant role in the development of Hezbollah. But the benefits that Hezbollah derives from its relationship with Syria are more than just the sum total of weapons and money received. Hezbollah has been able to utilize support from Syria in its escalation-counterescalation warfare with the Israeli military. For example, the Israel Defense Forces (IDF) noticed in the early 1990s that Hezbollah forces had begun to use remotely detonated explosive devices in southern Lebanon. Guerrillas would plant these bombs along the roads and detonate them as IDF patrols drove by. In response, the IDF began to detonate the bombs early, using the same radio frequency as Hezbollah. Rather than give up the tactic, Hezbollah went back to Syria to obtain a weapons upgrade. The result was a remote-detonated bomb with scrambling devices as well as a bomb detonated by a computer that provided multiple-frequency transmissions.[26] Additionally, analysts point out that Syria "checked" Hezbollah's guerrilla activities in southern Lebanon during peace talks between Syria and Israel in the late 1990s. Syria has also acted as arbitrator between Hezbollah and the rival Shi'ite movement Amal in the past.[27] These examples appear to demonstrate significant Syrian influence over Hezbollah's activities.

---

[25] See, for example, the 1998 interviews with IDF officials published in the *Jerusalem Report*. Leslie Susser, "IDF Plans to Beef Up Lebanon Intelligence," *The Jerusalem Report*, LexisNexis, September 14, 1998.

[26] For more information, see "Hizballah and Israelis Wage Electronic War in South Lebanon" (1995).

[27] Jaber (1997), pp. 210–211.

With regard to Iran, the hierarchical nature of Hezbollah is the result of its ties to Iran. For example, each unit has a "fighting cleric." Trained in religious and military warfare, these clerics derive their authority from Hezbollah's Shura Council and, to a certain extent, Iran.[28] Thus Hezbollah's core leadership can be assured that its orders will be followed, as ground units receive both spiritual and operational oversight. In addition, Fadlallah has strong ties with Iranian clerics. The strategic relationship between Iran and Hezbollah is perhaps best illustrated by the fact that Hezbollah followed Iran's example in its reaction to the 9/11 attacks, denouncing these attacks but continuing to support Palestinian terrorism.[29] Iran and Syria therefore appear to be the most significant external factors that influence Hezbollah's behavior.

Hezbollah also has demonstrated sensitivity to its support community in southern Lebanon. During the Israeli occupation, the IDF attempted to disconnect Hezbollah from its supporters by penalizing the latter. The IDF reasoned that the Shi'ite community would blame Hezbollah for its situation and reduce its support for the group. While this counterinsurgency strategy worked initially, Hezbollah soon developed an extensive relief and charity network in southern Lebanon.[30] Since May 2000, Hezbollah has used this network to strengthen its political base. In this context, Hezbollah's lack of Islamist-like goals within Lebanon could be attributed to attempts to broaden its support community. Lebanon, with a population of 3.5 million, has 18 different religious sects. The result is a fragmented society. To expand its support base to include Christians and Sunni Muslims, therefore, Hezbollah must tone down its Shi'ite ideology and rhetoric and emphasize its social and charitable activities. Nizar Hamzeh, a terrorism expert at the American University in Beirut, offered this explanation in 2000,

---

[28] Cragin interview, Hezbollah expert, Tel Aviv, April 2004.

[29] Sobelman (2001).

[30] Wege (1994), pp. 157–159; Saad-Ghorayeb (2002), pp. 7–33; and Bruce W. Nelan, "What's Peace Got to Do with It?" *Time,* August 9, 1993, pp. 32–33.

"Hizballah is pragmatic and has decided to perform a contract with the wicked, but the achievement of an Islamic state will always be there as a goal."[31]

Hamas: The Islamic Resistance Movement

The Islamic Resistance Movement, known by its acronym Hamas, has its organizational roots in Gaza's al-Mujamma al-Islami, also known as the Islamic Centre, which the late Sheikh Ahmad Yasin began in 1973. Sheikh Yasin used the Centre to draw together the eventual founders of Hamas, including Isa al-Nashshar, Dr. Ibrahim al-Yazuri, Abdulfattah Doukhan, Dr. Abdul Aziz Rantisi, Mohamad Hassan Shama'a, and Salah Shehade (Rantisi and Shehade, as well as Yasin, were killed in targeted assassinations). According to Hamas leaders and Israeli officials, this Islamic Centre was registered with the Israeli military authorities that administered the Gaza Strip in 1978.[32] This registration also explains a common argument made by Israeli authors that the Israeli government, in effect, "sponsored" Hamas in an effort to undermine Yasser Arafat and the PLO.[33] The spiritual-reformist organization sputtered to a halt in 1983 when Yasin was arrested for gun smuggling.[34] After that, the organization apparently focused its activities on building schools and mosques, scholarship programs for university students, and other charitable activities.

Hamas leaders have also said that around this time, Centre members began to consider an effort to launch militant activities against Israel.[35] It was not until 1988, after the beginning of the first intifada ,that the organization formally presented itself as "Hamas." Its military branch was named al-Qassam, after a Palestinian activist from

---

[31] Quoted in "Hizbullah Heroes Face the Test of Peace," *The Guardian*, June 1, 2000.

[32] For more information, see Charbel (2003). See also Israeli (1993).

[33] Charbel (2003); Israeli (1993).

[34] Charbel (2003); Israeli (1993).

[35] Charbel (2003).

the 1936 Arab Revolt. The original leader of al-Qassam was Salah She-hade; he was killed by the Israeli military in July 2002 and replaced by Muhammed Dief.[36]

Hamas derives its legitimacy from claims that it was the primary instigator of the first intifada, which began in December 1987. More likely, it managed to capitalize on this wider movement, along with Arafat and the PLO. For example, Hamas issued its charter in January 1988 and would subsequently publish 30 communiqués outlining its positions and philosophy over the subsequent eight months. These communiqués provided Hamas with the opportunity to establish itself as an Islamic alternative to the secular PLO. In addition, Hamas derives legitimacy from its local activism and charitable activities, which began in 1973 and continue today. The combination of these activities established Hamas as a credible player in the Palestinian political and militant arena.[37]

In May 1989 the Israeli government arrested Sheikh Yasin. Hamas's Gaza spokesman, Dr. Abdul Aziz Rantisi, and Yasin's acting deputy, Ismail Abu Shanab, assumed leadership of the group without much difficulty. This seamless leadership handover would eventually become a key characteristic of Hamas. Indeed, in December 1992, former Israeli Prime Minister Yitzhak Rabin deported over 400 Palestinian activists to the Marj al-Zahur camp in southern Lebanon. Although Hamas members—including Dr. Rantisi and former West Bank leader Salah Darwaza—made up a substantial portion of the deportees, Hamas continued its militant activities.[38] Some analysts argue that the deportations actually caused the organization to become more militant. Two years later, Hamas carried out its first suicide bombing when it attacked a bus in Afula, killing eight and injuring

---

[36] IDF Spokespersons Unit, "Salah Shehadeh—Portrait of a Hamas Leader," November 10, 2002, http://www.mfa.gov.il/mfa/government/communiques/2002/findings+of+the+inquiry+into+the+death+of+salah+sh.htm (as of March 10, 2006).

[37] For more information on the evolution of Hamas, see Mishal and Sela (2000).

[38] Jarbawi and Heacock (1993), pp. 32–45. See also Bedein (1999).

approximately 44 persons.[39] This attack marked the beginning of a violent campaign waged by Hamas against the Israelis, which also was intended to undermine the secular Palestinian Authority.[40]

Hamas's campaign of violence is aimed at the Israeli government and population, not the United States or other allies. Despite its opposition to the Oslo Accords, the Wye Agreement, and the Road Map for Peace, Hamas has remained aloof from bin Laden's appeal to join a global jihad, even though Sheikh Yasin expressed anger over the U.S. government's support for the government of Ariel Sharon, as well as the U.S.-led war in Iraq.[41] Indeed, many Palestinian Islamist leaders have been critical of bin Laden's use of the Palestinian cause in his rhetoric.

Ideological Foundation

Hamas's ideology, like that of many Islamic movements in the Arab world, is firmly grounded in the teachings of Egypt's Muslim Brotherhood (for more information on the Muslim Brotherhood, see the section in Chapter Three on al-Gama'a and the Egyptian Islamic Jihad). Indeed, Sheikh Yasin was the leader of the Gaza Strip branch of the Muslim Brotherhood in the 1970s and early 1980s.[42] One key ideological difference between the Brotherhood and Hamas is that Hamas believes in the use of violence in addition to passive resistance and charitable evangelism. Hamas's ideology is also strongly nationalistic, in contrast to the Brotherhood's pan-Islamism. Despite these differences, Hamas is still considered a militant faction of the wider Muslim Brotherhood movement in the West Bank and Gaza. As such, a number of Hamas's objectives—promoting traditional Islamic values and reducing Western influence—remain consistent with those of

---

[39] For more information on Hamas's terrorist activities, see the RAND Terrorism Chronology and the RAND-MIPT Terrorism Incident Database, http://www.tkb.org/Home.jsp.

[40] For more information on the conflict between the PLO and Hamas, see Saikal (1994), pp. 28–30.

[41] In October 2003, Sheikh Yasin expressed the view that the United States is lying to the world about weapons of mass destruction in Iraq and misinterprets Hamas's struggle with Israel. "Hamas Leader Talks Strategies," BBC News, October 29, 2003.

[42] Hroub (2000), pp. 32–36.

al-Qaeda and the broader Islamist movement. This belief system can be seen in an interview with Hamas's chief spokesman, Mahmud Zahhar, in 1994:

> A pebble tossed in a pool leaves a series of concentric circles. I live in the Rimal quarter. This quarter is in Gaza. Gaza is in Palestine. Palestine is in the Arab world. The Arab world is in the Islamic world. The error arises when you try to substitute a little circle for a bigger one, for instance, making the small circle of narrow nationalism a substitute for the large circle of the great community of believers.[43]

Thus, in many ways the ideological foundation of Hamas would seem to indicate a strong parallel between its interests and that of global jihadists. Hamas's leadership clearly views itself as one of many Islamist movements throughout the greater Islamic community. At the same time, the group has been reluctant to join the al-Qaeda network. Why? Hamas could benefit from al-Qaeda's support, especially given the cyclical attacks and counterattacks that have occurred during the most recent intifada. These continued operations have stretched Hamas's resources, even as Western governments have clamped down on its network of support organizations in the United States and Europe.[44] Additionally, the Israeli military has killed over 20 Hamas leaders since October 2000. Therefore, at this seemingly low point in Hamas's development, a tactical alliance with global jihadists would seem to have some appeal.

The charter published by Hamas in 1988 perhaps clarifies the group's reluctance to join the al-Qaeda network. It makes a clear distinction between global Islamist movements and the Hamas movement in Palestine:

---

[43] Quoted in "Interview with Mahmud Zahhar" (1995), p. 84.

[44] After 9/11, the U.S. government shut down a number of Hamas charities and has pressured other governments, especially the UK, to do so as well. This pressure appears to have affected Hamas because the quality of its weapons and explosive devices used shows a decrease over the past three years. In addition, Hezbollah has been attempting to augment the Palestinian uprising by providing its own weapons.

The Islamic Resistance Movement is an outstanding type of Palestinian movement. It gives its loyalty to Allah, adopts Islam as a system of life, and works toward raising the banner of Allah over every inch of Palestine. Therefore, in the shadow of Islam, it is possible for all followers of different religions to live in peace and with security over their person, property, and rights. In the absence of Islam, discord takes form, oppression and destruction are rampant, and wars and battles take place.[45]

So while al-Qaeda and Hamas have similar ideological roots, Hamas's interpretation of its role in the Islamic community is narrower and focused fundamentally on the Palestinian question. This narrow focus is an important element in Hamas's ideology. Moreover, the group has been consistent in its beliefs. Nevertheless, a shift in its focus toward the United States is possible under some circumstances, given Hamas's strategic and operational objectives.

Strategic and Operational Objectives

Hamas's fundamental objective is to establish an Islamic Palestinian state. That objective has two subsets:

- to create a separate Palestinian state
- to assert an Islamic form of government in that state.[46]

To achieve the first strategic objective, Hamas has focused its attacks on the Israeli government and citizens. A key tactic in this campaign is suicide bombings. Although Hamas was not the first Palestinian terrorist group to adopt the tactic of suicide bombings, it has perhaps been the most successful. Hamas initially conducted these attacks (the first, as mentioned above, took place in 1994) against bus passengers. Since the beginning of the Al-Aqsa intifada in 2000, Hamas has also targeted shopping malls, cafés, and pedestrian markets. Many terrorism scholars argue that Hamas uses this tactic because of

[45] Hamas charter, translated and published in the *Journal of Palestine Studies,* Vol. 22, No. 4, Summer 1993, p. 14.

[46] Hamas charter.

its shock and media value. While that argument seems logical, Hamas spokesmen continue to state that the purpose of these attacks is to retaliate for Israeli assassinations of its leaders. Hamas makes this argument not only through interviews with media representatives, but also with announcements over mosque loudspeakers in the West Bank and Gaza.

Hamas is careful to explain its motivations because the wider Palestinian community in the West Bank and Gaza has, at times, been highly critical of the use of suicide bombers. For example, after a series of suicide bombings in 1996, a public opinion poll taken in the West Bank and Gaza Strip indicated that a majority (59 percent) of Palestinians believed that the Palestinian Authority should take steps to stop the suicide attacks.[47]

Hamas's second strategic objective is the establishment of an Islamic Palestinian state. To achieve this objective, Hamas must oppose the Palestinian Authority and al-Fatah organization. The Hamas leadership, therefore, decided to abstain from Palestinian National Authority elections in 1995 and instead to focus on municipal elections in the Palestinian territories.[48] It continues to argue that it does not want a civil war in the territories and will pursue its Islamic agenda through democratic means after the creation of a Palestinian state. Yet there have been a number of clashes between Hamas and al-Fatah since 1988.[49] Similarly, Hamas has been criticized within and outside the wider Palestinian community for undermining the peace process and, with it, any chance of independence for the Palestinians. Mahmud Zahhar addressed this criticism in 1995:

> The problem is that we always use as our starting point international acceptance of power rather than the people's acceptance. What's the use of having a state that is accepted by the Arab and Western states if the people are against it? Isn't that the case of Algeria? Or Sudan? It seems that the world is looking for civil wars . . . What if the people support their state and the whole

---

[47] For more information, see Cragin and Chalk (2003).

[48] "Interview with Mahmud Zahhar." See also Mishal and Sela (2000), pp. 113–146.

[49] See, for example, Ahmad (1994); and Kattub (1992).

world is against it? Isn't the most important thing to be in har-
mony with one's people? What is the source of legitimacy—the
general will of the people or acceptance by America and the
Western powers? I leave you to choose which is preferable.[50]

Hamas, therefore, presents an interesting contradiction in strategic and operational objectives, especially when it comes to potential
shifts. On the one hand, evidence indicates that Hamas's leadership is
focused exclusively on Israel and ending the Israeli occupation of the
West Bank and Gaza Strip. This leadership appears to be pragmatic
enough to realize that widening the conflict may alienate its own support base, bring in a strong U.S. response, and harm its ability to compete politically with al-Fatah. That said, an argument could be made
that, from Hamas's point of view, the United States has not prevented
the Israeli government from pursuing a policy of targeted assassinations, bulldozing the houses of families linked to terrorist attacks, or
building the new security fence. It is also arguable that the Israeli government could not afford to continue these policies without military
and financial support from the U.S. government. So it is not unimagi-
nable that Hamas could shift some attention to U.S. targets, however
unlikely that may be.

Environmental Factors
Several environmental factors influence Hamas's choice of tactics,
targets, and strategic objectives. The primary influence, as discussed
above, appears to be its relationship with local Palestinian communities and, to some extent, the Palestinian diaspora. But there are other
important factors. For example, during the Gulf War, Arafat chose to
side with Saddam Hussein. Hamas leaders, in contrast, openly criticized Saddam's occupation of Kuwait. As a result, Hamas received
an influx of monetary support from charities and individuals in the
Gulf States in the early 1990s.[51] Though not rising to the level of state

---

[50] "Interview with Mahmud Zahhar."

[51] For examples of such reports, see Ramati (1993), p. 2; and Emerson, (1992), p. 27.

sponsorship (as in the case of Lebanese Hezbollah), these funds helped Hamas sustain its charitable and military activities.

More important is the Hamas relationship with al-Fatah and the Palestinian Authority. At the beginning of the second intifada, Palestinian secular and religious terrorist groups formed a unified command to help coordinate activities against Israel.[52] This relationship, more than any other, exemplifies the pragmatic nature of Hamas. Though it is an ideologically based group, it is willing to cooperate with potential antagonists if it will help further the group's long-term strategic or short-term operational objectives. Notably, in the spring of 2004 the cooperation between Hamas, al-Fatah, and the al-Aqsa Martyrs' Brigades (a terrorist group linked to al-Fatah) became strained. In part, this was the result of Hamas's declaration that it was ready to govern in Gaza after a unilateral Israeli withdrawal. Similarly, the al-Aqsa Martyrs' Brigade has begun to challenge the old power structure within al-Fatah. Internecine violence broke out in July 2004, which included kidnappings and violent riots in Ramallah as well as in the Gaza Strip.

Epilogue

The research for this study was conducted prior to the January 2006 Palestinian elections in which Hamas—or more correctly, Hamas's Change and Reform Party—won an outright majority (74 out of 132 seats) in the Palestinian Legislative Council. In those elections, Hamas's platform focused primarily on internal issues and corruption within Fatah and the Palestinian Authority. Indeed, since winning, Hamas leaders have continued to argue that they want to introduce domestic economic and political reforms before returning to the issue of the peace process. That said, international pressure may force Hamas to address the peace process before the group would prefer.

For the most part, the analysis provided in this chapter has held true even given those elections. Hamas's leaders have continued to balance an internal religious agenda with a pragmatic approach. For example, Hamas's leaders have made an effort to reach out to Fatah to

---

[52] For past coordination, see leaflets republished in Mishal and Aharoni (2004).

form a more cooperative government. Hamas also appointed an internal party personality, Ismail Haniyeh, as prime minister, and Abed al-Azia Duaik as the head of the Palestinian Legislative Council.[53] (The political head of the organization, Khaled Mashaal, is based in Damascus.) Duaik, in particular, is a well-respected academic in the West Bank. Thus, his appointment indicates a signal on the part of Hamas that its religious reforms are likely to be secondary to economic reforms at least in the early phases of its leadership. Fatah's leaders, for the most part, have rejected Hamas's efforts toward cooperation. The al-Aqsa Martyrs' Brigades and the Palestinian Islamic Jihad have continued their terrorist attacks, although at a reduced tempo.

Similarly, al-Qaeda's deputy leader, Ayman al-Zawahiri, released a statement in which he warns Hamas that "power is not an end in itself, but simply a stage on the path of implementing Sharia law" and called on the organization to continue the fight against Israel. In a public interview, Hamas's political leader Mashaal said the movement had "its own vision" and did not need al-Qaeda's advice.[54] A statement by a radical Kuwaiti cleric, Sheikh Hamed al-Ali, distributed to jihadi forums suggests that Hamas should hold steadfast to Islamic law, not deviate to fall into the "mirage of peace" and reject previous agreements signed by the Palestinian Authority. Sheikh al-Ali refers to three traps in which he believes the West and Israel want Hamas to be ensnared, including substitution of Islamic law for treaties such as Oslo and Camp David, laying down arms and then being led to the "slaughter of humiliation," and becoming a "toy" in the hands of the White House, the Kremlin, the European Parliament, and the "Enslavement Nations" (United Nations).[55] In another posting, Abu Yehia al-Libi, an

---

[53] Duaik was deported in 1992, along with 415 other individuals associated with various Palestinian terrorist groups. He returned to the West Bank and Gaza Strip approximately one year later but apparently did not actively participate in Hamas activities or decisionmaking.

[54] "Hamas Rejects al-Qaeda's Support," BBC News, March 5, 2006, http://news.bbc.co.uk/2/hi/middle_east/4776578.stm (as of April 23, 2006).

[55] SITE Institute, "A Statement from Sheikh Hamed al-Ali Addressing the Core of the Problem Between Ayman al-Zawahiri, Hamas, and the Chechen Mujahideen," March 8, 2006, http://siteinstitute.org/bin/articles.cgi?ID=publications154706&Category=publications&Subcategory=0 (as of April 23, 2006).

al-Qaeda operative who escaped with three others from the U.S. prison in Bagran, Afghanistan, in July 2005, writes of four "perversions and corrupt behaviors" that Hamas has manifested, including entering into an "infidel legislative council" and not making Islamic law paramount to all other concerns.[56]

The jihadist criticism of Hamas, as Stephen Ulph notes, lays bare the rift between the global jihadist movement, with its supra-national goals, and local groups and organizations that have more limited objectives and are open to tactical use of the political process. It has also exposed the fear that political progress, however limited, will compete with the jihadist program.[57] For the present, it appears that Hamas sees its own interests as separate from those of al-Qaeda and of the wider global jihadist movement.

---

[56] SITE Institute, "Hamas and the Impending Exposure by Abu Yehia al-Libi," April 17, 2006, http://www.siteinstitute.org.

[57] Ulph (2006).

CHAPTER THREE

Other Islamist Groups Outside the al-Qaeda Network

The Armed Islamic Group (GIA)

Terrorism and revolutionary violence have played a significant role in the modern history of Algeria. From 1954 to 1962, the Front de Libération Nationale (FLN) fought against the French colonial presence in this country and used terrorist attacks both in Algeria and in France as part of this war. Although the FLN was a predominantly nationalist organization, it used religious rhetoric in an effort to mobilize support. Once it came to power in Algeria, it began to restrict expressions of political Islam. Approximately 30 years later, an Islamist revolutionary organization, the Armed Islamic Group (GIA), would institute a campaign against the Algerian government now controlled by the FLN.

The GIA began in response to the Algerian government's decision to nullify the 1992 popular elections, which would have brought the Muslim party, the Islamic Salvation Front (FIS), into power. The FIS had gained momentum in the period between 1988 and 1992, partly in response to local factors and partly as a result of a wider Islamist movement across North Africa. The FIS established a social base in such urban centers as Algiers, Blida, Oran, Annaba, and Mostaghanem. In fact, it was the populations of these cities that rioted against the established order in October 1988 and contributed to the success of the FIS in the 1992 elections.[1]

---

[1] For more information see, Yaphe (2002), Chapter 2.

The GIA, in contrast to the FIS, was based in the countryside and has been one of the most extreme Islamist terrorist groups in history, often using tactics more brutal than those employed by some of the most savage terrorist organizations operating today. This extreme violence alienated the GIA from what could have been a wider popular base in both rural and urban areas and in recent years has caused a significant decline in its ability to conduct attacks both in Algeria and abroad.

Ideological Foundation

The ideological foundations of the GIA are similar to those of other Islamists emerging in the late 1980s. Its leaders were influenced by Egyptian Islamist theoreticians, such as Sayyid Qutb, and they saw the establishment of an Islamic government in Algeria as their primary goal.[2] Before the 1992 elections, Islamists might have thought that this revolution could be accomplished peacefully. Yet the military crackdown that prevented the FIS from coming into power ruled this possibility out.

GIA leaders believed that only an Islamic state could successfully take care of its citizens' spiritual and material wealth. Moreover, to achieve this revolution, political activities needed to be accompanied by violence. Indeed, many of the group's initial leaders and members had just returned from the Afghan war. These individuals had received a significant amount of religious indoctrination and training in the methods of guerrilla warfare. They had also witnessed the power of jihad to bring down even a "superpower," the Soviet Union.[3] Thus,

---

[2]   See Kepel (2002), pp. 159–173. Sayyid Qutb was one of the most significant figures in the development of modern radical Islamism. While in prison, before his execution by President Nasser's government, he wrote the influential book, *Ma'alim fi'l-tariq* ("Signposts for the Road"), a manifesto drawn from his vast, multivolume commentary on the Quran, *Fi zilal al-Qur'an* ("In the Shade of the Quran"). Qutb argued that the Muslim world was in a state of *jahiliyyah,* the ignorance that prevailed before Muhammad's revelation, and that the governments of Muslim countries were apostate and therefore illegitimate. He advocated the seizure of power by a revolutionary vanguard that would then impose Islamization from above.

[3]   Kepel (2002).

it was logical that their ideology would be rooted in beliefs similar to those of other returning jihadist fighters, such as members of al-Gama'a al-Islamiyya in Egypt or the Islamic Army of Aden Abyan in Yemen.

Until 1998, the GIA was the most powerful and active Islamic extremist group in Algeria. At that point, a splinter organization, the Salafist Group for Preaching and Combat (GSPC), eclipsed the GIA, as discussed in the first volume of this study as a result of popular revulsion at the GIA's use of extreme violence against civilians. The GSPC eventually joined the al-Qaeda network, whereas the GIA has remained largely independent and has relegated itself in recent years to conducting small-scale attacks inside Algeria.

Strategic and Operational Objectives

Throughout the 1990s, the GIA waged what many have considered to be an insurgent campaign against the Algerian government, using rural, mountainous hideouts to conduct strikes against Algerian police and security forces. The group complemented its rural insurgency with an urban terrorist campaign that focused on assassinating key government, intellectual, and cultural figures in Algeria, in addition, bomb attacks in restaurants and against other civilian targets.[4] In what some would describe as an act of desperation, the GIA turned to conducting large-scale civilian massacres. In some cases, the GIA conducted massacres of whole villages using mostly knives and machetes, in an attempt to force loyalty and support from Algerian Muslims. The massacres appeared as random acts of violence in which women and children were brutally killed. In fact, the GIA was targeting specific villages, families, and communities that it believed were providing support to rival Islamist factions.[5] The GIA was trying to send a message that if Algerian civilians did not provide support they would suffer the same fate as the villagers who had been massacred.

---

[4]   Kepel (2002), p. 70.

[5]   Kalyvas (1999), p. 244.

The GIA also adopted what one scholar calls an "apocalyptic" outlook that embodied the *takfir* ideology,[6] essentially the condemnation as apostates worthy of death of those Muslims who do not agree with the radicals' interpretation of Islam.[7] Eventually this tactic, in conjunction with other factors, such as a reconciliation program for Islamic militants instituted by Algerian President Abdelaziz Bouteflika in July 1999 (aimed at trying to contain the insurgency by offering amnesty in exchange for militants laying down their weapons), resulted in the GIA's decline.[8]

The Algerian regime was not the GIA's only target. The GIA began establishing cells in Europe and Africa in order to attack its other primary adversary, France. The group held the French responsible for propping up the Algerian regime and resented the influence of French culture on Algerian society, which it viewed as harmful to Islam and the Arabic language and culture.[9] As a result, the GIA waged a terrorist campaign inside France—primarily through these external networks—and relied heavily on the large Algerian expatriate population in France to provide support.

Some of the more noteworthy attacks inside Algeria include the massacre at Sidi Youssef in September 1997 in which 63 civilians were killed in a relatively protected area (Sidi Youssef is a neighborhood of Beni-Messous, an outlying suburb of Algiers which is home to a large military base. The security forces did not arrive until several hours after the attack, despite being stationed nearby).[10] In January 1998, the GIA conducted four separate civilian massacres in which over 400

---

[6] According to Reuven Paz, the *takfir* ideology is "the perception of the secular Muslim society as heretical, with the majority of the blame placed on the rulers of the Arabic and Islamic states." See Paz (2000).

[7] Takeyh (2003), p. 70.

[8] Takeyh (2003), p. 72.

[9] Takeyh (2003), p. 63.

[10] Takeyh (2003), p. 63.

people were killed in one night, raising the profile of these massacres with Western governments, which vowed to provide assistance to the Algerian government to stop the attacks.[11]

The GIA also threatened attacks against foreigners inside Algeria in 1993, warning them to leave or suffer the consequences. To date, the GIA is believed to be responsible for over 100 deaths of foreigners in Algeria, mostly Europeans.[12] One of the group's most shocking attacks was the killing of seven French monks in May 1996 after they were abducted from their monastery.[13] Outside Algeria, the GIA conducted a series of bombings in 1995 against the Paris metro, resulting in eight deaths and hundreds of wounded. The group also hijacked an Air France flight in Marseille in 1994 and bombed a Paris market in 1995, resulting in four deaths.[14] Notably, the GIA has not conducted any attacks outside Algeria since 1996.

Environmental Factors

The GIA sealed its own fate through the use of tactics inside Algeria that ultimately alienated any potential support base, both by conducting a campaign of civilian massacres and by attacking small business owners and the middle class—the economic backbone of the Muslim community in Algeria.[15] Unlike the GSPC, which splintered from the GIA in 1998 over its use of civilian massacres and its battlefield losses, the GIA never established a solid relationship with al-Qaeda outside the few members who were veterans of the Afghan war and who knew or had met bin Laden in that context. Although bin Laden took a special interest in supporting the Algerian extremists at the beginning of their campaign—probably because they contributed large numbers of

---

[11] "Hundreds Murdered in Widespread Algeria Attacks," International Policy Institute for Counter-Terrorism, January 6, 1998, http://www.ict.org.il.

[12] "Hundreds Murdered in Widespread Algeria Attacks."

[13] "Armed Islamic Group Attacks from 1998–Present," International Policy Institute for Counter-Terrorism, http://www.ict.org.il.

[14] "Armed Islamic Group," in U.S. Department of State (2003b); "Groupe Islamique Armee" (2003).

[15] Takeyh (2003), p. 70.

fighters to the Afghan war and were trying to establish an Islamic government in Algeria—he eventually turned his back on them because of their campaign of civilian massacres.[16]

The spiritual advisor for the GIA was Abu Qatada, an al-Qaeda leader now in British custody. Qatada issued a fatwa for the group in the mid-1990s authorizing attacks against women and children,[17] but he later denied he had done so after it became clear that many in the larger Islamic extremist world did not approve of such methods. The GSPC vowed not to attack civilians and was able to gain a following among Islamist supporters and disgruntled GIA members who had been alienated by the GIA's tactics.[18]

Al-Gama'a al-Islamiyya

The Egyptian al-Gama'a al-Islamiyya, an offshoot of the Egyptian Muslim Brotherhood, began in the early 1970s, not as an organized terrorist group, but as a student movement in Egyptian universities and prisons.[19] Although Muslim Brotherhood members assassinated Egyptian Prime Minister Nuqrashi Pasha in 1948 and attempted to kill President Gamal Abdel Nasser in 1954, the strategy and tactics of the organization evolved as it reached an informal accommodation with the Egyptian power structure. Al-Gama'a leaders rejected the Muslim Brotherhood's gradualist approach to change and instead based their ideology on principles enunciated by Sayyid Qutb.[20]

---

[16] Knights (2003).

[17] Michael Isikoff, Daniel Klaidman, and Evan Thomas, "Al Qaeda's Summer Plans for Americans," *Newsweek,* June 2, 2003, http://www.stevequayle.com/News.alert/03_Unrest/030526.al-Qaeda.summer.html (as of March 10, 2006); Terence McKenna, "Interview with Abu Qatada," CBC News, June 2002, http://www.cbc.ca/national/news/recruiters/qatada_interview.html (as of March 10, 2006).

[18] "Groupe Salafiste pour la Predication et le Combat (GSPC)" (2003).

[19] "Al-Gama'a al-Islamiyya (GAI)" (2003).

[20] "Al-Gama'a al-Islamiyya (GAI)" (2003).

Al-Gama'a began recruiting its mid-level leaders from the ranks of unemployed university students angry about the lack of economic opportunity, while poorer individuals in the southern rural regions of Assiut and Minya populated the group's rank and file.[21] Although the group had an early leadership structure that allowed it to make quick decisions, al-Gama'a ranks were loosely organized, allowing for maximum operational secrecy and effectiveness. After Sadat's assassination, the Egyptian government launched a massive crackdown on Islamic extremists and their supporters and jailed a large number of those believed to subscribe to extremist views. As a result, terrorist violence in Egypt was greatly reduced during the 1980s as many of the Islamic extremists who managed to escape imprisonment fled to Afghanistan to participate in the jihad against the Soviet Union. In Afghanistan, many of al-Gama'a's future leaders gained expertise in guerrilla warfare and terrorist tactics. Those same individuals returned to Egypt in the late 1980s ready to apply what they had learned to their struggle against the government of Hosni Mubarak.

Ideological Foundation

The ideological foundations of al-Gama'a are very much intertwined with the general emergence of political Islam in modern Egypt. Most scholars date a resurgence of political Islam in the Arab world to the crisis of secular nationalism following the 1967 Six Day War.[22] Yet the ideological roots of this political philosophy can be traced back to the fourteenth-century philosopher Ibn Taymiyya, who postulated that Muslims did not owe allegiance to impious rulers. Ibn Taymiyya's work is significant because his philosophy influenced the avatars of such modern radical Islamists as Hasan al-Banna, the founder of

---

[21] "Al Gama'a al-Islamiyya," International Policy Institute for Counterterrorism, http://www.ict.org.il/inter_ter/orgdet.cfm?orgid=12 (as of March 10, 2006).

[22] See, for example, Kepel (2002). See also Abu-Rabi (1996).

the Muslim Brotherhood;[23] Sayyid Qutb; and Maulana Abu al-Al'a Mawdudi.[24]

The "blind sheikh" Omar Abd al-Rahman and his followers represent another cleavage in the Egyptian Muslim Brotherhood. He eventually became the spiritual leader of al-Gama'a, providing the group with religious guidance and issuing fatwas when necessary. Abd al-Rahman was the ultimate decisionmaker on issues of strategy, and he encouraged members to use terrorist tactics to overthrow the Egyptian regime, even though he spent most of his time behind prison walls. Abd al-Rahman was imprisoned by the Egyptian government in 1981 for conspiring to kill President Anwar Sadat, released in 1984, and then jailed again in 1989 for incitement to riot. In 1990, he went to the United States to spread his message to Muslims in New Jersey but was jailed in 1995 for his involvement in the 1993 World Trade Center bombing. He remains in prison today.[25]

Strategic and Operational Objectives

Al-Gama'a reemerged in the early 1990s with a renewed sense of purpose after the return of its members from the Afghan jihad. Al-Gama'a leaders were energized by what they believed was a moral victory of Islamism in Afghanistan, and they were convinced that they could accomplish in Egypt what the mujahideen had achieved in Afghanistan by ousting the "illegitimate" governing power. As a result, al-Gama'a put its theories into practice in Egypt by attacking a wide variety of targets—Coptic Christians, banks, police, politicians, tourists, and

---

[23] Ibn Taymiyya's work was not revived until the Egyptian scholar Jamal al-din al-Afghani (1838–1897) began to express reservations about nationalism and modernity in the late nineteenth century and used Ibn Taymiyya's work to do so. Al-Afghani influenced later writings by Rashid Rida (1865–1935) along the same philosophical lines, which then influenced the following twentieth century political thinkers: Hasan al-Banna, Sayyid Qutb, and Muhammad al-Ghazali. Maulana Abu al-Al'a Mawdudi, a contemporary of Qutb from India, was also influenced independently by Ibn Taymiyya's work. Unlike his Arab contemporaries, he argued strongly that pan-Arabism was anti-Islamic. Mawdudi's work influenced Osama bin Laden and other pan-Islamic militants.

[24] Hallaq (1993); Black (2001), p. 155.

[25] Katzman (2005).

the media—with the goal of undermining Egyptian state power, secular institutions, and the economy and creating the perception that the Egyptian government was not able to protect its citizens.[26]

Two interrelated major splits developed over strategy within the organization. The first split occurred following the 1997 attack against Western tourists at Luxor; the second concerned whether the group should ally itself with bin Laden and al-Qaeda. The Luxor operation was allegedly organized by a group of renegade al-Gama'a members without the authorization of the group's leadership. The operation was designed to embarrass the Egyptian government by demonstrating that it was unable to protect foreigners. The al-Gama'a operatives who planned the attack were also hoping to get a boost in popular support from the success of the operation. Instead, there was widespread popular outrage over the incident, causing the group's historical leadership—who were imprisoned in Egypt—to call for a ceasefire to discuss the group's future direction and to repair existing disputes over strategy. Most of the group's active operational leaders were running the organization from outside Egypt.

The second split occurred shortly after al-Gama'a's call for a ceasefire when the group's operational leader, Rifa'i Taha Musa, signed bin Laden's 1998 declaration of war against "Jews and Crusaders."[27] Al-Gama'a was weakened both operationally and financially by the aftereffects of the Luxor attack and needed a boost to continue functioning as a viable terrorist organization. It is unclear whether Taha Musa actually agreed with bin Laden's views, wanted to seize power in al-Gama'a, or simply saw the financial and organizational benefits that al-Gama'a's rival terrorist group, the Egyptian Islamic Jihad (EIJ), reaped from making the decision to join al-Qaeda. Whatever the reason, Taha Musa courted bin Laden by making trips to Afghanistan and even appeared sitting next to him and EIJ leader al-Zawahiri in a videotape released

---

[26] "Al Gama'a al-Islamiyya," in U.S. Department of State (2003b).

[27] "Al Gama'a al-Islamiyya," in U.S. Department of State (2003b).

in September 2000 that threatened U.S. interests.[28] Nevertheless, Taha Musa was unable to recruit many of his cadres to support bin Laden and conduct attacks against the United States. Al-Gama'a witnessed how the EIJ had suffered significant setbacks because of its decision to join al-Qaeda. The group chose to go underground until it regained its strength. However, there are still al-Gama'a members who supported Taha Musa's desire to join al-Qaeda in attacking the United States, and those individuals could still participate in terrorist operations against U.S. targets.[29]

The historical leadership decided to call a unilateral ceasefire in 1999 once the group's spiritual leader, Abd al-Rahman, agreed, but this was done without the approval of the external leadership.[30] Despite Abd al-Rahman's cancellation of the ceasefire in June 2000, al-Gama'a has not conducted a terrorist attack either inside or outside Egypt since August 1998, and some suggest the historical leadership has struck a deal with the Egyptian government to lay down its arms in exchange for their release from prison.[31] In March 2002, the historical leaders issued a statement renouncing the use of violence. However, the external leaders have not appeared to abandon their commitment to jihad.[32]

Al-Gama'a has never attacked a U.S. target but has repeatedly threatened to attack Americans.[33] The group's most noteworthy attacks include the 1995 failed assassination attempt on President Mubarak in Addis Ababa, a 1995 car bombing in Rijeka, Croatia, that killed one

---

[28] Robert Windrem and Charlene Gubash, "Al-Zawahiri Statements Often Precede Attacks," NBC News, February 25, 2004. http://msnbc.msn.com/id/4358624 (as of March 10, 2006).

[29] "Al Gama'a al-Islamiyya," in U.S. Department of State (2003b).

[30] "Al Gama'a al-Islamiyya," in U.S. Department of State (2003b).

[31] "Al Gama'a al-Islamiyya," in U.S. Department of State (2003b).

[32] "Al Gama'a al-Islamiyya," in U.S. Department of State (2003b).

[33] "Al Gama'a al-Islamiyya," in U.S. Department of State (2003b).

and injured 29, a 1996 attack on tourists outside the Europa Hotel in Cairo that killed 18 foreign tourists, and the 1997 civilian massacre at Luxor in which 58 foreign tourists were killed.[34]

Environmental Factors

In the early 1990s, al-Gama'a was able to wage a sustained terrorist campaign, conducting attacks in multiple sectors and striking at high-profile targets. Because al-Gama'a appeared to many observers in the early to mid-1990s to pose a real threat to the regime, President Mubarak decided to use a consistently heavy hand against the group. The state of emergency that Mubarak instituted when he took office in 1981 allowed him to deploy an array of repressive measures against al-Gama'a to curb the threat, including detaining without representation individuals suspected of terrorist activity.[35] The measures taken by the state security services also succeeded in widening the splits within the leadership and driving down the group's threat potential.

Al-Wa'ad

Al-Wa'ad ("the Promise") is a shadowy Islamic extremist organization based in Egypt about which little is known. According to press reports of the trials of al-Wa'ad members in Egypt, the group formed in 1996. It is rather small and is made up largely of Egyptian citizens with dual nationality, including Russians (Chechens), Dutch, Germans, Canadians, and reportedly even Americans. The group was accused in a 2001 indictment of raising money for international jihadist causes, including Palestinian and Chechen groups, suggesting that al-Wa'ad subscribes to a pan-Islamic agenda.[36] Some of the militants arrested were businessmen or persons with a university education, a finding

---

[34] "Al-Gama'a al-Islamiyya (GAI)" (2003).

[35] "Egypt Imposes Another 3-Year State of Emergency," CBC News, February 25, 2003, http://www.cbc.ca/stories/2003/02/24/Egyptemergency030224 (as of March 10, 2006).

[36] "The Difficult Future of Holy Struggle," *The Economist,* January 31, 2002, http://economist.com/displayStory.cfm?story_id=966016 (as of March 10, 2006).

consistent with what we believe is the membership of other Egyptian extremist groups.[37] Much of the financing for the group's activities allegedly came from members who owned their own companies.[38] The Egyptian authorities, as well as various newspaper articles, have linked the group to al-Qaeda, but Western diplomats have reportedly questioned these links.[39] Al-Wa'ad has not plotted any attacks against U.S. targets thus far.[40] According to the trial testimony, the group was created from a fatwa issued by two prominent Egyptian clerics, Sheikh Fawzi al-Saeed of the al-Tawhid mosque and Nashaat Ibrahim of the Kabul mosque, both in Cairo, who are believed to be the key leaders of the group.

Strategic and Operational Objectives

Al-Wa'ad appears to have taken up the mantle of both the EIJ and al-Gama'a. Starting in November 2001, an Egyptian military court tried at least 94 al-Wa'ad members in 2001 and 2002 for attempting to overthrow President Mubarak and threatening the state's security. The initiation of this trial followed a major crackdown on extremists by the Egyptian government after the September 11 attacks. The trial, which concluded in September 2002, resulted in reduced sentences of 2–15 years for more than 40 defendants believed to have played a key role in terrorist planning.[41] The rest of the individuals who were initially indicted were acquitted and released. Although the arrests may have eliminated or reduced the potential al-Wa'ad threat, some press reports indicate that at least two new terrorist groups have formed in Egypt as

---

[37] Khaled Dawoud, "Trying Times for Islamists," *Al-Ahram Weekly* Online, January 10–16 2002, http://weekly.ahram.org.eg/2002/568/eg6.htm (as of March 10, 2006).

[38] "Egypt: Trial of Al-W'ad Group Adjourned," Cairo MENA, FBIS AFP20020106000116, January 16, 2002.

[39] Karl Vick, "Political Repression Spawns Extremism in Arab World," *The Washington Post,* October 30, 2001, http://www.commondreams.org/headlines01/1030-03.htm (as of March 16, 2006).

[40] "Egypt: Verdicts Issued Against Defendants in Tanzim al-Wa'd case," MENA, FBIS GMP20020909000103, September 9, 2002.

[41] "Egypt: Verdicts Issued . . . ."

of this writing—the Jihad Group for the Victory of Muslims at Home and Abroad; and Jundullah, a faction of EIJ.[42]

Al-Wa'ad militants were reportedly organizing attacks against public buildings in Egypt, Muslim and Christian clergymen, artists, writers, and foreigners in Egypt, as well as plotting to assassinate Mubarak.[43] The individuals whom al-Wa'ad was targeting for assassination were all known for their secular views and opposition to Islamic extremism.[44] According to trial testimony, two of the militants put on trial in Egypt after September 11 were trained as pilots in Texas. No specific evidence was revealed, however, that they planned to use their expertise in a terrorist attack. At least one operative from Dagestan was considered to be an explosives expert who trained other members of the group. Militants from al-Wa'ad also reportedly traveled overseas and trained with other extremists to apply the skills they learned to their jihad in Egypt.[45]

South Africa: People Against Gangsterism and Drugs (PAGAD)

PAGAD was formed in 1996 as a Muslim community group fighting drugs and violence in South Africa.[46] By early 1998, the group had also become violently antigovernment and anti-Western. It is closely associated, if not intertwined, with the South African Islamic group Qibla. PAGAD uses several front names, including Muslims Against Global

---

[42] Abduh Zaynah, "Egyptian Authorities Reportedly Apprehend New Fundamentalist Group," Al-Sharq al-Aswat, FBIS GMP20030828000164, August 28, 2003.

[43] Dawoud, "Trying Times . . . ."

[44] Dawoud, "Trying Times . . . ."

[45] Dawoud, "Trying Times . . . ."

[46] According to the 2001 South African census, there are approximately 665,000 Muslims in South Africa, or 1.5 percent of the population (2.5 percent of the population is of South Asian origin, the ethnic background of most of South Africa's Muslims), making Islam the third-largest religion in South Africa (after Protestant and Catholic). Thus, Muslims are a significant part of South African society—a central place they have occupied historically in South Africa's development (CIA, 2004).

Oppression and Muslims Against Illegitimate Leaders, when launching anti-Western protests and campaigns.[47] PAGAD operates mainly in the Cape Town area, South Africa's foremost tourist venue.[48] While PAGAD's and Qibla's overall strength was last estimated (in 2001) at several hundred members, PAGAD's G-Force (Gun Force), which operates in small cells, probably contains fewer than 50 members and is the PAGAD element believed to be responsible for carrying out acts of terrorism.[49] PAGAD has not been active since 2002.

Ideological Foundation

PAGAD and its ally Qibla, founded and led by Achmat Cassiem since 1979,[50] advocate a greater political voice for South African Muslims.[51] Though distinct, the two groups are often treated as one by the media. According to an extensive study by the Centre for the Study of Violence and Reconciliation in South Africa, PAGAD originated

> in a network of hitherto disparate and isolated anti-drug, anti-crime groups and neighborhood watches frustrated by their inability to tackle problems whose roots extended far beyond their individual localities.

While its ideology was "predominantly, but by no means exclusively Muslim" from the beginning,

> PAGAD's development . . . cannot be seen simply as the unfolding of a master plan conceived and executed by a small group of Islamic radicals. Rather it has to be viewed as the outcome of the

---

[47] U.S. Department of State (2003b); Potomac Institute for Policy Studies, TerrorismCentral, http://www.terrorismcentral.com (both as of March 16, 2006).

[48] Potomac Institute for Policy Studies.

[49] U.S. Department of State (2003b).

[50] Qibla was founded in 1979 and inspired by the Iranian Revolution. The group's aim was either to defend and promote Islam in South Africa or to establish an Islamic state in South Africa. Cassiem was vocal in the struggle against apartheid and was imprisoned at on Robben Island at age 17.

[51] "Appendix C: Background Information on Other Terrorist Groups," in U.S. Department of State (2003b).

interplay between many internal and external forces—of action by PAGAD and its constituent elements and reaction by the State and its agencies in the specific political, social and economic context of the Western Cape.

PAGAD is perceived by the South African state and the United States as "an urban terror group threatening not just the State's monopoly on the use of coercive force but the very foundations of constitutional democracy."[52]

Led by a national coordinator, Abdus Salaam Ebrahim, PAGAD and Qibla view the secular South African government as a threat to Islamic values.[53] According to one study, PAGAD's ideology stems from "belief in essentialist notions of a historical truth encapsulated in Islam . . . a number of stands converge at this level without any coherent distinction between them, and one can simultaneously belong to more than one stream"—indicating an organization that has common interests but not necessarily homogenous beliefs. It desires to "protect the new South Africa from the 'scourge' of democracy and liberalism which is essentially a Western principle." Its leader maintains that Islam is "the true meaning of the democratic principle of 'the people shall govern.'"[54]

PAGAD states that it was originally founded to "eradicate gangsterism and drugs from our society, thereby restoring morality and social order to the communities that have lost hope of combating this lethal social evil."[55] Over time, however, its outlook has evolved to become sharply antigovernment and anti–United States, with deep Islamic influences. Authorities suspect that in addition to Qibla's initial Iranian inspiration, PAGAD has ties to Islamist extremists in the

---

[52] Dixon and Johns (2001).

[53] Potomac Institute for Policy Studies; "Appendix C: Background Information on Other Terrorist Groups."

[54] "Organisation and Structure of Pagad," PAGAD, South Africa: UniTech—University of Zululand, online at http://www.duc-uz.co.za/PAGAD%5B2%5D.htm.

[55] PAGAD: http://www.pagad.co.za/nethome.htm (no longer available).

Middle East.[56] This suspicion goes hand in hand with a growing belief that Saudi-financed imams were active in Cape Town's mosques, propagating and inspiring militant Islam. However, they do not appear to have made widespread inroads. As Morrison and Lyman stated in early 2004, there "is little evidence of other terrorist sympathies among South Africa's Muslim population."[57] Nevertheless, a number of South African academic experts have made accusations that PAGAD and Qibla are affiliated with al-Qaeda. This has been difficult to prove, although Cassiem did maintain in an October 2001 interview that he had recruited—via Muslims Against Illegitimate Leaders—"1000 young volunteers to fight in Afghanistan."[58] While it is doubtful that this statement is true, it does reinforce the possibility that Qibla and PAGAD may look beyond their immediate interests in the Western Cape and South Africa to be part of the global Islamist struggle.

Strategic and Operational Objectives
When PAGAD was first formed in early 1996, it worked with the South African authorities to combat organized crime and narcotics in the Western Cape area. However, following a number of increasingly violent attacks perpetrated by PAGAD in late 1996, the South African government outlawed the group. There is evidence to suggest that PAGAD underwent a split in October 1996, similar to that between the "Provisional" Irish Republican Army (IRA), which wanted to abandon violence and return to peaceful means of struggle against the British, and the "Real" IRA, which wanted to continue the violence. In January 1997, three of PAGAD's founding members, Farouk Jaffer, Nadthmie Edries, and Mohammed Ali "Phantom" Parker, left the main organization and registered PAGAD as a nonprofit commu-

---

[56] Although increasingly anti-Western and anti-U.S., PAGAD had not been designated as a foreign terrorist organization by the U.S. government as of 2003 (U.S. Department of State, 2003a). However, PAGAD was listed on the Terrorist Exclusion List in 2001 (U.S. Department of State, 2002b).

[57] Lyman and Morrison (2004), p. 82.

[58] "Islam—A South African Perspective: An Interview with Achmat Cassiem," Carte Blanche MNET, October 1, 2001, produced by Sophia Phirippides, http://www.mnet.co.za/CarteBlanche/Display/Display.asp?Id=1808.

nity organization under South African law. The remaining members of PAGAD effectively became Qibla's strong-arm wing through the G-Force. Indeed, Parker complained that PAGAD had been "taken over by Qibla" in the months leading up to this split.[59] Currently, PAGAD's Web site appears to be that of a community-empowering organization, with no mention of Islam.

This split could explain why the two factions of PAGAD appear to have two very different targeting practices: that of assassinating drug dealers and crime lords, and that of bombing symbols of globalization. Indeed, the official PAGAD has condemned attacks on people unconnected with drugs and gangsterism but has also stated time and again that the South African government's failure to curb drug dealing and crime is the entire driving force behind PAGAD's actions.

In addition to the few hundred estimated criminal victims of PAGAD's targeted violence, PAGAD's bombing targets have included South African authorities, moderate Muslims, synagogues, gay nightclubs, tourist attractions, and Western-associated restaurants. PAGAD is believed to have carried out the August 25, 1998, bombing of the Cape Town Planet Hollywood restaurant. PAGAD members are also thought responsible for nine additional bombings in the Cape Town area in 2000.[60] These nine bombings resulted in some 30 injuries. Of the nine attacks, five were car bombings that targeted South African authorities, public places, and restaurants and nightclubs with Western associations. According to the U.S. government, these attacks included larger bombs triggered by more sophisticated remote detonation devices than had been previously witnessed in South Africa. Police arrested several suspects affiliated with PAGAD in November 2000 and confiscated several pipe bombs. There were no further bombings or inci-

---

[59] "Organisation and Structure of Pagad."

[60] "Appendix C: Background Information on Other Terrorist Groups"; Potomac Institute for Policy Studies.

dents after the arrests.[61] Notably, PAGAD did not take credit for these attacks and, instead, maintained that the bombings were actually the responsibility of the South African police.[62]

In early 2002, PAGAD was suspected of being behind a bomb attack at the Cape Town International Airport, which coincided with the trial of two of its members on a charge of illegal possession of explosives. This followed a similar attack, on January 12, at the courthouse where the trial was slated to begin. Although PAGAD denied any involvement in the incident, it was the second time the trial had been postponed on account of bomb attacks.[63]

Environmental Factors

Since 2001, PAGAD's activities have been severely curtailed by law enforcement and prosecutorial actions against leading members of the organization. There were no urban terror incidents from September 2000 through 2001, compared to nine bombings in the Western Cape in 2000 that caused serious injuries, and a total of 189 bomb attacks since 1996. Although South Africa undertook a number of counterterrorist actions during 2001–2002 in support of the war on terrorism,[64] Morrison has warned that "the South African government has been too ill-informed, and ill equipped, to bring effective controls upon radical Islam within its borders."[65]

---

[61] "Africa Overview," U.S. Department of State (2001).

[62] This statement was made on PAGAD's Web site, http://www.pagad.co.za (no longer available). It should be noted that, in the past, the apartheid government frequently carried out "pseudo-operations" involving government-initiated attacks made to appear to be those of the liberation movements in a number of Southern African countries.

[63] Information about these and other terrorist attacks can be found in the RAND-MIPT Terrorism Incident Database, http://www.tkb.org/Home.jsp.

[64] South Africa enacted legislation establishing a financial intelligence unit, which targets money laundering. A draft antiterrorism law was approved by the cabinet and informally submitted to the Parliament. South Africa provided support to the United States by extraditing a member of the Symbionese Liberation Army. South Africa is also a party to five of the 12 international conventions and protocols relating to terrorism. "Africa Overview," in U.S. Department of State (2003b).

[65] Morrison (2001), p. 19.

This points to the danger that, as the militancy of PAGAD's and Qibla's followers has evolved—particularly after September 2001, if Cassiem is to be believed—there will be an increasing pool of potential recruits for militant Islamic activity both inside and outside South Africa. If the security and policing services are unable to confront this problem—and U.S. authorities are deeply concerned that this is the case already[66]—then the potential that South Africa could become a center of Islamist terrorism and terrorist support could increase (although most South African analysts are skeptical about this possibility, given South Africa's historic involvement of Muslims in society). Moreover, while South Africa generally has a history of militant, often violent, protest against authority, it is unlikely that the same levels of anti-apartheid violence would be seen in any antiestablishment protests conducted by South Africa's Muslim communities.

This is not to say that South Africa—as the most advanced country in Africa and with a very large Muslim population—could not become a support-base for externalized jihadist activities. The danger was highlighted by the April 2004 arrests of five alleged al-Qaeda suspects in South Africa. The South African police chief stated that those arrested were part of "an al-Qaeda-linked plot to disrupt the country's third democratic elections" and that the arrests led directly to other arrests in Jordan, Syria, and the United Kingdom.[67]

Whether any of these individuals were involved with Qibla (which is unlikely, given that they were all foreign nationals) or whether they were developing an independent jihadist cell in South Africa remains

---

[66] Interview with senior U.S. Department of Defense Africa official, Washington, D.C., July 2004.

[67] The police chief stated that those arrested in the UK were found in possession of "boxes and boxes of South African passports," raising serious concerns that someone in South Africa's Home Affairs Ministry might have supplied them. "SA Action Led to Arrest of al-Qaeda Suspects: Selebi," SAPA, May 27, 2004; "SA Police Foils Al-Qaeda Plot to Disrupt Elections," Panafrican News Agency (PANA) Daily Newswire, May 27, 2004; Michael Wines, "South Africa Says It Deported 5 Terror Suspects Before Vote," *The New York Times,* May 28, 2004, p. 12.

unclear. Nevertheless, leaders of the South African Muslim community maintain that the overwhelming majority of South African Muslims are

> people emotionally identifying with Al-Qaedah's rhetoric against the United States of America, but in another part of their hearts, condemning wholesale the kind of violence that Al-Qaedah has undertaken around the world.[68]

The same sources stated that foreign jihadists coming into South Africa would not be able to blend into the South African Muslim community because

> they would be identified immediately by people within the community . . . the news would get out. It's not very easy to hide in the South African Muslim community if you're a foreigner. You're going to be identified almost immediately.

Eritrean Islamic Jihad/Eritrean Islamic Reform Movement

The Eritrean Islamic Jihad Movement (EIJM), Harakat al Jihad al Islami (also known as the Abu Sihel Movement), is a Sunni Islamist group that changed its name in 2003 to the Eritrean Islamic Reform Movement (EIRM) (also called the Islamic Salvation Movement).[69] The group has been active in the Horn of Africa in various guises since the mid-1970s. It seeks the violent overthrow of Eritrea's secular government and its replacement with an Islamic government.

---

[68] "SAFRICA: Analyst, Muslim 'Authority' Discuss Deportation of Al-Qaeda Suspects," BBC Monitoring International Reports (Radio 702, Johannesburg, in English, May 27, 2004).

[69] http://web.lexis-nexis.com/universe/document?_m=3b10ee425f375821178bacd87541ecf 1&_docnum=6&wchp=dGLbVzz-zSkVb&_md5=dfe6f1d0d3d3896dd4ab74f1b0d86083.

The group is led by its Secretary-General, Sheikh Mohamed Amer, and his deputy, Amir Abul Bara Hassan Salman.[70] It has been named by U.S. officials as being "one of al-Qaeda's main allies in the Horn of Africa."[71] However, the true nature of EIRM's external relationships is far more complicated, and far less obvious, than this. The EIRM appears to be an amalgam of a number of different organizations, interests and factions, combining moderate and radical Islam. Its methods combine *da'wa* (propagating Islam) and jihad.[72]

Eritrea, the EIRM's main target, has complained that Sudan is backing the group to advance Khartoum's wider Islamic agenda across the Horn.[73] Eritrea, in turn, is believed to support the Sudanese opposition group National Democratic Alliance, which has the stated objective of overturning the current National Islamic Front government in Khartoum.[74] It is also alleged that, in the summer of 2001, Ethiopia sponsored a conference of Eritrean exile terrorist groups, which included the EIJM, in the Ethiopian city of Gonder. Thus it appears that regional governments use terrorist groups in the Horn for their own geopolitical ends.

Following the conference in Gonder, a new group was formed in March 2003 called the Eritrean National Alliance (ENA), or the Alliance of the Eritrean National Forces, a coalition of thirteen Eritrean opposition groups led by Heruy Tedla Biru and dedicated to the overthrow of Eritrean president Isaias Afewerki's government. The ENA is

---

[70] Interview with the Deputy Amir of the Eritrean Islamic Jihad Movement—Abul Bara' Hassan Salman: "The Governing Regime Is a Terrorist Regime Which Acts with Enmity Against the Eritrean People," *Nida'ul Islam,* Issue 22, February–March 1998, http://www.fas.org/irp/world/para/docs/eritrea.htm (as of April 23, 2006).

[71] Victoria Ward, "Warning to Travellers After British Geologist Killed in Eritrea," *PA News/The Scotsman,* April 18, 2003, http://www.dehai.org/archives/dehai_news_archive/apr-may03/0284.html (as of March 16, 2006).

[72] Iyob (2004).

[73] Support for this theory comes from a news conference held by EIRM's Secretary-General Amer in Khartoum in mid-1998. Interview with the Deputy Amir of the Eritrean Islamic Jihad Movement; United Nations Development Programme (1998).

[74] http://web.lexis-nexis.com/universe/document?_m=9d00794b6fab0f9b6ee0588c13a017&_docnum=1&wchp=dGLbVtz-zSkVb&_md5=8df17f6fc5cf681f0edc01e7a0c76be0.

believed to include the EIRM; Eritrean Islamic Salvation, also called the Arafa Movement; the Eritrean Democratic Resistance Movement (Gash-Setit); the Eritrean Liberation Front–Revolution Council; and other groups and factions.[75]

Some questions remain as to whether the EIRM is fully integrated into the ENA or continues to operate alongside it. The ENA, unlike the EIRM, does not espouse an Islamic ideology but rather a secular one comprising elements of Afro-Marxism, Maoism, and Ba'athism. Many EIRM supporters do not appear to subscribe to the group's militant Islam but rather support it because of resentment over the ruling Popular Front for Democracy and Justice (PFDJ) and PFDJ's curtailment of Islamic political activity. (The Eritrean government also curtails Christian evangelism out of concern that it might disturb the balance between Islam and Christianity in the country and threaten national unity.)[76] A January 2004 U.S. Institute of Peace report noted that "the EIJM's continuity as an organization is fed by the PFDJ regime's unwillingness to contemplate real versus virtual political participation of Eritrea's multicultural citizens."[77]

The ENA has stated that it would not attack the Eritrean military but rather "strategic targets such as television and radio centres," as it wanted to "win over" the military. Heruy also indicated that it would not attempt to assassinate President Afewerki because "the problems [assassinations] produced later are too big to handle." Ethiopia, Sudan, and Yemen, according to Heruy, had promised "material support" to

---

[75] See http://www.theodora.com/wfb2003/eritrea/eritrea_government.html; IRIN, "Horn of Africa: Armed Factions and the Ethiopia-Eritrea Conflict," May 14, 1999, http://www.fas.org/irp/world/para/docs/19990514.htm (both as of March 17, 2006).

[76] See Christian Solidarity Worldwide, Eritrea, at http://www.cswusa.com/Countries/Eritrea.htm (as of June 8. 2006).

[77] Iyob (2004).

the ENA. Heruy stated that "We wish to get rid of the dictatorship in our country and the natural thing to do is to ally ourselves with our immediate neighbours."[78]

Ideological Foundation

The EIRM has not been designated as a foreign terrorist organization by the U.S. Department of State.[79] Indeed, while the EIRM has been accused of being an al-Qaeda affiliate in Eritrea, there is little evidence of any links between the group and al-Qaeda. The leadership of the EIRM and ENA has indicated that it sees its struggle against Afewerki's government within the wider context of al-Qaeda's professed push for a new Islamic caliphate, but it is clear that the EIRM's operational view remains focused on the situation in Eritrea, with some concern over Sudan and Ethiopia as well. Indeed, an April 2003 communiqué from the then-EIJM blamed the Eritrean government for using the September 11 attacks to attempt to link the Eritrean jihadists to al-Qaeda and of fabricating evidence that the Eritrean "mujahideen" were targeting civilians. The EIJM communiqué stated,

> We do not target civilians and innocent people of Eritrea or the foreign[ers] visiting or residing in Eritrea. We, in our fighting are targeting the Afewerqi regime and its military machinery and that Jihad in Eritrea is not terrorism against innocents, but has been launched for a sublime end and a legitimate goal, that is lifting tyranny and grievance suffered by the Eritrean people in general, and by Muslims in particular, from that dictatorial ruling regime and resisting the (state terrorism) carried out by Afewerqi Chauvenic [sic] regime.[80]

---

[78] "New Rebel Force in Eritrea: An Alliance of 13 Eritrean Opposition Groups Says It Is Setting Up a Military Wing to Topple President Isaias Afewerki," BBC News, May 2, 2005, http://news.bbc.co.uk/go/pr/fr/-/1/hi/world/africa/2995873.stm (as of March 17, 2005).

[79] The EIRM/EIJM is not even mentioned in the State Department's *Patterns of Global Terrorism 2002*; see U.S. Department of State (2003a).

[80] Eritrean Islamic Jihad Movement General Secretariat, April 17, 2003, http://www.meskerem.net/eritrean_islamic_jihad_movement.htm (as of June 2004).

Strategic and Operational Objectives

As noted, the EIRM maintains that its actions are directed only against the Eritrean government and not against civilians. It is clear that such statements need to be treated with some skepticism, especially because there is a lack of clarity regarding the EIRM-ENA relationship when it comes to attacks against the Eritrean military. The EIRM has claimed various "military successes" against the Eritrean armed forces. For example, in August 2003, the EIRM's "military secretariat" released a communiqué stating that its "mujahideen" had successfully carried out five attacks during July and August 2003, and claimed 44 Eritrean military personnel killed, with the loss of only three "mujahideen."[81]

Nevertheless, the Eritrean government has blamed the movement for civilian deaths, including the murder of British geologist Timothy Nutt in April 2003.[82] The government believes that such attacks are aimed at deterring foreign investment in Eritrea, but the EIJM has denied any involvement, stating that its policy was "only to attack government targets in Eritrea."[83] Another attack in August 2003, in which two local employees of the U.S.-based aid group Mercy Corps International were killed in the northern Red Sea region of the country, was similarly blamed by the government on the EIJM.[84] In November 2003, two UN aid trucks in Tesseney near the Sudanese border were destroyed by remote-control devices placed under each truck. There were no casualties.[85]

In March 2004, the Eritrean government blamed Sudan and Ethiopia for backing "terrorists"—notably the EIJM—who allegedly

[81] Awate Team, "EIRM's 'Military Communiqué' & Our Commentary," August 18, 2003, http://www.awate.com/artman/publish/article_2025.shtml (as of March 17, 2006).

[82] Ward, "Warning to Travellers."

[83] "New Rebel Force in Eritrea."

[84] "US Told Suspected al-Qaeda Affiliate Killed Aid Workers in Eritrea," AFP, October 6, 2003, 12:40PM PDT, http://quickstart.clari.net/qs_se/webnews/wed/cx/qus-eritrea-unrest.r2lw_do6.html (as of June 2004).

[85] Jonah Fisher, "UN Assesses Security in Eritrea," BBC News, November 24, 2003, http://news.bbc.co.uk/go/pr/fr/-/1/hi/world/africa/3234378.stm (as of March 17, 2006).

bombed a hotel, also in Tesseney,[86] killing three people. It was not clear whether the dead at Tesseney were civilians or military. While both Ethiopia and Sudan denied the accusation and accused Eritrea of blaming them for its internal problems, Eritrean Foreign Minister, Ali Said Abdella, also claimed the group "had been trained and armed by al Qaeda head Osama bin Laden during the 1990s."[87]

Environmental Factors

The focus of the EIRM (and the ENA) remains firmly fixed on the Eritrean government, but there is a possibility that other regional factors could push it toward militancy outside Eritrea's borders. Although it is unlikely that the EIRM would suddenly refocus its violence against wider Western targets outside Eritrea, the EIRM could become involved with other like-minded Islamic organizations throughout the Horn of Africa to promote common interests and perhaps seek to establish an Islamic federation in the Horn. This is a possibility as long as the interests, actions, and legacies of most of these groups, their supporters, and targets, remain interwoven in an almost indistinguishable pattern of relationships.

A multitude of groups and factions, each with its external supporters, abounds across the Horn. For a description of these groups, see the box on the next page.

---

[86] Tesseney is believed to be central to the EIJM's operations because it is the Eritrean base for refugee repatriations from the Sudan and so has a significant UN presence.

[87] "Eritrea Says Sudan and Ethiopia Behind Hotel Blast," Reuters, March 10, 2004, http://eri24.com/news4651.htm (as of April 23, 2006).

Other Groups Across the Horn of Africa

Djibouti: The Afar Front pour la Restauration de l'Unité et la Démocratie (FRUD) and the separate FRUD–"Dini/combatant faction."

Eritrea: The little-known Red Sea Afar Democratic Organisation (RSADO) and Afar Liberation Front [Party].

Ethiopia: The ethnic Somali Ogadeni clan occupies much of southeastern Ethiopia, and its preeminent political party, the Ogadeni National Liberation Front (ONLF), has resisted attempts by the Addis Ababa government to have it join the Ethiopian Somali Democratic League, which is a multi-clan umbrella party affiliated with the ruling Ethiopia People's Revolutionary Democratic Front (EPRDF). The ONLF is also believed to be linked to the United Front for the Liberation of Western Somalia (UFLWS) in Somalia. Finally, there are the Oromo Liberation Front, the United Oromo People's Liberation Front, the Oromo Peoples' Liberation Organisation, and the Oromo Peoples' Democratic Organisation, the latter a member of the EPRDF coalition.

Somalia: The many factions and groups include the United Somali Congress–Patriotic Movement and the Rahanweyn Resistance Army, both allegedly supported by Ethiopia; the Somali National Front, a Marehan group split between pro- and anti-Ethiopia factions; Mohamed Hussein's ruling Somali National Alliance, supported by Eritrea; and the previously noted al-Itihaad al-Islamiyya (covered in the first volume, *Part 1, the Global Jihadist Movement*) and its affiliated UFLWS, which is believed to receive support from Ethiopia.

Finally, there is also the question of the Afar region which, following the de facto independence of Eritrea in 1991, found itself straddling three states: Ethiopia, Eritrea, and Djibouti. Afar rebels fighting in Ethiopia are known as the Ugogomo, or revolutionary party, and are believed to be supported by the ruling EPRDF, which includes the Afar Revolutionary Democratic Front (ARDUF) in Ethiopia. The ARDUF and Ugogomo are thought to be closely associated. (IRIN, "Horn of Africa.")

CHAPTER FOUR

The Iraqi Insurgency

The nonaffiliated part of the Iraqi insurgency, that is, the component that is outside the al-Qaeda and al-Zarqawi networks, is diverse and widespread. It is composed of groups of both nationalist and religious provenance.[1] The insurgency is almost exclusively Sunni. Both the Shi'ite and Kurdish communities have continued to rally around their new national leaders and, until the February 2006 bombing of the al-Askari mosque in Samarra—one of the holiest Shi'ite shrines[2]—refused to engage in sectarian revenge.

We do not place the Shi'ite militiamen associated with Muqtada al-Sadr in the insurgent category because even though al-Sadr's militiamen, organized in the so-called Mahdi's Army, share the Sunni hostility toward the United States and have engaged in violent activities, these activities generally do not rise to the level of Sunni terrorism. Moreover, al-Sadr must operate within the broader framework of Shi'ite politics in Iraq. In this context, al-Sadr's movement has to take account of the political and religious authority of the Iraqi Shi'ite hierarchy headed by Ayatollah Ali al-Sistani—which limits the al-Sadr movement's freedom of action and ability to mount a sustained insur-

---

[1] This chapter reflects information provided by CJTF-7 personnel in Baghdad; Kathleen Ridolfo, "A Survey of Armed Groups in Iraq," RFE/RL Iraq Report, June 4, 2004; "Iraqi Insurgency Groups," http://www.globalsecurity.org/military/ops/iraq_insurgency.htm (as of March 17, 2006); and surveys of open press sources.

[2] The shrine, built in 944, is the site of the tombs of the Tenth and Eleventh Imams, Ali al-Hadi and his son, Hassan al-Askari. Samarra is also the place where, according to Shi'a tradition, the Twelfth or "Hidden" Imam, Muhammad al-Mahdi, went into occultation.

gency with popular support. Al-Sadr's movement participated in the January 2006 general elections as part of the United Iraqi Alliance, the Shi'ite coalition, and emerged as a power broker in the formation of a new Iraqi government.

The insurgency under discussion is certainly one of the most complex and challenging ever faced by the United States. It presents no single coherent enemy against which American forces can mass their superior strength. The insurgency's various components fight for their own reasons, having little in common other than a desire to remove the U.S. and coalition presence from the country. In general, they seek to create a crisis between the Iraqi government and the Iraqi people in the hopes that outside support for the government will wane, forcing the withdrawal of foreign forces.[3] The insurgency is far larger than the 5,000 guerrillas previously thought to be at its core. One indication is the sheer number of suspected insurgents—some 22,000—who have cycled through U.S.-run prisons. Most have been released. Indeed, some U.S. commanders in Iraq have expressed concern that the Abu Ghraib prison has become a "jihad university"—a breeding ground for extremist leaders and a school for terrorists.[4]

At least 28 different insurgent groups have formed in 2003 through 2005, some but not all based in the Sunni triangle north and west of Baghdad. Some of these groups are increasingly embracing tactics imported by foreign fighters, such as the car bombings of civilian targets.[5] It goes without saying that the universe of insurgent groups in Iraq is very dynamic and fluid. Groups appear, change, merge, divide, and disappear. They operate under different names and sometimes

---

[3] "Defeating the Insurgency in Iraq," U.S. Institute for Peace Workshop, May 16, 2005.

[4] Jim Krane, "U.S. Officials: Iraqi Insurgency Bigger," *Philadelphia Inquirer,* July 9, 2004; Thom Shanker, "U.S. Fears Abu Ghraib Is 'Jihad University,'" *International Herald Tribune,* February 15, 2006.

[5] Edward Cody, "Sunni Resistance to U.S. Hardens," *The Washington Post,* July 7, 2004, p. 1.

under no name at all.[6] Therefore, our intention is not to provide a comprehensive portrayal of the Iraqi insurgency but to identify its key components, trajectory, and likely prospects.

Ideological Foundation

As noted in the preceding discussion, the myriad groups engaging in armed activity in Iraq have little in common other than a desire to remove the U.S. and coalition presence from the country. The Sunni groups—the backbone of the insurgency—want the new Iraqi government to fail, but beyond that, they exhibit wide differences. By contrast, Shi'ite militants—including al-Sadr's movement—back the idea of a new government that is representative of the majority Shi'ite population, even if they compete over control of that government. (The al-Sadr movement and the Supreme Council for the Islamic Revolution in Iraq are fierce competitors for dominance in the Shi'ite-majority southern provinces.)

For the moment, nationalism is the glue that holds the Sunni-based insurgency together. Sheikh Abdul-Satar Abdul-Jabbar of the Council of Islamic Scholars, Iraq's preeminent Sunni organization, has said that the main, Sunni-based insurgency is likely to rage as long as Iraqis' sense of nationalism is bruised by the presence of U.S. military forces on their soil.[7]

In the wake of the turnover of authority from the Coalition Provisional Authority (CPA) to the Iraqi government, and especially after the first round of elections in January 2005, tensions appeared to be rising between the homegrown Iraqi resistance and the foreign Islamist fighters. There has been evidence of sniping between groups on Arabic television and Web sites and in interviews with Iraqi and American officials, as well as from members of the insurgency and people with close ties to it. All speak of rising friction between nationalist

---

[6] Ahmed Hashim, "Iraqi Insurgency Is No Monolith," *The Daily Star* (Lebanon), July 28, 2003, http://www.lebanonwire.com/0307/03072815DS.asp (as of March 17, 2006).

[7] Cody, "Sunni Resistance to U.S. Hardens."

fighters and foreign-led Islamists over goals and tactics, with some Iraqi insurgents indicating revulsion over the car bombs and suicide attacks in cities that have caused hundreds of civilian deaths.[8] The split took a dramatic turn in July 2004, when masked men calling themselves the Salvation Movement released a videotape containing threats to kill al-Zarqawi.[9] The next day, a statement posted on an Islamist Web site, claiming to be signed by al-Zarqawi, lashed out against the Council of Islamic Scholars. The statement accused the group of weakness for offering a ransom to prevent the beheading of Nicholas Berg, the American killed in May 2004.[10] More recently, in the run-up to the ratification of the new Iraqi constitution in the fall of 2005, jihadists have publicly executed Sunni clerics who advocated participation in the October 2005 referendum on the constitution. Since then, there have been reports of armed clashes and executions of foreign jihadists by Iraqi Sunnis. (As this book was going to to print, the news was received that al-Zarqawi and several of his associates had been killed in a U.S. air strike on their hideout on June 7, 2006.)

Strategic and Operational Objectives

The strategic and operational objectives of these groups vary widely. The most senior official from Hussein's regime still at large is the former vice-chairman of Saddam's Revolutionary Command Council, Izzat Ibrahim al-Douri, who specialized in internal security. He may

---

[8]   Ian Fisher and Edward Wong, "Iraq's Rebellion Shows Signs of Internal Rifts," *The New York Times,* July 11, 2004, p. 1.

[9]   In the video, three men with rocket-propelled grenades and other weapons, flanked by an Iraqi flag, delivered the threats. The man speaking had a clear Iraqi accent. "We have started preparing . . . to capture [al-Zarqawi] and his allies or kill them and present them as a gift to our people. This is the last ultimatum to those who give him shelter. This is the last warning. If you don't stop, we will do to you what the coalition forces have failed to do." By issuing its threat on a tape released to the satellite channel al-Arabiya, the group has copied the tactics of al-Zarqawi himself, who has repeatedly used that network and the al-Jazeera channel to publicize its terrorist attacks (AP, July 7, 2004).

[10]   Ian Fisher and Edward Wong, "Iraq's Rebellion Shows Signs of Internal Rifts," *The New York Times,* July 11, 2004, p. 1.

be directing some of the attacks.[11] Former regime loyalists believe that they have no option but to continue fighting and are also convinced that the United States and its coalition partners will tire long before they do.[12] These groups are trying to apply the experiences of other guerrilla and terrorist organizations to their operations. Their objective, as noted earlier, is to return the old order, or vestiges of it, to power.

Nationalists do not necessarily support the return of the Ba'ath party (some actively oppose it), but they resent what they consider to be the U.S. occupation of Iraq and are angered by the coalition's failure to restore law and order, as well as security, and by U.S. operational methods that are seen as deliberately humiliating the Iraqis and their honor. These individuals or groups are relying heavily on kinship and tribal ties to provide them with shelter and succor as they plan and execute their operations.

Iraqi Islamists have emerged after decades of suppression by the Ba'thist regime. At the beginning of Operation Iraqi Freedom, many were amateurs. Others have proven to have considerable military experience. All of them have learned quickly, and they have the experiences of other Islamist organizations to help them. Their objective is the establishment of an Islamic state. As discussed in Part 1, foreign Islamist fighters have infiltrated into Iraq to fight the United States, its allies, and the Iraqi government and have provided the bulk of the suicide bombers who have caused the largest number of casualties in the conflict.

Insurgent elements are employing an increased range of weapons in their attacks. Iraqi militants employed Katyusha rockets for probably the first time in an October 28, 2003, attack in Kirkuk. Other relatively advanced weapons reportedly used by, or newly available to, the insurgents include 160-millimeter mortars; shoulder-fired surface-to-air missiles; an improvised, though not crude, multiple rocket launcher (used to attack the Rashid Hotel in Baghdad); and improvised explosive devices (IEDs) and antitank mines (both used to damage heav-

---

[11] Cody, "Sunni Resistance to U.S. Hardens."

[12] Sergio Ramazzotti, "Iraqi Rebel Vows to Kill 'Lying' Americans, Distances Resistance from al-Qa'ida," *La Repubblica,* January 24, 2004, pp. 33–38.

ily armored coalition vehicles). Of course, the insurgents continue to attack with their original means—including rocket-propelled grenades (RPGs) and smaller IEDs—while adding new weapons, allowing them to engage more difficult coalition targets from longer ranges.

Environmental Factors

The early dissolution of the CPA in June 2004 clearly threw off the insurgents and their plans, forcing them to redirect their target selection from primarily U.S. and coalition to Iraqi targets and creating a split in their ranks.[13] The split between native Iraqi insurgents and foreign fighters played into former interim Prime Minister Iyad Allawi's strategy of seeking to divide the insurgency by appealing to Iraqi fighters to reject the presence of foreigners. Allawi and other officials of the former interim government met with former Ba'ath Party members and Sunni tribal leaders to convince them that their interests and those of foreign fighters were not the same.[14]

The high turnout in the January 30, 2005, elections and the prospect of a sovereign Iraqi government dominated by Shi'ite and Kurdish parties appears to have caused some sectors within the Sunni insurgency to doubt their strategy. The February 28, 2005, issue of *Time* magazine revealed direct contacts in Baghdad between senior insurgents, including former members of the Saddam regime, and U.S. officials. The goal of the insurgents participating in the talks, according to the article, was to establish a political identity that would enable them to represent disenfranchised Sunnis and to negotiate an end to the U.S. military offensive in the Sunni triangle.[15]

The expectation of U.S. officials and some sectors of the Iraqi government is that Sunnis will eventually channel their discontent into political action rather than continue to take up arms. A move in this

---

[13] Edward Wong, "Undeterred, Insurgents Keep Up Deadly Attacks Across Iraq," *The New York Times,* July 2, 2004.

[14] Fisher and Wong, "Iraq's Rebellion Shows Signs of Internal Rifts."

[15] "Talking with the Enemy," *Time,* February 28, 2005.

direction could further widen the rift between local insurgents and foreign fighters. But the reality is that the Sunni Arabs are a minority in the country and will probably be a small or nonexistent presence in the highest echelons of the new Iraqi government, even though they had governed the area that is now Iraq since the days of the Ottoman Empire. Shi'ite politicians have been remarkably conciliatory after their success in the January 2005 elections, despite continued violence against Shi'ites. Nevertheless, Shi'ite parties could block constitutional amendments desired by the Sunnis, thus alienating Sunnis even further (the possibility of such amendments was left open at the time of the approval of the Iraqi constitution as an incentive for Sunnis to participate). Moreover, there is strong sentiment within Shi'ite political sectors to resume the policy of "de-Ba'athification" that had been deemphasized by the Allawi government. That, of course, would render an agreement to end the insurgency harder to achieve.

Security is a major environmental factor shaping Iraqi political dynamics. The interim Iraqi government displayed a single-minded focus on issues of security. At his first cabinet meeting, interim Prime Minister Allawi kept the discussion centered on ways to combat the tenacious insurgency. His first public appearance after his appointment was at a military recruiting center. His first out-of-town trip was to an Iraqi army base. And his first official order was a new national security decree allowing him to exercise broad powers of martial law in rebel strongholds.[16] The offensives to retake Fallujah and to pacify the area known as the "triangle of death" southwest of Baghdad were major initiatives to reduce insurgent sanctuaries. The successor government of Ibrahim al-Ja'afari has continued this emphasis, and it can be expected that the government elected after the adoption of a permanent Iraqi constitution will support a continued U.S. military presence until an adequate level of security is restored.

---

[16] Danica Kirka, "Iraq Vows 'Sharp Sword' vs. Attackers," *The Boston Globe,* July 13, 2004.

Future Trajectory of the Insurgency

At this writing, the Iraqi insurgency is in a transitional stage. It is evolving in response to wider political events in Iraq, which center, of course, on the rise of the Shi'ites to a dominant position in the state. Sunni-Shi'ite dynamics, therefore, will likely become more significant. Even as the original political goals of the insurgency become less attainable, changes that might occur in the future could include the rise of more competent insurgent units and the emergence of more skilled leaders. The effect could be more sophisticated and more skillfully conducted attacks against government and civilian targets; increasing attacks on armored vehicles; systematic efforts to restrict air and road mobility; and the destruction of oil infrastructure.

For the short to medium term, the insurgency may persist as long as coalition forces remain visible in Iraq. Iraqi forces have provided the American military with intelligence for air strikes on rebel safe havens.[17] How often the Iraqi government asks for American airpower to achieve tactical goals may affect the pace and scope of the insurgency. U.S. and British commanders have been careful to emphasize their partnership with the new Iraqi security forces, but they acknowledge that Iraqi units still lack the training, equipment, and motivation to take on the insurgency.[18] That can be expected to change, of course, as Iraq resumes full sovereignty and builds up its armed forces.

In the end, terror alone cannot guarantee success for the insurgents. Despite the uncertainty about the future of Iraq, there can be no doubt that the January 2005 election, the approval of the Iraqi constitution, and the January 2006 election for a permanent Iraqi government drove a nail in the coffin of Sunni political supremacy in Iraq. The insurgency can continue to wreak havoc, but doing so will become an exercise in political futility. In these circumstances, three general scenarios are possible:

---

[17] Edward Wong, "New Law in Iraq Gives Premier Martial Powers to Fight Uprising," *The New York Times,* July 7, 2004, p. 1.

[18] Richard Lloyd Parry, "Coalition Could Act Alone over Rebels," *The London Times,* July 1, 2004.

In the most benign case, significant elements of the Sunni community realize that a return to the status quo ante is no longer viable. They accept a minority role within a democratic Iraq. The Sunnis might find a common interest with the Kurdish parties in balancing Shi'ite predominance. A rough balance of power could develop, allowing for what might be called "democracy with Iraqi characteristics."[19] Over the medium to long term, the insurgency, increasingly isolated from its Sunni base, would eventually subside.

In the second scenario, the representatives of the Sunni community are too alienated or terrorized to enter into a political arrangement with the Shi'ites and the Kurds. The insurgency could continue, perhaps at high levels of violence, but would be unable to transcend its narrow social base or to prevent the nascent government from gradually consolidating its control over the country.

In the third and least favorable scenario, if the new government is unable to contain the insurgents and terrorists or to win broad support among the diverse ethnic and religious communities in Iraq, it will be no match for local warlords and will have to contend with the growth of terrorist infrastructures. A failure of central authority could lead to a formal or de facto partition of the country.[20]

The wild card in Iraq's political evolution is external interference. Elements of the former Saddam regime are believed to be directing the insurgency from Syria. Tens of thousands of Iranian pilgrims, smugglers, drug runners (hashish and heroin), and illegal immigrants have entered southern Iraq, which contains Shi'ite pilgrimage sites in Najaf and Karbala. The influx also includes Iranian intelligence operatives and agents attempting to promote Iranian influence. Iranian activity is not just limited to the southern part of Iraq. Two Iranians were caught in Baghdad in the summer of 2004 attempting to detonate a

---

[19] See Rabasa, Benard, Chalk, et al. (2004), p. 53. Different Iraqi scenarios are discussed in more detail on pp. 53–54.

[20] Robin Wright, "In Iraq, Daunting Tasks Await," *The Washington Post,* July 7, 2004, p. 14.

car bomb.[21] In June 2004, eight British Marines were seized by the Iranian military while navigating the river border with Iran. And at least twice in July 2004 machine guns were fired at night from the Iranian side of the border toward Iraqi workers prospecting for oil on their own side.[22]

These Iranian actions may be part of a long-term strategy by Tehran to create an Iranian sphere of influence in southern Iraq. Matters are complicated by the existence of Shi'ite political parties in Iraq with varying degrees of loyalty to Iran. The key question is whether they will identify themselves as Shi'ites first, united with their Iranian brethren, or as Iraqis, threatened by Iranian encroachment. In addition, key periods of religiosity—the annual Karbala pilgrimage and the hajj—can help bring radical Islamists into and out of Iraq and the Arabian peninsula. The final answer may not be clear for years.

---

[21] Richard Lloyd Parry and Richard Beeston, "Iranian Bombers Held in Baghdad," *The Times* (London), July 6, 2004.

[22] Richard Lloyd Parry, "Iraq Struggles to Stem New Incursion," *The Times* (London), July 19, 2004.

CHAPTER FIVE

Non-Islamist Groups

Categories of Non-Islamist Groups and Insurgencies

Non-Islamist terrorist and insurgent groups fall into two basic categories:

- *Marxist insurgencies, most of them Maoist, that follow a strategy of "people's war" as defined in the writings of Mao Zedong and the Vietnamese revolutionaries.* There are, of course, variations, and each of these insurgencies has its own specific characteristics, but they generally follow the same model.
- *Separatist groups.* Although some claim to be Marxist or Islamic, the separatists' primary goal is to establish independent ethnically defined entities. This category includes such groups as the Liberation Tigers of Tamil Eelam (LTTE), also known as the Tamil Tigers; Basque Fatherland and Liberty (ETA); and the Moro Islamic Liberation Front (MILF), among others.

The Revolutionary Armed Forces of Colombia and National Liberation Army

Ideological Background

The Revolutionary Armed Forces of Colombia (FARC) and the National Liberation Army (ELN) are Marxist armed groups that have operated in Colombia since the 1960s. The FARC originated as the military arm of the Moscow-line Colombian Communist Party and has an orthodox Marxist-Leninist ideology, although its military approach is derived from Maoist and Vietnamese "people's war" doctrine. The ELN, on the other hand, was inspired by the Cuban Revolution and was infused with a strong dose of Marxist-oriented Catholic "liberation theology." Both advocate armed revolutionary struggle to overthrow the Colombian government and replace it with a socialist system. A third actor in the Colombian conflict, the United Self-Defense Forces of Colombia (AUC), the so-called paramilitaries, opposes the Marxist groups. AUC is in the process of demobilizing pursuant to an agreement with the government of President Álvaro Uribe.[1]

Strategic and Operational Objectives

The FARC has not deviated from its original strategy of "protracted people's war" that it reaffirmed at its landmark Seventh Conference in 1982. The strategy, based on Maoist, Vietnamese, and Farabundo Marti National Liberation Front (FMLN) precepts, involves gradually extending the organization's presence and control in the countryside and eventually isolating the government forces in the major cities. This strategy of territorial control is linked to the FARC's involvement in the drug trade that generates much of the revenue that funds the organization's operations (the other main sources of funds are extortion, kidnappings, and cattle rustling).[2]

FARC methods and tactics include bombings, assassinations, kidnappings (which have political as well as financial utility), and hijackings. The FARC also carries out guerrilla and main force military action against Colombian political, military, and economic targets, including the electrical infrastructure. It has increasingly conducted support operations outside Colombia. It has logistical facilities on the

---

[1] For a survey of the ideology of the FARC and ELN, see Rabasa and Chalk (2001). Colombia's Fundacion Seguridad & Democracia has published a valuable series of reports on the demobilization of several AUC units in 2005 and on numerous other aspects of the political-military situation in Colombia, found at the foundation's Web site, http://www. seguridadydemocracia.org (as of March 17, 2006).

[2] Some have argued that the FARC has in fact simply become a criminal cartel, but this perception underestimates the group's political agenda. See Rabasa and Chalk (2001).

Panamanian side of the inhospitable Darien border region, as well as camps in Venezuela and Ecuador. Still, FARC targets have been almost exclusively domestic. However, in March 1999, a FARC unit executed three U.S. Indian rights activists on Venezuelan territory after it kidnapped them in Colombia. Foreign citizens, as well as Colombians, often are targets of FARC kidnapping for ransom.[3]

Both the FARC and the ELN have entered into periodic negotiations with successive Colombian governments. President Andrés Pastrana's government (1998–2002) attempted to come to terms with the FARC. The negotiation process involved giving the FARC control of a 42,000-square-kilometer territory in central Colombia known as the *despeje,* a demilitarized area. The negotiations broke down in February 2002, and the government abrogated the agreement that gave the FARC free rein in the despeje. The Uribe government, which came to office in July 2002, has pursued a more aggressive counterinsurgency strategy that has sought to reduce the FARC's influence in its operational areas. Ongoing operations have succeeded in dismantling a significant part of the FARC infrastructure in its base areas in the departments of Meta, Caquetá, and Guaviare, in southeastern Colombia.[4] The FARC has attempted to counter with diversionary attacks in areas of limited government presence. Colombian analysts debate whether the Uribe government's campaign has successfully eroded the FARC's hold over its base areas or whether the group has implemented a tactical move to lower its profile in order to build up its strength and regain the strategic initiative at a later date.[5]

In recent years, the ELN has declined in importance and become more amenable to a negotiated political settlement. Although the group retains a strong presence in the oil-producing department of Arauca,

---

[3] See Chapter Seven.

[4] Rabasa conversation with senior Colombian army officer, Washington, D.C., August 2005. See also the data on combat operations in Fundacion Seguridad y Democracia (Bogotá), "Coyuntura de Seguridad, Enero–Marzo 2005," http://www.seguridadydemocracia.org/ docs/pdf/boletin/boletin8completo.pdf (as of March 17, 2006).

[5] The latter is the opinion of Colombian insurgency expert Alfredo Rangel Suarez, "Un campanazo de alerta: las lecciones de Putumayo," *El Tiempo* (Colombia), August 12, 2005.

in eastern Colombia, it has suffered from inroads by the FARC and the paramilitaries into its former strongholds on the Atlantic coast and Magdalena valley.[6]

Environmental Factors

The FARC sees itself as part of the anticapitalist and antiglobalist movement. For example, the group is a member of the Sao Paulo Forum discussed in Chapter Six, and it has stated that it will now target U.S. forces and economic interests in Colombia. The more active role of the United States in providing military assistance and training to Colombian government forces, including the training of specialized units for the protection of a critical oil pipeline in northeastern Colombia, could produce a shift in FARC strategy toward directly targeting U.S. personnel and assets.

Numerous incidents point to the presence of Middle Eastern actors in Colombia and FARC-controlled territory. An Egyptian terrorist belonging to al-Gama'a al-Islamiyya, who was wanted in connection with the 1997 massacre of Western tourists at Luxor, entered Colombia illegally in 1998 to hold talks with the FARC. He was arrested and turned over to the United States via Paraguay.[7] In October 1998, FARC and Iranian officials signed an agreement allowing the construction of an Iranian meatpacking plant and slaughterhouse in the "demilitarized zone" in southern Colombia that was then controlled by the FARC.[8] In 2004, there were reports of FARC personnel forming suicide squads to

---

[6]   See Espejo and Garzon (2005).

[7]   "La Frontera de 'Los Caballitos,'" http://historicos.elespectador.com/periodismo_inv/2001/noviembre/nota1.htm (as of March 17, 2006).

[8]   "U.S. Pressured Bogota to Stop Iranian-Funded Meat Plant," ABC News, January 6, 2000.

attack government as well as American facilities and personnel. These reports could be false or misguided, however, because the FARC has yet to conduct a definitive suicide operation.[9]

Maoist Insurgencies

Ideological Foundation

Maoist groups throughout the world—prominently in Peru, Nepal, India, Bhutan, and the Philippines—are committed to seizing power using the concept of "people's war" and instituting Maoist forms associated with The Great Proletarian Cultural Revolution in China.[10]

In India, a growing number of states—most prominently Bihar and Andrah Pradesh—have experienced a steadily escalating level of Maoist insurgent violence. So concerned has New Delhi become that in September 2005, it convened a strategy coordination session of the chief ministers from Maoist-affected states. Indian Maoism, previously the senior partner in the Coordination Committee of Maoist Parties and Organizations of South Asia, now finds itself overshadowed by its Nepalese counterpart. Indeed, using a combination of terror, guerrilla warfare, and main force action, the Communist Party of Nepal (Maoist), or CPN(M), has come to dominate much of the countryside in a struggle that now has cost more than 12,000 lives. Viewed by the Revolutionary Internationalist Movement (RIM) umbrella organization as the premier Maoist force active in the world today, the CPN(M) has increasingly made common cause with like-minded Indian groups. Joint pronouncements cite Indian and American imperialism as the leading enemies of mankind. In Bhutan, the activities

---

[9] "Militiaman Reportedly Training Guerrillas to Carry Out Suicide Attacks Captured," *El Espectador,* March 18, 2004; Frank Monteverde, "Interview with FARC spokesman Raul Reyes," New Colombia News Agency, November 29, 2003. In January 2003, FARC members appeared to conduct a suicide operation as they self-detonated a vehicle that pulled alongside a military convoy. Yet given the lack of any further suicide-like attacks, the death of the perpetrators might have been unintended.

[10] The definition is from Thomas A. Marks's review of this report, August 2005. For a authoritative study of Maoist insurgencies, see Marks (1996).

of Ngolops (armed Nepalese dissidents) pose a serious threat to the country's security. Ngolops, referred to by Bhutanese authorities as "antinationals," are people of Nepalese origin who claim that they are Bhutanese citizens forcibly evicted by the Royal government of Bhutan into refugee camps.[11] In the state of Assam, India, Ngolops formed the United Liberation Front of Asom and the National Democratic Front of Bodoland as their political arms. In the Philippines, the Maoist Communist Party of the Philippines (CPP) remains active, with its New People's Army thought to field some 13,000 combatants. Reports of the CPP collaborating with Islamic groups such as the MILF have yet to be confirmed.[12] Peru's Shining Path (Sendero Luminoso, or SL) once held the leading role in RIM now ascribed to the CPN(M). Characterized by the extreme brutality of its attacks, Shining Path steadily grew after its founding in the early 1960s. The group suffered a near-fatal blow with the capture of its leader Abigail Guzmán in 1992, but the kidnapping of 71 oil workers in June 2003 and the ambush of a military patrol in July 2003 demonstrate that remnants remain active.[13]

Strategic and Operational Objectives

Maoist groups emphasize violence in rural areas to mobilize a "counterstate" capable of challenging urban-based government power. Although each group has its peculiarities, all generally follow the strategy and tactics developed in the writings of Chinese and Vietnamese revolutionaries. Maoist strategy involves first gaining control of the countryside through a variety of tactics, of which terror against "class enemies" is an essential component, and eventually isolating and defeating the government forces in the urban centers. The operationalization of this approach takes a predictable form. As the armed political movement projects itself into local areas, resistance is neutralized by terror. Appeals for help from victims or their relatives are answered by the armed local representatives of the state, the police. The police are ambushed, forced

---

[11] "Bhutan Assessment, 2003," http://www.satp.org/satporgtp/countries/bhutan/index.html (as of March 17, 2006).

[12] Cronin (2004).

[13] McDermott (2004a).

to seek refuge in their stations, and then systematically eliminated. The result in affected areas is a population dominated by the insurgents. Seeking to reverse the tide, the government commits the main force units of its military. As these forces disburse to reclaim lost population, they are themselves attacked by insurgent main force units formed from "regularized" guerrilla formations. "Mobile warfare," in Maoist terminology, ensues, with force-on-force action designed to produce equilibrium. This is to be followed by "war of position," as government forces are routed and captured "positions" held. In the end, the counter-state, the alternative society formed under the Maoists, is to become the state.

Environmental Factors
Maoist groups connect not only through organized meetings but also by reading accounts of one another's exploits and duplicating models for organizing, training, and equipping. Although "anti-imperialist," these groups by and large direct their attacks against domestic enemies and have not attacked the United States directly.

Although not a direct threat to the United States, Maoists use terrorism as an integral component of their strategy of people's war and are inherently hostile to the international order. They may thus find common interests with al-Qaeda and its associates. They have, as opportunity has presented itself, participated in narcotics trafficking. Nepal serves as a hub for hashish trafficking in Asia.[14] SL deals in drugs, and coca farmers are being organized into support bases for SL.[15] The Philippines' New People's Army derives much of its revenue from marijuana trafficked to urban areas and the production of hashish oil exported to Europe through crime syndicates in Manila.[16] Clearly, Maoist groups thrive in countries where there is corruption, lawlessness, transnational crime, and the discontent produced by broken political systems. Key factors that could move the Maoists to become a larger

---

[14] McDermott (2004a).

[15] McDermott (2004a).

[16] Rabasa, discussion with Intelligence Service, Armed Forces of the Philippines, Manila, August 2005.

threat include U.S. support for governments under attack by Maoists, spillover effects from insurgency, and recruitment and indoctrination of native peoples against urban elites and governments.[17]

Liberation Tigers of Tamil Eelam

Background and Ideological Foundation

The Liberation Tigers of Tamil Eelam (LTTE) is a terrorist insurgency that has waged a bitter war for the creation of a separate Tamil Eelam state in Sri Lanka's northern and eastern provinces for the past four and one-half decades. The group emerged in the wake of renewed intercommunal antipathy and violence between the country's majority Sinhalese and minority Tamil populations during the 1970s.[18] The LTTE developed as an extremist outgrowth of the Tamil United Liberation Front, a social-political movement that was prepared to advance Tamil demands through the accepted channels of the Sri Lankan state. Rejecting this stance, a hard core of militants formed a variety of underground guerrilla organizations dedicated to armed struggle against the Colombo government during the mid-1970s. Initially, 42 militant groups were created, although five quickly achieved dominance. These were: the Tamil Eelam Liberation Organisation; the People's Liberation Organisation of Tamil Eelam; the Eelam People's Revolutionary Front; the Eelam Revolutionary Organisation of Students; and the Tamil New Tigers (TNT).[19] Of these, it was the TNT that was to assume the early mantle of the Tamil struggle.

Led by Chetti Thanabalasingham, the TNT embarked on a particularly intensive campaign of assassination and violence in 1974 that

---

[17] Davis and Bedi (2004).

[18] For further details on the roots and genesis of the ethnic conflict in Sri Lanka, see Gunaratna (1993a, 1993b, 1998); Little (1994); Rupesinghe, ed. (1998); Rotberg, ed. (1999); Bullion (1995); Hellmann-Rajanayagam (1994); Venkatachalam (1987); Manogaran (1987); Misra (1995); De Silva (1986, 1995); and Suryanarayan (1991).

[19] Gunaratna (1993b), p. 27.

was variously designed to silence pro-government Tamils,[20] eliminate informants, and disrupt police investigations into terrorist incidents and related criminal activities perpetrated under the group's auspices. Velupillai Prabhakaran, the TNT's second in command, assumed leadership of the organization in 1976 when Thanabalasingham was arrested. He renamed the group the Liberation Tigers of Tamil Eelam and set about to reconfigure it in a manner consonant with his own ambitious intentions and ideological designs. Affirming the legitimacy of the Tamil struggle for independence on the basis of the Thimpu Principles[21] and specifying that it was only through the LTTE that these objectives could be achieved, Prabhakaran fashioned a uniquely elite, ruthlessly efficient, and highly professional fighting force[22] that emphasized selective recruitment (a policy that continues to this day) and an institutional ethos of unswerving dedication to the Eelam cause.

Over the course of the intervening 28 years, the LTTE has gained a reputation as one of the most sophisticated and deadly terrorist insurgencies in the world. At the time of writing, the Tigers had successfully driven the Sri Lankan government to the negotiating table and effec-

---

[20] Significantly, attention was drawn precisely to this LTTE policy in a 1998 analysis of the group by the U.S. State Department. Included within a synopsis of the Tigers' "political objectives" was "eliminate moderate Tamils and other Tamil militant groups that compete with the LTTE for influence within the Sri Lankan Tamil community." See U.S. Department of State (1998).

[21] The Thimpu Principles affirm the following five nonnegotiable demands: (1) recognition of Tamils as a nation; (2) recognition of the existence of an identified homeland for the Tamil people; (3) recognition of the right of the Tamil people to self-determination; (4) recognition of the right of the Tamil people to a separate citizenship; and (5) recognition of the fundamental right of all Tamils to look on the north and eastern provinces of Sri Lanka as their country. See Kumar Ponnambala, "The Only Possible Solution to the Tamil National Problem," TamilCanadian.com (as of March 21, 2006).

[22] "We fight while others merely talk" was how the LTTE both defined and distinguished themselves from other Tamil militant organizations. Cited in Wijesekera (1993), p. 310.

tively forced it to accept terms for a ceasefire that have since allowed the group to set up a mini Eelam state covering roughly 15 percent of the country's entire geographic territory.[23]

Current estimates of the LTTE's overall on-ground strength in Sri Lanka vary between a low of 12,000 to a high in excess of 20,000.[24] The true figure likely lies somewhere between these two approximations, although a recent split in Tiger ranks resulting from the defection of the group's special commander for the Eastern Batticaloa-Amparai District, Vinayagamoorthi Muralitharan (alias Colonel Karuna), has complicated the picture somewhat, reducing the number of cadres available to Prabhakaran by an estimated 5,500.[25] Although Karuna's departure represents a potentially serious blow to the LTTE, it probably will not significantly dent the group's overall human resource and operational capabilities, for three reasons. First, most Tamil forces are concentrated in the Prabhakaran-loyal districts of northern Sri Lanka. Second, virtually all the specialist units at the center of past militant

---

[23] The ceasefire was brokered by Norway on February 22, 2002, and has since led to several rounds of talks between the LTTE and Colombo over the last two years. At the time of writing, the Tigers had put forth their own blueprint for home rule, which calls for the establishment of a so-called Interim Self Governing Authority covering eight Tamil-majority districts in the northeast and a subsequent plebiscite (five years later) on self-determination. Prabhakaran has given explicit warning that if this proposal is not taken seriously, the LTTE will once again take up arms against the central government. Many in Colombo believe that the Tiger leader has no interest in peace and is merely using the current period of relative stability to rearm, recruit additional cadres, and consolidate control over the north. Chalk interviews with Sri Lankan intelligence and military officials, Colombo, May 2004.

[24] RAND fieldwork and interviews, Sri Lankan Armed Forces (SLAF) and Internal Intelligence Bureau (IIB), Colombo, May 2004. According to one source, the LTTE's strength breaks down as follows: military strength, 11,000–15,000 (depending on the numbers of Karuna supporters that have yet to be integrated back into the group); intelligence cadres, 2,500; Black Tigers, 350; total strength including political and logistical support cadres, 21,000.

[25] RAND fieldwork and interviews, SLAF and Western diplomatic official, Colombo, May 2004. See also B. Rahman, "Split in LTTE: The Clash of the Tamil Warlords," South Asia Policy Institute Topical Paper No. 942, March 2004; "Rebel Commander Willing to Meet LTTE Top Leadership," Associated Press, March 11, 2004; IISS, "Sri Lanka's Peace Process in Jeopardy"; Chris Kamalendran, "Inside the Karuna Fortress," *The Sunday Times* (Sri Lanka), March 14, 2004; Bandula Jayasekera, "Prabhakaran Smuggled in 11 Arms Shiploads During Truce—Karuna," *The Island* (Sri Lanka), April 9, 2004.

activities—including the Black Tigers, the Leopards Division, and the intelligence wing—remain fiercely loyal to the LTTE and, just as important, view Prabhakaran's continued leadership as absolutely essential to the success of the Eelam struggle. Third, the immediate threat from Karuna was silenced after his forces were decisively defeated in a sustained Tiger offensive at the Verugal River (just south of Trincomalee in eastern Sri Lanka) on April 9, 2004; of those who survived the onslaught, the bulk have since returned to their local villages and show no sign of taking up arms again.[26]

Operations and Tactics

As noted, the LTTE remains one of the most adept terrorist insurgencies in the world. The group has effectively fought the Sri Lankan armed forces (SLAF) to a standstill and currently exercises effective control over significant stretches of northeast Sri Lanka. The Tigers have also repeatedly demonstrated an ability to operate along the entire guerrilla conflict spectrum from selective assassinations and targeted terrorist strikes to mobile hit-and-run attacks as well as full-scale, multiple battalion-sized assaults.[27] Much of this success is due to a highly dynamic learning process that has taken advantage of the inherent weaknesses in Colombo's military and security establishment.

In many ways, the SLAF has yet to emerge as a professional force that truly understands the nature and type of war it has been fighting. The majority of commanders have never seen any action, with many promoted purely on the basis of seniority or as a result of political connections, personal loyalties, and friendships. Compounding the situation is the wholly inadequate training and support that is given to

---

[26] Interviews, SLAF, Colombo, May 2004. Although Karuna's defection is unlikely to prove a major challenge to Prabhakaran, the incident does demonstrate the potential costs to a group of centralizing under the authority of a single leader that demands and expects complete subordination. Karuna was an extremely experienced guerrilla fighter and highly revered figure among the Tamils of eastern Sri Lanka. His loss will undoubtedly complicate the LTTE's challenge of establishing and consolidating control over this part of Sri Lanka (which is, itself, an integral component of the Eelam state that the Tigers ultimately seek to create).

[27] RAND fieldwork and interview with SLAF, Colombo, May 2004.

regular soldiers. Some recruits have been dispatched to the front line after only four weeks of basic combat training, and troops regularly cite shortages in such basic equipment as modern assault rifles, ammunition, and field radio sets.[28]

On a strategic level, the SLAF tends to rely on outdated doctrines that place a premium on taking and holding static lines of defense through maximum force as opposed to more nuanced (and relevant) counterinsurgency operations that combine civil campaigns to win hearts and minds with directed disruptive missions behind enemy lines. Indeed the one positive initiative to create a permanent special forces body able to undertake unconventional missions of this type—the Long Range Patrol Group (LRPG)[29]—was reversed in 2003 after Prime Minister Ranil Wickremesinghe dismantled the group following unsubstantiated claims that the squad was involved in a plot against his ruling coalition.[30]

The weaknesses and associated failings of the SLAF have provided the LTTE with a useful benchmark of what *not* to do in terms of combat readiness and effectiveness. Indeed the makeup of the group's military structure is exactly contrary to that of the Sri Lankan army. Tiger commanders are promoted purely on merit and all retain extensive battlefield experience. Regular cadres undergo intensive training that is specifically geared to the Sri Lankan context (see below). And LTTE tactics emphasize small teams, deep penetration, and pseudo-style operations, generally taking on a more conventional footing (of which the LTTE is perfectly capable of mounting) only when theater conditions are most conducive to this style of fighting.[31]

---

[28] RAND fieldwork and interviews, senior Western diplomat and SLAF, Colombo, May 2004.

[29] The LRPG, a U.S.-trained unit, was established in 1996.

[30] Iqbal Athas, "Safe House Raid: Heads Roll as Army Chief Cracks the Whip," *The Sunday Times* (Sri Lanka), January 25, 2004. Some observers have gone even further, claiming that the decision to dismantle the LRPG was deliberately orchestrated to keep the LTTE at the negotiating table and ensure that Prabhakaran continued to view the Norwegian-led peace process as beneficial. Comments made during the World Alliance for Peace in Sri Lanka (WAPS) conference on "Road Maps to Peace in Sri Lanka," Oslo, August 20, 2004.

[31] RAND fieldwork, Colombo, May 2004.

Tactically, the LTTE has conspicuously exploited the outmoded doctrines of the SLAF to repeatedly confound Sri Lankan military offensives. Indeed, one of the main reasons the army has failed to secure much of the north and east is due to its overwhelming reliance on set-piece, trench warfare. The Tigers quickly recognized that the best way to defeat this type of warfighting stance was first to monitor the combat readiness and deployment size of known defense lines using long-range reconnaissance and sabotage teams and then, based on this intelligence, to hit them with overwhelming artillery fire and battalion-sized attack forces. Between 1995 and 2002, roughly 60 percent of all Sri Lankan field casualties resulted from this adaptive combination of low- and high-level assault modalities.[32] On an "unconventional" level, the LTTE has developed highly effective (and feared) suicide wings to carry out selective assassinations, urban bombings, and sea-borne attacks. Located in both the Black Tigers and Sea Tigers, these cadres have been responsible for well over 200 strikes since 1987, the vast bulk of which have been successful in achieving their primary aim. Table 5.1 details some of the most well known of these instances. Indeed until recently, the LTTE was unique among militant substate entities around the globe in specifically institutionalizing martyrdom as a signature mode of attack and establishing this form of violence as not only "normal" and positive but also the sine qua non of operational effectiveness.[33]

---

[32] RAND fieldwork and interviews, SLAF and senior Western diplomats, Colombo, May 2004. The LTTE is currently thought to be in the possession of a battery of new-age missiles with an accurate firing range of 40 miles.

[33] By comparison, at the height of the Lebanese Shi'ite campaign against American diplomatic and military targets in Beirut during the 1980s, suicide bombings accounted for fewer than 20 percent of all Hezbollah/Islamic Jihad terrorist operations. See Merari and Braunstein (1984), p. 10.

Table 5.1
Prominent LTTE Suicide Attacks, 1987–2002

Date	Target	Purpose	Remarks
1987	Tamil University taken over by SLAF	Destroy strategic military location	Attack modeled on the 1983 Hezbollah truck bombing in Beirut; 75 people died in the assault.[a]
1991	Rajiv Ghandi (Indian prime minister)	Political assassination	Ghandi was assassinated for his decision to curtail Indian support for the LTTE and lead a peacekeeping force to stabilize the situation in Jaffna. This is the only act of concerted terrorism that the LTTE has carried out beyond the Sri Lankan theater. Eleven others were killed in the attack.[b]
1991	Joint Operations Center (JOC), Ministry of Defense	Destroy strategic military location	The blast killed over 20, wounded 50, and destroyed vehicles as far away as 300 yards from the JOC premises.[c]
1993	Ranasinghe Premadasa (Sri Lankan president)	Political assassination	Premadasa was killed by a deep penetration mole who had been on the presidential staff for several years. He was targeted for his endorsement of the 1987 Indo–Sri Lankan Peace Accord. The attack killed 17 and wounded over 60.[d]
1994	Gamini Dissanyake (opposition leader running in the 1994 presidential elections)	Political assassination	Dissanyake was targeted for his key role in arranging the details of the 1987 Indo–Sri Lankan Peace Accord; an additional 50 people were killed in the attack (which bore strong resemblances to the Ghandi assassination).[e]
1995	Naval gunboats (SLNS *Suraya* and SLNS *Ranasuru*)	Destroy strategic naval asset	Both ships were completely destroyed in the twin assaults, which left 11 sailors dead (the two ships were berthed with skeleton crews at the time of the strikes). It has been speculated that al-Qaeda's attack on the USS *Cole* was modeled on this operation.[f]

Table 5.1—continued

Date	Target	Purpose	Remarks
1995	Ceylon Petroleum Corporation oil facility	Destroy strategic economic target	Four oil storage tanks were destroyed, triggering one of the largest fires ever seen in Colombo. Twenty-one persons were killed in the operation.[g]
1996	Central Bank	Destroy strategic economic target	This is the most destructive act of terrorism to have ever taken place in Sri Lanka, killing 91 and injuring in excess of 1,400.[h]
1997	Colombo World Trade Center	Destroy strategic economic target	The WTC was hit just one week after it opened. The attack, which killed 15 and injured over 100, was thought to be in retaliation for the U.S. decision to designate the LTTE as a terrorist organization (the bombing is one of the few conducted by the Tigers that has made no attempt to limit foreign casualties).[i]
1999	Chandrika Kumaratunga (Sri Lankan president)	Political assassination	Kumaratunga was targeted for her hard-line stance against the LTTE and (then) refusal to negotiate with the group. Although the president survived the attack, which was carried out by a male Black Tiger dressed as a woman), she suffered damage to her face and lost her right eye. Fourteen other people were killed, including a top officer in charge of Kumaratunga's security.[j]
2001	Bandaranaike International Airport	Destroy strategic economic target and hub of critical transportation infrastructure	Twenty-six civil and military aircraft were destroyed in the attack; it is estimated that losses to Sri Lankan Airways exceeded $350 million.[k]

[a] Amal Jayasinghe, "Tiger Bombers Primed for a Repeat," *The Australian*, February 8, 1996; Amy Waldman, "Suicide Bombing Masters: Sri Lankan Rebels," *The New York Times*, January 14, 2003.

[b] "Tigers Suspect in Gandhi Assassination," *The Daily News* (Sri Lanka), May 25, 1991; "Tiger Terror," *The Times* (London*f*), August 10, 1995.

[c] Daryll de Silva, "Car Bomb Wrecks JOC Headquarters," *The Daily News,* June 22, 1991.

[d] Amal Jayasinghe and Anosh Ahamath, "President Assassinated," *The Sunday Observer* (Sri Lanka), May 2, 1993; "Tiger Terror."

Table 5.1—continued

[e] "Gamini Killed in Bomb Blast," *The Daily News,* October 24, 1994; "Tiger Terror," *The Times* (London), August 10, 1995.

[f] Author interview, Western diplomatic official, Colombo, May 2004; Panduka Senanaysake and Nicholas Candappa, "LTTE Blasts Two Navy Gunboats," *The Daily News,* April 20, 1995; Panduka Senanayake, "LTTE Claims Responsibility over Blasts in Trinco," *The Observer* (Sri Lanka), April 19, 1995.

[g] Sarath Malalasekera, "Tiger Hitmen Go for Oil Facility," *The Daily News,* October 21, 1995.

[h] Vijitha Yapa, "Tamil Lorry Bomb Rips Apart Central Bank in Colombo," *The Independent* (UK), February 1, 1996; Amal Jayasinghe, "Tiger Bombers Primed for a Repeat," *The Australian,* February 8, 1996.

[i] Niresh Eliatamby, "Tigers Take Carnage to Heart of Colombo," *The Courier-Mail* (Australia), October 16, 1997; John Stackhouse, "Terrorists Rip Sri Lankan Peace," *The Globe and Mail* (Canada), October 16, 1997; John Burns, "Tamil Bombing Tied to U.S. Terror Listing," *The International Herald Tribune,* October 17, 1997.

[j] "Wounded Sri Lankan President Calls on Tamils to Join Fight Against Terrorism," CNN.com, December 20, 1999, http://www.time.com/time/asia/magazine/99/1227/srilanka.iv.wickramasinghe.html; Dilshika Jayamaha, "Bombing Wounds Sri Lankan President," *The Washington Post,* December 19, 1999.

[k] Rohan Gunaratna, "Intelligence Failures Exposed by Tamil Tiger Airport Attack," *Jane's Intelligence Review,* September 2001, p. 16; "The Tigers Pounce," *The Economist,* July 28, 2001; "Tamil Rebels Raid Sri Lankan Airport," *The Washington Post,* July 25, 2001.

Boosting its tactical and operational base is part of the LTTE's active and innovative R&D agenda. The group has demonstrated remarkable skill in this regard, particularly in the realms of suicide devices, standoff resources, and marine attack munitions. The Tigers have developed numerous technologies to avail martyr operations, ranging from bomb vests complete with primary, secondary, and even tertiary detonation switches—including one version that explodes when the wearer raises his or her arms in surrender—to specially equipped suicide boats, bicycles, and motorbikes. These delivery media are repeatedly tested and reconfigured in secure Tiger camps and are only actively deployed after they have demonstrated a high degree of effectiveness (generally upward of 90 percent).[34]

LTTE has been even more adroit with surface and underwater combat innovation. The group is known to have fabricated at least two types of submersible, timer-activated explosive: a cylindrical bomb

---

[34] RAND fieldwork and interviews, Western diplomatic official and Internal Intelligence Directorate (IID), Colombo, May 2004.

(roughly 60–90 centimeters in height) that can be suspended from a ship's propeller or rudder shaft and an improvised RDX slab that can be attached to a vessel's hull with a black glycerol mixture. The Sea Tigers have also manufactured a variety of attack, logistics, personnel, and multipurpose craft as well as stealth suicide boats especially equipped with angled metallic superstructures to reduce their radar cross-section.[35] However, perhaps the most creative R&D effort has been the attempt to construct two-man mini-submarines for releasing divers inside Sri Lankan harbors. Revelations that the LTTE were making concerted moves in this direction first broke in 2000 when a partially completed prototype was discovered at a Tamil-owned shipyard in Phuket. According to informed sources, the five-meter vessel, while rudimentary, was capable of remaining submersed for up to six hours (at speeds up to five knots) and could very well have served as a prototype for more advanced versions to attack operational naval surface ships.[36]

Environmental Factors
Although the LTTE does not presently threaten the United States, it does provide a benchmark for the sophistication that a substate insurgency can achieve given the right combination of circumstances. Moreover, there is always the danger that the group could contract out its expertise to other groups that are of more immediate relevance to the ongoing global war on terror, including jihadists in South and Southeast Asia, or could itself come to view Washington as an obstacle to the attainment of Tamil objectives in Sri Lanka. According to one source in Colombo's Internal Intelligence Directorate (IID), the LTTE has already made contact with al-Qaeda through Pathmanathan Kumaran, the Tigers' weapons procurement chief, who allegedly traveled to Kabul between 2000 and 2001 to try to arrange the procure-

---

[35] Campbell and Gunaratna (2003).

[36] Interview, IIB, Colombo, May 2004. See also "Lanka Suspects Submarine in Thailand to be LTTE's," Associated Press, July 16, 2000; Davis (2000), p. 28. It is not currently known whether the LTTE has been able to successfully introduce submarines into its overall battle armory.

ment of surface-to-air missiles (munitions that the group had already demonstrated a proven capacity to employ, using them to bring down two Sri Lankan transport planes and a helicopter gunship during the 1990s). It is not known whether these munitions were ever supplied to the Tigers or, indeed, if this initial contact was followed with subsequent meetings. The same IID source also explicitly referred to the residual threat of attacks being directed against U.S. warships visiting the port of Trincomalee should Prabhakaran begin to view Washington's stance in the current peace process as unalterably opposed to the notion of an independent or at least fully autonomous Tamil homeland.[37] For these reasons, the United States needs to be aware of how the LTTE has evolved and how learning has affected its organizational capabilities and the corresponding threat levels that those capabilities represent.

Basque Fatherland and Liberty (ETA)

Ideological Foundation

Founded in 1959, ETA is a Marxist group that uses terrorism in hopes of forming an independent Basque state in parts of northern Spain and southwest France.[38] ETA stands for Euskadi ta Askatasuna, which means "Basque Fatherland and Liberty." In the past, ETA has received assistance from the Cuban and Libyan regimes, and some of its members have found political asylum in Mexico and Venezuela. It has had links with other militant left-wing movements in Europe and elsewhere, such as the Provisional Irish Republican Army (PIRA).[39] Although ETA's aim is to establish an independent Basque state based on Marxist principles, there have been ideological splits in the organi- zation as to whether there should be class war or national war, as well

---

[37] RAND fieldwork and interview, IID, Colombo, May 2004.

[38] Some analysts today downplay the salience of the ideology in motivating the group. Thomas A. Marks's review of this manuscript, July 2005.

[39] See, for instance, Mariano Rajoy, "Está absolutamente probado que ETA se entrenó en algunos países con terroristas islámicos," *El Mundo,* Madrid, October 21, 2001, p. 26.

as splits within the ETA over the level of violence the group should use to achieve its goals.[40]

Strategic and Operational Objectives
ETA's goal is the establishment of an independent Basque state through the use of violence. Like the PIRA, which is linked to a political movement (Sinn Fein), ETA has a political arm, Herri Batasuna, which is in fact a coalition of various nationalist factions. ETA's goal is complicated by the fact that only about half of the population of the Basque country is of Basque origin. In the 2001 regional elections, Batasuna received only about 10 percent of the vote. Batasuna was declared illegal in 2003 and is listed as a terrorist organization by the United States and the European Union.

ETA conducts assassinations of national and regional officials and attacks on government buildings in Spain. In 1973, ETA operatives killed Generalissimo Francisco Franco's apparent successor, Admiral Luis Carrero Blanco, by planting an underground bomb that exploded as he was being driven to mass at a Madrid church. In 1995, an ETA car bomb almost killed José María Aznar, then leader of the conservative Popular Party, who later became Spain's prime minister. The same year, investigators disrupted a plot to assassinate King Juan Carlos. And in 1999, Spanish investigators foiled a truck bombing of Madrid's Picasso Tower, a skyscraper designed by the architect of the World Trade Center.[41]

ETA finances its operations through kidnapping, extortion, robbery, arms trafficking, and "taxes," as well as with money leaking from its political counterpart Batasuna.[42] ETA operatives have reportedly trained in Algeria, Libya, Lebanon, and Nicaragua. Mexico, Cuba, and several South American states harbor ETA operatives.[43]

---

[40] Drake (1998), p. 56; Perez-Agote (1999).

[41] Steven Adolf, "Taliban van Baskenland Onder Druk Door Antiterreur," NRC Handelsblad, October 1, 2001, p. 5.

[42] Cronin (2004).

[43] Miro (2003).

Environmental Factors

A dispute within the ETA over the future course of the movement resulted in an extremely small faction willing to work with Osama bin Laden's terrorist network. Journalistic sources claim that up to 80 members of ETA were in Iraq prior to Operation Iraqi Freedom, and two of them were arrested on February 29, 2004, transporting explosives to Madrid.[44] Moreover, al-Qaeda has had a lengthy presence in Spain. In November 2001, Spanish authorities arrested eight men suspected of being al-Qaeda operatives involved in the September 11 attacks, and one of these men reportedly had past links with Batasuna.[45] Although there has been no evidence that ETA has considered targeting Americans, connections with the al-Zarqawi terror network and European al-Qaeda networks could induce members of this organization to join in attacks on U.S. interests in Europe.

Some Conclusions Regarding Groups Outside the al-Qaeda Universe

We began this volume by discussing three categories of alternative groups and alternative threats in the ongoing struggle against terrorism: (1) Islamist groups that articulate a politico-religious agenda for their own country and are not directly linked to the al-Qaeda network; (2) Islamist terrorist groups whose agendas are primarily ethnonationalist and that present a reasonable challenge to U.S. allies; and (3) highly capable, non-Islamist, terrorist groups. Table 5.2 separates the groups we examined into these three categories. Notably, of the Islamist groups outlined, only two—al Wa'ad and the Iraqi insurgents—developed after 1998, when Osama bin Laden issued his fatwa calling for a global jihad against "Jews and Crusaders."

---

[44] Magdi Allam, "Patto di sangue Eta-integralisti—In Iraq anche le brigate basche," *Corriere della Sera,* March 15, 2003; Richard Giragosian, "The al-Qaeda Franchise," *Asia Times,* March 17, 2004.

[45] Sumario (Proc. Ordinario) 0000035/2001 E, Juzgado Central de Instuccion No. 005, Madrid, Spain, September 17, 2003, pp. 366 and 577.

Table 5.2
Categories of Groups Outside the Global Jihadist Movement

Group	Islamist with Politico-Religious Agenda	Islamist with Ethno-Nationalist Agenda	Highly Capable, Non-Islamist
Hezbollah	X		
Hamas	X	X	
GIA	X		
Al-Gama'a	X		
Al-Wa'ad	X		
PAGAD	X		
EIJM	X		
Iraqi insurgents	X	X	X
LTTE			X
FARC			X
ETA			X
Maoist insurgencies			X

The other groups were already well established and active and had articulated their agenda prior to al-Qaeda's emergence in the international arena. The majority of the Islamist groups we have discussed interpret their jihad much more narrowly than groups affiliated or associated with al-Qaeda. Hezbollah's interests center on Lebanon and its immediate vicinity; Hamas is focused on the Palestinian problem; and the GIA seeks to overthrow the Algerian government. Even for the groups to which affiliation or association with al-Qaeda might be operationally attractive, external and internal factors have held such tendencies in check. Hezbollah appears to be influenced by its ties to Syria and Iran, as well as by its involvement in Lebanese politics. Al-Gama'a al-Islamiyya appears to be concerned about the views of its support communities in Egypt.

Nevertheless, these groups should not be dismissed as unthreatening just because they have not joined the global jihadist movement.

These organizations—which we refer to as *regional threats*—endanger U.S. regional security interests and U.S. friends and allies, and some, such as Hezbollah, could emerge as global threats.

Potential Dangerous Shifts Ahead

Some analysts have argued that after the September 11 attacks and the onset of the global war on terror, Islamist terrorist groups have begun to move toward al-Qaeda. The logic behind this argument is that the success of these attacks caused a shift in the worldview of many like-minded groups, turning them away from their local agendas to a more global, anti-America outlook. This view has some merit. It is clear from our previous discussion that many of the nonaffiliated Islamist groups have at least considered some involvement with al-Qaeda or expansion toward a more pan-Islamic agenda. Importantly, the interaction among these groups so far appears to have been motivated by both ideology and pragmatism.

In this context, even some of the non-Islamist groups could decide to cooperate with al-Qaeda or other Islamist groups for their own reasons. For example, many of the militant groups now maintain representatives in the criminal and black market world. This interconnectivity allows terrorists to acquire weapons as necessary, perhaps even to expand their capabilities. We discuss the nexus between transnational criminal organizations and militant groups in Chapter Seven. At this point, it is important to stress that some terrorist groups could shift their worldview, thus adopting an agenda similar to that of al-Qaeda. Alternatively, others could simply capitalize on a perceived trend toward anti-U.S. attacks, shifting the focus of their own attacks toward U.S. targets—either to increase their potential through alliances with more capable al-Qaeda affiliated groups or simply to gain greater recognition.

A recent RAND study analyzed factors that caused terrorist groups to adjust their intentions (e.g., their ideology or worldview) and capabilities. The study isolated three key factors that cause terrorist groups to shift from their chosen paths: (1) counter-attacks by security forces; (2) external support from states or other militant organizations; and (3) gain or loss of popular support.[46]

Significantly, the global war on terrorism has affected a number of the terrorist organizations discussed in this study in all three areas. We mentioned earlier that a potentially dangerous shift can be seen in the emerging Hamas-Hezbollah nexus, as illustrated by the March 14, 2004, attack in the Israeli port of Ashdod.[47] Given the qualitative leap in Hamas's efforts, it might not be a surprise that Hezbollah financed and, indeed, allegedly planned this attack. Yet this degree of aid and coordination is greater than anything prior in the Hamas-Hezbollah relationship. From an Israeli viewpoint, some security officials have stated that this attack motivated the Israeli government to assassinate Sheikh Yasin.[48] Indeed, the Israeli security apparatus has methodically assassinated both existing and emerging Hamas leaders and many experts believe it may take years for Hamas to rebuild, if it ever can recover.[49]

But the Ashdod attack also holds other, and more global, implications for the war on terrorism. First, it demonstrates that Sunni and Shi'ite militants *will* work together, given a mutual enemy. In this case, the enemy is Israel, but this does not preclude cooperation between Sunni and Shi'ite militants against the United States. Second, up to this point, Hamas was facing significant counterterrorism pressure from the Israeli government. In addition, tightening security and the fence around Palestinian territories all served to make it more difficult for Hamas to carry out its operations in Israel. Thus it could have been more willing to take strategic guidance from Hezbollah—not just aid

---

[46] For more information, see Cragin and Daly (2004).

[47] Cragin and Daly (2004); Cragin interviews, Israeli counterterrorism experts, April 2004.

[48] Cragin interviews, Israeli counterterrorism experts, April 2004.

[49] The IDF also reportedly was responsible for an attack against a Hezbollah leader, Ghaleb Awali, in Beirut on July 19, 2004. It is likely that this attack was also linked to the Ashdod bombing, perhaps as a warning for Hezbollah not to get too involved in the Israeli-Palestinian conflict.

but actual suggestions for types of attacks and targets. Parallel counterterrorism efforts by the United States and its allies in the war on terrorism could provoke other nonaffiliated terrorists to accept guidance from al-Qaeda in the future, as Hamas apparently did from Hezbollah. Finally, in the case of Hezbollah, a potential explanation for the shift in its aid toward Hamas is that Hezbollah may be struggling to sustain attention and support since Israel pulled out of southern Lebanon. Greater involvement in the Palestinian resistance could help Hezbollah increase its momentum and support. It is thus possible that Muslim anger at the U.S. presence in Iraq could similarly provoke shifts in the agendas of Hezbollah or other groups vis-à-vis the United States, as these groups continue to vie for local recruits and support.

CHAPTER SIX

Antiglobalization Movements

During the past ten years, political movements based on ideologies opposed to the spread of global capitalism, the destruction of the natural environment, and the growth of such transnational bodies as the European Union (EU) have taken root in Western Europe and North America, where the presence of international media has given these oppositionists a vast forum. At its core, this nascent ideological movement opposes corporate power and the assumed socioeconomic dislocations that may follow in the wake of the spread of globalized capitalism across the world.

It is in this context that several commentators have described the antiglobalization movement as a de facto "New, New Left," drawing comparisons to the international radical upheaval that swept France and other countries in 1968. Although antiglobalization radicals have been associated with marches and demonstrations, the real importance of the movement in terms of terrorism and national and international security considerations lies in its effect on organizations that have shown, in varying degrees, an explicit penchant for violence.

This chapter provides an overview and assessment of anarchist groups, the "New, New Left," and right-wing extremists in Europe and North America; antiglobalization populist movements and radical indigenous people's movements in Latin America; and ecoterrorists and other niche extremists on the even farther fringe of the movement. It should be noted that this analysis is not intended to be comprehensive. The fluid and overlapping nature of the groups, along with their often secretive and frequently opaque nature, makes it difficult to arrive at authoritative judgments. These evaluations should be viewed as a first step in a more long-term process to assess potential terrorist threats.

Anarchism, the "New, New Left," and the Extreme Right in Western Europe and North America

Anarchists

During the 1880s and 1890s, prime ministers, presidents, and monarchs were frequent targets of anarchist bombs and guns. A series of spectacular terrorist attacks in Europe and North America, including those that took the lives of Czar Alexander II of Russia in 1881, French President Marie-François Sadi Carnot in 1894, and U.S. President William McKinley in 1901, led to widespread fears of a worldwide anarchist conspiracy and a transatlantic campaign to eradicate the movement.[1] From the time of the 1917 Russian Revolution until the collapse of European communism in 1989, Marxism-Leninism eclipsed anarchism as the premier left-wing anticapitalist ideology.[2] In the postsocialist world, activists opposed to global capitalism, militarism, nuclear power, and other perceived ills have rediscovered anarchism and embraced it as a framework for explaining and changing the political, economic, and social order.

Nowhere has anarchism enjoyed a greater resurgence than in Germany, Spain, and Italy, the ideology's traditional Western European homes. Chronically high levels of unemployment, disillusionment with mainstream politics, and a deep reservoir of opposition to globalization have made Western European audiences receptive to anarchism. Recently, violence has been associated with anarchist militants. Beginning shortly before Christmas in 2003, Romano Prodi, president of the European Commission; European Central Bank chairman Jean-

---

[1]   For more on this campaign, see Jensen (2001). For more on anarchism in Europe during this period, see Miller (2001), pp. 41–58.

[2]   Except possibly in Spain during the Spanish Civil War, when anarcho-syndicalists were the dominant force in the Catalunya region until suppressed by the communists in 1938.

Claude Trichet; and EUROPOL, the continent's police coordinating body, received packages containing small amounts of explosives. No one was hurt by these bombs. They were "little more than a symbolic gesture," according to the Public Prosecutor's Office in Bologna.[3] An organization known as the Informal Anarchist Federation (*Federazione Anarchica Informale*), numbering an estimated 350 members, took credit for the parcel bomb sent to Prodi.[4] A communiqué delivered to the offices of a Roman newspaper explained the purposes of the attack, namely, to strike out at the "control and repression structures . . . of the new European order," and, ultimately, "the destruction of the state."[5] At the tactical level, anarchist goals include the release of imprisoned comrades and, more broadly, the abolition of jails and prisons.[6]

The anarchist "galaxy," according to Italian officials, includes "insurrectional-anarchists." Numbering no more than 100, this subset of activists is highly elusive and dangerous, according to Italian authorities.[7] "They do not claim responsibility for their attacks [and] they act suddenly," according to one magistrate.[8] Since 1996, their targets have included railway building sites, the offices of the center-left Democrats of the Left party, and international corporations, such as McDonalds and Blockbusters.

---

[3] Luigi Spezia, "Prodi: Spate of Searches," *La Repubblica* (Rome), December 29, 2003, FBIS. "Gunpowder may not have been used, just chlorate-based weedkiller, which 'does little more damage than Christmas sparklers, because this was no lethal device,' one detective said."

[4] "Letter Bombs Addressed to EU Officials Panic Europe," National Public Radio, Weekend Edition Sunday, January 25, 2004.

[5] Luigi Spezia, "Bologna, Explosives Claim: 'Prodi Was Our Target,'" *La Repubblica* (Rome), December 24, 2003, FBIS.

[6] Emanuela Fontana, "A Subversive Thread from Rovereto Leads to Riva del Garda," *Il Giornale* (Milan), December 9, 2003, FBIS.

[7] Fabrizio Roncone, "The Map: Although They Are Few and Disorganized, They Now Feel Like Protagonists," *Corriere della Sera* (Milan), November 12, 2003, FBIS.

[8] Roncone, "The Map . . . ."

Italian anarchists have forged links with anarchists in other European countries, such as Spain, Greece, Germany, and France.[9] The Internet has been a boon to anarchist groups by allowing dispersed individuals to share information, plan operations, recruit new members, and, allegedly, to share bomb-making recipes.[10] Germany has proven to be a particularly fertile ground for anarchist recruitment. Within the so-called "autonomist scene," there are as many as 5,000 activists and supporters, according to Germany's internal intelligence agency, the Office for the Protection of the Constitution (*Bundesamt für Verfassungsschutz*, or BfV).[11] In the autonomists' view, acts of counter-violence are a necessary response to the "structural" violence embodied in the German state and society. Recent violent actions by the autonomists include arson, attacks on neo-Nazis, militant demonstrations against nuclear power, and the disruption of road and rail transport. During street protests, autonomists typically don combat gear, wear masks, and form into "black blocs" to smash windows, assault police, and carry out other violent acts. In the view of the German authorities, such actions cross the line from protest into terrorism. Indeed, according to the BfV, these groups "have posed a threat to internal security in Germany."[12]

In Italy, some observers have claimed that the upsurge in terrorist violence heralds a return to the "days of lead" (*giorni di piombo*) of the 1970s, in which Italian society was paralyzed by frequent ter-

---

[9]   Claudia Fusani, "Counteroffensive at Viminale: 'We Know All the Names,'" *La Repubblica* (Rome), December 30, 2003, FBIS.

[10]   Sophie Arie, "Berlusconi Says Basta! to Violence," *Guardian* (London), November 6, 2003, http://www.guardian.co.uk/elsewhere/journalist/story/0,7792,1079040,00.html (as of March 21, 2006).

[11]   BfV, Annual Report of the Office for the Protection of the Constitution 2002, Cologne: BfV, n.d., p. 108.

[12]   BfV, Annual Report, p. 97. The BfV also alleges that other groups on the extreme left are willing to use violence to achieve their goals. Most notable are activists with links to remnants of the Red Army Faction (*Rote Armee Fraktion*, or RAF), the Marxist-Leninist terrorist movement that dissolved in 1998. BfV, Annual Report, fn. 115, p. 239.

rorist bombings, assassinations, and violent street protests.[13] Similarly, the Council of the European Union has concluded that the possibility exists for the "resurrection" of extreme left-wing and anarchist terrorism across the continent.[14] Recent events would seem in some ways to bear out this judgment. In Italy, in addition to the violent anarchists, other terrorists have emerged, including those claiming to be successors to the Red Brigades, which splintered in 1984. Extremist groups such as the Revolutionary Proletarian Initiative Nuclei (*Nuclei di Iniziativa Proletaria Rivoluzionaria*), which claimed responsibility for a bomb attack in 2002 near the Interior Ministry in Rome, have no more than a dozen members,[15] although some observers claim such groups are attracting increasing support.[16]

That said, the claim that Italy is returning to the "days of lead" seems overstated. Anarchist groups are small, and while they have carried out acts of terrorism, they cannot be compared to the violence of the late 1970s. At first glance, the left-wing extremist threat in Germany might appear to be larger, since the number of violent activists is greater. However, most of the terrorist incidents described by the German authorities are really little more than glorified vandalism. Window breaking, minor arson, and rock throwing, rather than assassination, are the order of the day. Moreover, what is considered "anarchist" violence by European authorities may not always be the responsibility

---

[13] See, for example, "Return to the 'Days of Lead,'" *Weekend Australian* (Sydney), March 23, 2002, p. 15.

[14] Council of the European Union, "Situation in the Terrorist Activity in the European Union: Situations and Trends," document no. 5759/02, January 31, 2002, p. 9.

[15] U.S. Department of State (2003b), p. 142.

[16] See, for example, "Nuclei di Iniziativa Proletaria Rivoluzionaria (NIPR)," *Jane's World Insurgency and Terrorism* 16, October 2002.

of anarchist groups. In both Italy and Germany, there is a long tradition of labeling incidents of political violence as "anarchist" when in
fact other groups on the right have been responsible.[17]

An assessment of the terrorist potential of the anarchist groups
presents a mixed picture. Factors that could contribute to terrorism include highly efficient communications and transportation networks, elite alienation, impatience with conventional political organizing, and membership with a strong commitment to the cause and a
willingness to take risks. Countervailing factors include the apparent
willingness of the state to take actions against suspected terrorists, the
lack of concrete grievances, and the existence of traditional and non-
violent outlets for expressing political grievances.

The "New, New Left"

During the past decade, once-staid meetings of international financial and political institutions—the International Monetary Fund, the
World Bank, the Group of Eight (G-8)—have been transformed into
arenas of street protest, civil disobedience, and occasionally violence.
To some outsiders, the antiglobalization movement (or, as many activists prefer to call it, the global justice movement) appears to be an
inchoate collection of a wide variety of causes ranging from international debt, to global capitalism, to freedom for Mumia Abu-Jamal,
the former Black Panther on death row in Pennsylvania for the murder
of a police officer. Sometimes described as the "New, New Left,"[18] the
movement, while still highly diverse, has begun to fashion a coherent
worldview.

---

[17] Statewatch, "EU Definition of Terrorism: Anarchists Targeted as Being 'Terrorists'
Alongside Al Qaeda," Analysis No. 10, February 2002, p. 3, http://www.statewatch.org/
news/2002/feb/terrdef.pdf (as of March 22, 2006); and Paul Berman, "The Passion of
Joschka Fischer," *The New Republic,* September 3, 2001, p. 36.

> There is an extensive history in Italy of anarchists or "left-wingers" appearing as suspects
> in the early stages of investigations, being arrested and later being shown to be innocent.
> In 2000 and 2001 two trials concerning explosions during the so-called 'years of lead'
> originally blamed on anarchists resulted in convictions for right-wingers acting with
> state collusion." (Statewatch, "EU Definition of Terrorism," p. 3.)

[18] Bob von Sternberg, "Call It Anarchism or New New Left, It Has a Big Voice," *Star
Tribune* (Minneapolis), May 21, 2000, p. 25A.

At the movement's core, as mentioned earlier, is opposition to global capitalism. Globalization, according to the Act Now to Stop War and End Racism (ANSWER) Coalition, "is in fact a form of class war by the rich and powerful against the poor. It is a form of corporate violence against working people and their labor unions."[19] The global justice movement, in the words of a leading theorist, "is the only major channel through which we can engage the most critical issues," such as climate change, poverty, and environmental degradation—issues that are allegedly ignored in mainstream political discourse.[20]

Opposing "globalization," or international financial institutions, is no longer at the movement's cutting edge. Like the anarchists, global justice movement activists are turning their energy to opposing what they consider illegitimate concentrations of public and private power. According to one movement polemicist, a "genuine, global revolution is underway," sparked by the belief that

> Political freedom without economic freedom is meaningless. This shared understanding is one of the rallying points for this new international gathering force of dissidents, conjured into existence by a capitalism more powerful and unchecked than anything we have seen for a century. . . . Freedom—sovereignty—is about the right to decide your economic, as well as your political destiny.[21]

The potential for these movements to pose a violent threat to the political, economic, and social order beyond isolated excesses—that is, the potential to cross the line from protest to terrorism—is unclear. It is not at all certain, for example, that today's movements will follow the trajectory of the left-wing, largely student-based movements of the 1960s and 1970s, from which violent extremists emerged in West Germany, Italy, France, and the United States.[22]

---

[19] ANSWER fact sheet, October 2, 2003, http://www.internationalANSWER.org.

[20] George Monbiot, "Stronger Than Ever: Far from Fizzling Out, the Global Justice Movement Is Growing in Numbers and Maturity," *Guardian* (London), February 28, 2003, p. 19.

[21] Paul Kingsnorth, "The Global Backlash," *New Statesman,* April 28, 2003.

[22] Berman (1996), p. 96.

The Extreme Right

On the other end of the political spectrum, extreme right-wing activists also profess an opposition to global capitalism, international financial bodies, Third World debt, and other manifestations of globalization. The British National Party, for example, claims that the "bosses of the banks" have used "bribery or economic pressure to encourage the corrupt rulers of unfortunate Third World states to take out huge loans their people can never repay."[23] In the discourse of some right-wing extremists in Germany, globalization is an American-led conspiracy, conducted by, and for the benefit of, Jewish capitalists.[24] Other right-wing extremists oppose globalization on the grounds that it undermines national sovereignty. In the words of one writer, "Pro-White Nationalists are natural enemies of Globalization for racial, economic and sovereignty reasons."[25] The National Alliance, one of North America's largest neo-Nazi groups, has set up an "Anti-Globalism Action Network," and claims that "White Nationalists are . . . anti-capitalist and anti-establishment and pro-environment . . . [they] are the true revolutionaries."[26]

Much of this railing against the evils of globalization is probably opportunistic—done in the hopes that it will attract recruits rather than as a result of new interpretations of events. However, the use of anti-globalization rhetoric may also reflect deeper trends within the extreme right, specifically, a growing ideological convergence with some parts of the far left. This is not an entirely new phenomenon, of course. During the previous century, political extremists ostensibly at odds with each

---

[23] British National Party, "Cults, Jets and Greed—The Frantic Rush to 'One World,'" http://www.bnp.org.uk/articles/rush_globalism.htm (as of March 22, 2006).

[24] BfV, *The Significance of Anti-Semitism in Current German Right-Wing Extremism,* p. 9, http://www.extremismus.com/vs/antisemitism-e.pdf (as of March 22, 2006).

[25] Walter Nowotny, "Pro-White Nationalism Versus Globalization," *Pro-White Forum,* July 17, 2002, http://www.churchoftrueisrael.com/nsforum/ns7-17.html (as of March 22, 2006).

[26] Quoted in Anti-Defamation League, "Deceptive Web Site Attempts to Lure Anti-Globalization Activists to Neo-Nazi Movement," http://www.adl.org/NR/exeres/D512AD57-27F3-44B0-AA18-14D136259DCF,0B1623CA-D5A4-465D-A369-DF6E8679CD9E, frameless.htm (as of March 22, 2006).

other in fact shared a common outlook. In Weimar Germany during the 1920s, some members of the extreme right described the Soviet Union in approving terms as an anticapitalist, antiliberal beacon for the world.[27] During the 1960s, the American Nazi Party, violently opposed to racial integration, found common cause with the Nation of Islam, whose leader, Elijah Muhammad, praised white opponents of "race mixing."[28] In recent years, opposition to Israel and Zionism has also emerged as a common theme for the extreme right and the New, New Left. The leader of France's leading Jewish organization has decried the emergence of a "brown-green-red" alliance that attacks Jews and Israel in racist, anticapitalist, and anticolonialist terms.[29]

An Extreme Right–Islamist Alliance?

The possibility of a tactical alliance between white supremacists and Islamist extremists cannot be discounted. The National Alliance has staged pro-Palestinian demonstrations outside the Israeli embassy in Washington, and Louis Beam, a prominent anti-Semitic agitator, has publicly praised the "liberation movements" of Syria, Libya, Iran, and Palestine.[30] Echoing a favorite Islamist trope, the National Alliance denounces "American and allied forces which have repeatedly made war on Moslem states in response to the demands of the Jewish lobby."[31] The global war on terrorism, according to the National Alliance, is "just a new name for the same game of killing when the Jewish lobby says 'kill.'"[32]

---

[27] Furet (1999), p. 203.

[28] Clegg (1997), pp. 152–153.

[29] "Le CRIF dénonce une alliance antisémite 'brun vert rouge,'" Accueil TF1, January 27, 2003, http://www.col.fr/judeotheque/archive.web/CRIF%20Cukierman%20fustige%20l%E2%80%99alliance%20brun,%20vert,%20rouge.htm (as of June 2005); and Strauss (2003), pp. 61–65.

[30] Anti-Defamation League, "Louis Beam," http://www.adl.org/learn/Ext_US/beam.asp?xpicked=2&item=beam (as of March 22, 2006).

[31] National Alliance, "Make Your Neighborhood a Terror-Free Zone," http://www.natall.com/leaflets (as of March 22, 2006).

[32] "Real Homeland Security," *Free Speech*, Vol. VIII, No. X, October 2002, p. 8.

Al-Qaeda, according to some press accounts, has shown some interest in reaching out to non-Islamic militant groups, with anti-Semitism, anti-Americanism, and anti-Westernism serving as a common ground.[33] An alliance between the global justice movement and either neo-Nazis or Islamic radicals is harder to imagine. Certainly the movement's libertarian elements (and the movement's anarchist fringe) would be unlikely to support linkages with politically and theologically totalitarian groups. Although neo-Nazis, Islamists, and the New, New Left share an anti-Zionist stance (and a deep well of anti-Semitism), opposition to Israel remains a relatively minor component of the global justice movement's agenda, and so is unlikely to serve as the foundation for any real partnership.

Neo-Marxist and Radical Populist Movements in Latin America

Antiglobalist movements are not part of the universe of terrorism, and some claim to be democratic—although they generally reject definitions of Western liberal democracy. Nevertheless, they threaten U.S. security interests because they threaten the stability of key countries and take countries where they seize power into destructive detours into irrational economic and political policies.

The antiglobalization movement in Latin America is unique in that many of the regional leftist movements and parties are linked in an international structure known as the São Paulo Forum. The São Paulo Forum was established under the auspices of Fidel Castro in 1990 in the Brazilian city of São Paulo. The forum brings together about 120 Latin American leftist political parties and organizations, including the two major Colombian guerrilla organizations—the FARC and the ELN—as well as the Cuban Communist Party, Venezuelan President Hugo Chávez's V Republic political movement, Nicaragua's Sandinistas, the FMLN of El Salvador, the National Revolutionary

---

[33] Paolo Pontoniere, "Al Qaeda Reaching Out to Non-Islamic Militant Groups," Pacific News Service, November 16, 2001.

Union of Guatemala, former Haitian President Jean-Bertrand Aristide's Lavallas Movement, Mexico's Zapatista National Liberation Army, and the United Left Movement of Peru.

The goal of the forum's organizers was to develop a post-Soviet strategy for the Latin American revolution. The fall of the Berlin Wall and the subsequent Soviet collapse were traumatic events for the extreme left in Latin America. Nevertheless, the more optimistic radicals argued that the end of communism in the Soviet Union and Eastern Europe did not signify the end of the socialist camp. According to a document of the VI Conference of the São Paulo Forum, "China, Vietnam, Laos, North Korea, and Cuba remain on their feet, and are working to develop their own political strategies to advance the socialist alternative."[34]

The forum's political program centers on a strong critique of "neoliberalism," which it describes as an economic model that allows the elites to accumulate even greater wealth at the expense of the poor. Globalization, according to the forum, is "pillage on a planetary scale." The forum believes that the contradictions between the wealthy few and the exploited many cannot in the long term be sustained and that the neoliberal economic model will collapse sooner rather than later.

At the strategic and tactical levels, the forum concluded that the antiglobalization forces needed to develop "new forms of struggle." It was necessary to move beyond the social sectors that had supported the left in the past, and capture "popular organizations that have emerged in response to the injustices of the modern capitalist model." Among the new forms of struggle that were recommended was taking advantage of the democratic opening in a number of Latin American countries, particularly in those where "democratic and popular fronts" were viable alternatives to unpopular neoliberal governments. Although the method of struggle was to be the democratic process, the forum's goal remains revolution. This was clearly stated in the Base Document of the IX Encounter of the forum, held in Managua, Nicaragua, in February

---

[34] Cited in Alejando Peña Esclusa, "A los diez años de su fundación: radiografía del Foro de São Paulo," forums.terra.com/foros/actualidad/ actualidad_C5/actualidad_venezolana_F100/foro_P532013 (as of November 2001).

2000: "Our goal is revolution. That is, a profound transformation of society, which should be accomplished by reaffirming and recreating democracy, an essential aspect of any alternative political project."[35]

In recent years, political forces backed by the São Paulo Forum have gained some notable successes. By the mid-1990s the strategy has brought to elected office throughout Latin America 291 deputies or legislative chamber members, 51 senators, 10 governors, and several hundred mayors affiliated with the São Paulo Forum.[36] The most spectacular success of the antiglobalization Latin American left was the election of Hugo Chávez as president of Venezuela in December 1998, but Chávez's election was not an isolated case. Other antiglobalist populists have been elected, or have come close to being elected, in a number of South American countries. Lucio Gutiérrez, a former military officer who led a coup against the government of President Jamil Mahuad in 2000, won the presidential election in Ecuador in November 2002 (although Gutiérrez has since sought to govern as a centrist). Evo Morales, the longtime leader of the Bolivian coca farmers, came in second out of eleven candidates in the June 2002 Bolivian presidential election, and his Movement Toward Socialism (MAS) gained the second-largest number of seats in the Bolivian parliament. Morales was elected president of Bolivia in December 2005.

The goal of the Cuban government and its allies in the São Paulo Forum of reversing the so-called neoliberal reforms in Latin America currently focuses on derailing the Free Trade Area of the Americas (FTAA), which would remove trade barriers among all Western hemisphere countries except Cuba. In January 2004, the Cuban government hosted the third "Hemispheric Meeting Against the FTAA," attended by 1,200 antiglobalization activists from 32 countries. In their final declaration and action plan, the anti-FTAA forces took credit for the ousting of Bolivian president Gonzalo Sánchez de Lozada

---

[35] "IX Encuentro del Foro de São Paulo: Capitalismo contemporaneo y debate sobre la alternativa," http://www.geocities.com/nuestrotiempo/25foro.htm.

[36] Institute for Cuban and Cuban-American Studies (ICCAS), University of Miami, Cuba Transition Project, "Cuban Foreign Policy in Latin America," No. 51, January 22, 2004, p. 2.

in 2003 and agreed to a coordinated strategy to defeat any and all trade liberalization agreements with the United States, including a modified North American Free Trade Agreement (NAFTA), as well as bilateral accords. The first battle is to be waged against the U.S.– Central America Free Trade Agreement (CAFTA), which is pending ratification by the legislatures of Costa Rica, El Salvador, Guatemala, Honduras, and Nicaragua.[37] Havana and its anti-FTAA allies are well poised to obstruct or reverse movement toward the FTAA, the most important U.S. policy objective in the hemisphere. Venezuela, Brazil, and Argentina walked out of the World Trade Organization talks in Cancun, Mexico, in 2003, and are delaying negotiations on the final draft of the FTAA treaty.

Radical Indigenous Peoples' Movements in the Andean Region

Radical indigenous peoples' movements throughout the Andean region have been a major transmission belt for Cuban and Venezuelan influence and general antiglobalization activity. These movements include leftist and populist groups, such as those led by Evo Morales and Felipe Quispe in Bolivia, the Pachakuti in Ecuador, and Uruguayan, Argentine, and Mapuche Indian groups in Chile (see below). The emergence of these movements is related to broader social and political trends in the Andean region, most notably the collapse of traditional governing arrangements that permitted small Spanish-origin elites to monopolize political power and exclude the indigenous majorities, and the reaction against the effects of neoliberal economic policies.

In Bolivia, economic reforms—privatizing state enterprises, reducing subsidies, and encouraging foreign investment—were implemented in the 1980s and 1990s but stalled toward the end of the 1990s as a result of a downturn in the price of Bolivia's mining output. A coca eradication program spearheaded by the United States led to the near-elimination of coca cultivation in the Bolivian lowlands but deprived

[37] ICCAS, "Cuban Foreign Policy in Latin America, Part II, Cuba Transition Project," No. 52, February 3, 2004.

tens of thousands of peasants in the lowlands of an income.[38] The result was the growth of the MAS, started by the coca farmers' leader Evo Morales, and the radical indigenous people's movement led by Felipe Quispe. Morales, who came in second in the June 2002 presidential election, despite (or because of) open opposition by the U.S. ambassador, has proposed a "participatory democracy" model for Bolivia based on elements of the Cuban model and Chávez's "Bolivarian Revolution." In April 2003, Morales and leaders of indigenous peoples in Ecuador and Honduras met with Chávez in Caracas and agreed to create an alliance extending beyond indigenous peoples to other "dispossessed" groups in Latin America.[39] Felipe Quispe, the founder and leader of the Pachakuti Indian Movement (MIP), was imprisoned from 1992 to 1997 for his role in the Tupac Katari Guerrilla Army, a Bolivian terrorist organization. In the 2002 election, MIP came in third in the capital city of La Paz. The MIP's long-term goal is to abolish Bolivia and other Andean states and restore the Tahuantinsuyo, the pre-Colombian indigenous state. In the short term, the movement seeks to replace its authority for the state's authority in the areas it controls—that is, to create a parallel state structure based on communitarian values.[40]

Antiglobalization forces in Bolivia scored a spectacular victory when they overthrew the U.S.-backed government of President Sánchez de Lozada in October 2003. The conflict began soon after Sánchez de Lozada announced his decision to export natural gas to the United States and Mexico. An estimated 74 people were killed in a month of protests against the government's free-market economic policies before President Sánchez de Lozada resigned and left the country.[41] Sánchez

---

[38] Marc Lifsher, "The Andean Arc of Instability," *The Wall Street Journal,* February 24, 2003.

[39] "Bolivia, indigenismo y vasos comunicantes," *Destaque Internacional—Informes de Coyuntura,* Año V, No. 113, Buenos Aires, October 23, 2003.

[40] "Felipe Quispe: de 'terrorista' a líder parlamentario," http://www.redvoltaire.net/article454.html; and "El Mallku Speaks: Indigenous Autonomy & Coca," January 15, 2002, http://www.narconews.com/felipe1eng.html (both as of March 22, 2006).

[41] Jose de Cordoba, "Indians Agitate for Political Goals," *The Wall Street Journal,* January 8, 2004.

de Lozada's successor, Vice President Carlos Mesa, resigned in June 2005, after weeks of escalating street demonstrations and violent confrontations, conceding that he was no longer able to govern. Mesa's resignation opened the way for Morales's election in 2005. A powerful anti-U.S. and antiglobalization indigenous movement has also emerged in Ecuador. In January 2000 thousands of indigenous protesters and young army officers overthrew the government of president Jamil Mahuad and announced the creation of a new government, including a "Parliament of the People" and a three-man governing junta. However, the coup was defused when the country's military chief took a seat in the junta but then dissolved it and turned over power to Vice President Gustavo Noboa. In the November 2002 election, former colonel Lucio Gutiérrez, a leader of the 2000 revolt, defeated the incumbent Noboa. Although he appeared very much in the Chávez mold—a former coupmaker who campaigned as a populist—Gutiérrez has moderated his stance since taking office and has sought to cooperate with the United States and international financial institutions.[42] The antiglobalization movement, however, remains capable of threatening or even bringing down his government.

In Peru there have been signs of the revival of the Shining Path. Although its leaders, including its chairman Abigail Guzmán, are in prison, the group never completely disappeared. There have been reports of kidnappings and killings in the Upper Huallaga Valley, the organization's traditional stronghold, since 2001.[43] With the increase in coca cultivation in the area as a consequence of U.S. eradication efforts in Colombia, Shining Path remnants may be able to access the resources that they need to fund a renewed insurgency.

---

[42] "Ecuador's Gutierrez Boosts His Image in U.S. Tour," *The Wall Street Journal,* February 21, 2003.

[43] See "Peru's Shining Path Starting to Show Signs of New Life," *The Miami Herald,* June 15, 2001.

CHAPTER SEVEN

The Convergence of Terrorism, Insurgency, and Crime

During the Cold War, many of the insurgent and terrorist organizations that proliferated throughout what was then known as the Third World were largely dependent on great power support. Even when these groups developed within a specific local context, they were quickly assimilated into one global camp or the other. The Soviets and the Cubans backed a number of so-called liberation movements in Africa and Central America, as well as Middle East terrorist organizations; while the United States supported groups such as the National Union for Total Independence of Angola (UNITA) in Angola, the Afghan mujahidin, and the anti-Sandinista forces in Nicaragua.

The end of the Cold War brought an effective end to external support for these groups. The Soviet Union disappeared and the United States simply lost interest in the fate of many of its former clients. For many of these groups, making the adaptation to a new environment was a matter of survival. Their post–Cold War survival strategies hinged on their ability to generate new sources of revenue to support their operations. Some groups were unable to make the transition and disbanded or made peace with the governments that they were seeking to overthrow, as in the case of the Salvadoran and Guatemalan rebels.

Other groups, however, tapped into locally available sources of revenue and grew in strength. The most successful in making the transition were those that operated in countries that produced high-value commodities, legal or otherwise—for instance, diamonds in West Africa; minerals in Central Africa; cocaine and heroin in Colombia; and opium and heroin in Southwest Asia and the "Golden Triangle."

Still other groups were able to fund themselves successfully by means of smuggling and arms trafficking, kidnapping and extortion, piracy, compact disc counterfeiting, and a variety of other criminal activity.

These activities provided easy targets of opportunity for terrorist or rebel movements. The groups had the firepower to deal themselves into the trade. They could trade the commodities themselves, as in the case of the Liberia-backed Revolutionary United Front of Sierra Leone and "conflict diamonds"; or protect and "tax" them, which is the FARC's preferred approach to the cocaine industry;[1] or set themselves up as middlemen in human and arms trafficking.

The activities of these groups tend to weaken and corrupt political and social institutions, particularly when they involve trafficking in a lucrative and social destructive commodity such as cocaine. To the extent that these groups are successful, they also displace state and government institutions, usually weak to begin with, in the areas where they establish a foothold. Unchecked, the groups will expand their resource base, increase their recruiting pool, and generate greater capacity at the expense of the state. Therefore, there is a high correlation between the development of these groups and failed or failing states.

To illustrate the operation and evolution of these linkages, we will analyze several case studies. These include the Tamil Tigers in Sri Lanka; the Abu Sayyaf Group in the Philippines; the FARC and ELN in Colombia; the activities of al-Qaeda, Hezbollah, and the Revolutionary United Front (RUF) in West Africa; and Hezbollah and other Middle Eastern extremist groups in North America and the tri-border region of Paraguay, Brazil, and Argentina.

---

[1]   The FARC is involved in the drug trade at all stages of production and transportation; however, most commentators concur that the bulk of the FARC's income from drugs is derived from taxing production as opposed to profits earned through trafficking.

The Tamil Tigers' Widespread International Criminal Network

One factor that has considerably benefited the LTTE insurgency over the past three decades is the group's sophisticated international support network. While much of this infrastructure is a result of legitimate fundraising activity among the Tamil diaspora and political lobbying designed to discredit the Sinhalese Colombo government, a significant component has been criminal in nature, involving human smuggling, drug trafficking, and gunrunning.

Human Smuggling

The trade in human beings is thought to constitute an important part of LTTE financial procurement, providing a consistent and long-term source of operational income (as well as a convenient way to establish arms procurement agents around the world—see below). According to intelligence officials in Canada, Australia, and the UK, the group is playing a pivotal role in smuggling illegal migrants and refugees out of Sri Lanka and India to the West, charging anywhere between $18,000 and $32,000 per transaction.[2] The overall scope of this trade is difficult to determine. However, in June 2000, the Sri Lankan Criminal Investigation Department (CID) uncovered one major LTTE smuggling ring involving an estimated 600–700 people who had been trafficked to the EU on forged Schengen state visas.[3] Even after taking overhead costs into account, the net profits from such an operation would have been substantial, running into the millions of dollars.

The Tigers allegedly make considerable use of Thailand for human trafficking—both as an identification forgery hub and as a staging point for onward journeys. The group is thought to have established a small

---

[2] Chalk interviews with defense and intelligence officials, London, Ottawa, Bangkok, and Canberra, November–December 2000.

[3] With a Schengen visa, a person may travel freely, with no internal border controls and few stops and checks, in the 15 European countries that are party to the Schengen agreement. See "CID Bust Another Multi Billion Rupee Human Smuggling LTTE Operation," *Daily News* (Sri Lanka), May 17, 2000; and "Human Smuggling Racket Busted," *Daily Mirror* (Sri Lanka), June 26, 2000.

but highly effective cadre of intermediaries in Bangkok and Chiang Mai. They are used to facilitate the actual movement of migrants across national borders. Such a modus operandi is also seen as a viable way of distancing senior LTTE members from possible prosecution in the event that a smuggling ring is broken up or otherwise penetrated by law enforcement authorities.[4]

Canada constitutes the main destination of choice for the bulk of the LTTE's human cargo because of its large Tamil diaspora (which facilitates rapid local integration into the adopted society) and Canada's liberal immigration laws.[5] Once in the country, the migrants quickly go underground and generally take on low-paying menial jobs that have been prearranged by the LTTE. This effectively ensures that the new arrivals remain semipermanently indentured to the group. In the current context, this essentially means acting as local Tiger henchmen or debt collectors.[6]

Drug Trafficking

Apart from human smuggling, there have been additional claims about the group's involvement in drug-running operations from South Asia's Golden Crescent. According to the Toronto-based Mackenzie Institute, some of the most profitable LTTE activities have been in the form of heroin trafficking, particularly since the 1980s when Afghan and Pakistani producers started to use smuggling routes through southern

---

[4]   Personal correspondence between Chalk and Sri Lankan High Commission officials, Bangkok, December 2000. See also Davis (2003c), p. 32.

[5]   Police and intelligence officials believe that the LTTE-Canadian smuggling route operates according to a basic procedure. Clients first travel to Bangkok, often on stolen passports that have been doctored for the purpose, where they await the provision of forged identity documents such as passports, driver licenses, and residency cards. Onward journeys to Canada are then arranged. Personal correspondence between Chalk and Sri Lankan intelligence officials, Bangkok, December 2000. See also Joshi (2000); and "Underground to Canada," *The National Post* (Canada), March 25, 2000.

[6]   Personal correspondence between Chalk and Canadian and Sri Lankan intelligence officials, Ottawa and Bangkok, November–December 2000.

India and Sri Lanka more frequently.[7] Officials in Colombo agree; one senior official asserted that collections from the Tamil diaspora pale compared to the group's narco-based revenue.[8]

Definitive proof linking the LTTE to an official policy of drug trafficking has yet to materialize. In Canada, for instance, both the Royal Canadian Mounted Police (RCMP) and the Canadian Security Intelligence Service (CSIS) have failed to implicate the group conclusively in heroin smuggling operations in Montreal, Toronto, and Vancouver, despite conducting intensive and protracted investigations into the trade over the past two years.[9]

Sri Lankan government sources insist that this merely reflects the tightly organized and compartmentalized nature of LTTE trafficking networks in general, which, as with human smuggling, has effectively insulated the group and its senior membership from prosecution.[10] Western organized crime specialists tend to adopt a similar line, further pointing out that, at least on a circumstantial level, definite indicators do exist suggesting a connection between the LTTE and the heroin trade:

---

[7] "Funding Terror: The Liberation Tigers of Tamil Eelam and Their Criminal Activities in Canada and Western Europe," Mackenzie Briefing Notes, The Mackenzie Institute, Toronto, 1995. See also "Narco-Terrorism Alliance in India, Sri Lanka," *The Hindu* (India), May 17, 1998.

[8] Personal correspondence between Chalk and Sri Lankan intelligence and law enforcement officials, Colombo, March 1999. It should be noted information derived from Sri Lankan officials concerning this matter must necessarily be viewed with a degree of caution and circumspection.

[9] Personal correspondence between Chalk and officials with the Canadian Security Intelligence Service (CSIS), Ottawa, November 2000.

[10] Personal correspondence between Chalk and Sri Lankan High Commission officials in Ottawa, Bangkok, and Canberra, November–December 2000.

- There have been numerous arrests of Tamils on drug-related charges over the last fifteen years, many of whom have had at least some links with militant organizations.[11]
- The LTTE supreme leader, Velupillai Prabhakaran, is known to have met the legal costs of many of these Tamils and has occasionally authorized "sustenance payments" to their family members while they served their prison terms.[12]
- Several organized gangs operating in the greater Toronto metropolitan area and engaged in the importation and distribution of number 3 heroin ("brown sugar") retain important symbolic links with the LTTE, including the VVT gang;[13] the Jane Finch, Kipling, Sooran, Seelapul, and Mississauga gangs; and the Gilder Tigers.[14]

Gunrunning

Finally, the LTTE is known to run a highly proficient gunrunning operation. The group's weapons and munitions network, which spans the globe, is headed by Tharmalingham Shanmugham, alias Kumaran Pathmanathan and colloquially known simply as "KP." Second to Prabhakaran and with a half-million-dollar bounty on his head, he is currently the second-most-wanted man in Sri Lanka. Most members of his weapon procurement team—the "KP Department"—have no criminal record and have not been involved in active guerrilla or terrorist operations. The reliance on noncombatants is a deliberate tactic that is designed to minimize the possibility that those involved with

---

[11] See, for instance, Athas (1999); Anthony Davis, "Tiger International," *Asiaweek.com*, http://www.pathfinder.com/asiaweek/96/0726/cs1.html (as of March 22, 2006); "To Catch a Tiger," *The Island* (Sri Lanka), May 25, 1998; "Funding Terror: The Liberation Tigers of Tamil Eelam and Their Criminal Activities in Canada and the Western World," pp. 5–6.

[12] Correspondence between Chalk and South Asian terrorism specialist, June 1997.

[13] A west Toronto Tamil gang named for Valvettithurai, a northern Sri Lankan town.

[14] RCMP Directorate for Criminal Intelligence, "The Use of Organized Criminal Activity for Profit by Extremists Operating in Canada," internal document supplied to Chalk, January 20, 2000.

gunrunning operations will be known to either Sri Lankan or overseas intelligence and law enforcement agencies.[15]

Facilitating the movement of arms is a highly active merchant shipping network known as the Sea Pigeons. Apart from the PIRA and the PLO, the LTTE is the only insurgent-terrorist group that is known to have at its disposal a viable maritime capability for logistical purposes. Today, the fleet numbers at least 11 deep-sea freighters, the majority of which reportedly sail under Honduran, Panamanian, or Liberian flags of convenience.[16] The LTTE has effectively exploited the notoriously lax registration requirements of shipping bureaus in these countries, allowing the group to confound international tracking and monitoring attempts by repeatedly changing the names, manifest details, and duty statements of the vessels used, which has also been an integral part of the so-called "phantom ship" phenomenon (see below).[17]

LTTE munitions procurement draws on a variety of sources. Much of the group's overseas arms purchases come from the booming post–Cold War arms bazaars that have emerged in Southeast and Southwest Asia—especially Cambodia, Burma, Pakistan, and, until the U.S.-led Operation Enduring Freedom, Afghanistan. The Tigers have also moved to establish major weapons trading centers in Bulgaria, the Czech Republic, North Korea, Ukraine, Croatia, and South Africa.[18]

Thailand has emerged as the main logistical interface between these various international source countries, both with regard to weapons bound for the Sri Lankan theater and for subcontracted deals involving other insurgent and criminal actors. The LTTE Thai net-

---

[15] Byman, Chalk, Hoffman, et al. (2001), p. 119.

[16] LTTE vessels sail under a number of additional flags. Three ships, the *Sun Bird*, the *Amazon,* and the *Golden Bird,* for instance, are respectively known to have been registered in Cyprus, New Zealand, and Malta.

[17] Chalk interview, Canberra, September 1998. See also Mike Winchester, "Ship of Fools: Tamil Tigers' Heist of the Century," *Soldier of Fortune,* Vol. 23, No. 8, August 1998, p. 39; "Tiger Arms Ship in High Sea Drama," *The Sunday Times* (Sri Lanka), May 9, 1998; and "Armed to the Teeth," *India Today,* January 11, 1996.

[18] Byman, Chalk, Hoffman, et al. (2001), p. 119.

work involves the recruitment of locally based Tamils who are used to open and staff front companies based in Trang and Phuket on the Andaman Sea coast as well as in Bangkok, notably around Naret Road and the General Post Office.[19]

Rationale for Convergence with Organized Crime

The LTTE's involvement in organized crime essentially relates to changing geopolitical decisions and calculations undertaken by the Indian government in the 1980s. During the early stages of the Tamil insurgency in Sri Lanka, the LTTE had benefited greatly from the backing and support of New Delhi, which was acutely aware of the risk of ignoring the sympathetic ethnic proclivities of its own Tamil population in Tamil Nadu. Moreover, the Indian government was actively prepared to support the Tamil separatist war as a way of indirectly pressuring Colombo to remain within its sphere of influence. Between 1983 and 1987, India's Research and Analysis Wing, the agency charged with advancing India's clandestine foreign policy goals, provided sanctuary and arms to the LTTE as well as insurgent training in paramilitary camps located in the south of the country.

Although the Indian government was instrumental in supporting the Tamil insurgency during the early 1980s, by 1987 New Delhi was beginning to fear that the creation of an independent Tamil state in Sri Lanka could spark secessionist demands in its own Tamil Nadu. Moreover, the presence of armed Tamil militants in the country had begun to cause a growing problem in the south, compounding already serious strains brought about by the number of Tamil refugees fleeing from Sri Lanka's Jaffna peninsula.[20] As a result, the Indian government terminated its support for the LTTE and actively began looking for a

[19] See Davis (2003c), p. 30.

[20] Gunaratna (1998), p. 117. By 1987, the total number of Tamil refugees in Sri Lanka had risen to an estimated 13,000.

federalist solution to Sri Lanka's growing ethnic crisis, something that Colombo was equally keen to achieve given the increasingly violent and costly nature of the insurgency.[21]

New Delhi's subsequent efforts to disrupt the Tigers' munitions supply chain represented a significant blow to the group, requiring the development of a more secure and independent line of weapons funding and acquisition. Accordingly, the LTTE moved to develop its own logistical network—one that would be self-sustaining, specific to the needs of the group, and, most importantly, insulated from the changing strategic imperatives of a sole state backer. To a certain extent, the LTTE could rely on remittances and contributions from sympathetic members of its extensive diaspora in such countries as the United Kingdom, Australia, Canada, Switzerland, and Norway.[22] However, this represented only a finite, effectively capped source of assistance that was contingent on the mobilization of communities that may have little opportunity or willingness to support an insurgency being fought on the other side of the world. The move to organized criminality reflected the need for larger, more consistent injections of support, as well as the requirement for battle-related materiel that could only be supplied through the shadowy world of underground arms trading.

The LTTE has strenuously sought to play down any suggestion that it is involved in organized crime for any reason other than self-preservation. A considerable component of the group's overseas publicity and propaganda effort entails portraying the Tigers as a bona fide organization engaged in a fully justified and legitimate war of national liberation. More to the point, the LTTE political leadership seeks to

---

[21] In July 1987, Colombo and New Delhi signed the Indo–Sri Lankan Peace Accord, which provided for a complete cessation of hostilities and the surrender of all weapons by the Tamil militants; the amalgamation (subject to a referendum) of the Northern and Eastern Provinces into one, Tamil-dominated administrative unit with its own elected provincial council; co-equal status for Tamil and English as official languages; the prevention of the use of Indian territory by Tamil militants for military or propaganda purposes; and the repatriation of Tamil refugees. New Delhi also agreed to send a peacekeeping force (IPKF) to Sri Lanka, sparking a bloody secondary guerrilla war with the LTTE that eventually led to a humiliating Indian withdrawal in March 1990. For further details of this period see Singh (2001).

[22] Overall, the LTTE has a relatively sizable diaspora in 54 countries from Bangladesh to Botswana.

impress on the international community that, should the organization succeed in winning control of a separate state, it would exercise its duties in a responsible manner consistent with democratic norms of civilized behavior.[23] Obviously any overt attachment to organized criminality—particularly drug trafficking, which the United States has portrayed as one of the most threatening transnational dangers currently confronting the global community—would run counter to this objective.

A related consideration has to do with the Tamil diaspora. As noted above, contributions from expatriates do not constitute a self-sustaining source of income for the LTTE. They nevertheless remain an important source of supplementary income. Donations from the UK, Australia, and Canada, for instance, are collectively estimated to net up to $1.5 million a month for the group's cause, most of which is derived from a standard baseline "tax" that is imposed as a minimum moral obligation on families living in the respective host state.[24] To a large extent, the LTTE's ability to procure this funding has been indicative of its general invisibility to law enforcement by shunning unnecessarily explicit criminal behavior.[25]

These public relations considerations have acted as a self-regulating brake on the LTTE's overall convergence with organized crime. The group has conspicuously sought to cover its tracks at every juncture (as noted above, very few cadres have ever been charged on drug-related offenses) and has generally engaged only in those endeavors that are directly related to its war effort and that offer a reasonably secure line of funding and support. Consequently, the LTTE has not morphed into the type of criminal-terrorist entity seen in other parts of the world. Crime remains an adjunct to its wider political goals rather than its central purpose.

---

[23] See, for instance, Chalk (2000).

[24] See, for instance, Davis, "Tiger International," p. 35; "Tamil Expatriates Finance LTTE Terror," *Daily News* (Sri Lanka), June 8, 1998; "A Tamil Tiger Primer on International Arms Bazaar," *The International Herald Tribune,* March 10, 1998; and "The LTTE Rides High in Norway," *Lanka Outlook,* Summer 1998, pp. 24–25.

[25] Chalk interview, Ottawa, October 17, 2002.

The Abu Sayyaf Group: An Islamic Terrorist-Criminal Group

Mindanao has been the locus of a prolonged and bitter Moro Islamic separatist conflict since the mid-1970s. Historically, the Moro National Liberation Front (MNLF) represented the main vehicle for this struggle. However, the group made peace with Manila in 1996,[26] and since then two entities have been at the forefront of militant activities in the southern Philippines: the Moro Islamic Liberation Front (MILF) and the Abu Sayyaf Group (ASG). Of the two, it is the latter that has established the most concerted ties to organized criminal activity.

Abu Sayyaf is a self-styled Islamic insurgent movement that first emerged in 1989 with the assistance of Mohammed Jamal Khalifa, Osama bin Laden's brother-in-law and personal representative in the Philippines.[27] Its original founder was Abdurajak Janjalani, an ultra-fundamentalist veteran of the anti-Soviet campaign in Afghanistan who fought under the command of the mujahidin commander Abdul Rasul Sayyaf and was influenced by bin Laden. Under Janjalani's tutelage, the ASG developed a highly radical ideological agenda that aimed for the creation of an independent and exclusive Islamic state in Mindanao. In pursuit of this objective, the group has advocated the deliberate targeting of all non-Muslims in the southern Philippines and

---

[26] The MNLF signed a peace agreement with Manila in 1996, known as the Davao Consensus, which created a limited Autonomous Region of Muslim Mindanao and provided for peace and development efforts in the south. For an overview of the accord see Chalk (1997).

[27] At its inception, the ASG was known as al-Harakat al-Islamiyya (Islamic Movement); in 1992, the group renamed itself the Mujahidin Commando Freedom Fighters before settling on Abu Sayyaf in 1993.

has repeatedly defined its intentions as intimately tied to an integrated effort aimed at asserting the global dominance of Islam through militant armed struggle.[28]

Although the ASG was originally founded as a committed and closely coordinated jihadist movement, it has progressively degenerated into a network of loosely based territorial commands concerned more with money than political or religious goals. The main factor accounting for this structural and ideological fragmentation was the death of Janjalani, who was killed during a Philippine police ambush in December 1998.[29] Not only did his elimination trigger an acute leadership crisis within the group (which has never been resolved), more importantly it removed the chief driving force behind the ASG's former Islamic zeal.[30] The combined effect of these two factors was the gradual infusion of outside criminal tendencies and imperatives, the principal thrust of which has been piracy and kidnapping.

Piracy

The ASG has carried out numerous pirate attacks off Mindanao and nearby islands, particularly between Tawi-Tawi, Sulu, Basilan, and the Zamboanga Peninsula. The group essentially has free run of these waters, because of both the absence of joint Philippine-Malaysian maritime patrols (essentially reflecting interstate tensions arising from ongoing territorial disputes and issues of maritime sovereignty) and the difficulty of instituting a comprehensive monitoring regime of the Philippines' extensive archipelagic coastline.

---

[28] Turner (1995), p. 15; Concepcion Clamor, "Terrorism in the Philippines," paper presented before the Council for Security Cooperation in the Asia Pacific's Working Group on Transnational Crime, Manila, May 1998, p. 5; "Validation of the Existence of the ASG," internal document prepared for the Philippine National Intelligence Coordinating Agency, February 14, 1997; "Separatist Rebellion in the Southern Philippines," *IISS Strategic Comments,* Vol. 6, No. 4, May 2000, p. 2.

[29] See, for instance, Jose Torres, "The Abu Sayyaf Ten Years After," ABS-CBN News, n.d., http://www.abs-cbnnews.com/images/news/microsites/abusayyaf/abu10.htm (as of March 22, 2006).

[30] Comments made during the INR Workshop on Radical Islam in Southeast Asia, Washington, D.C., October 31, 2003.

ASG cadres, usually operating in teams of between two and ten, mainly target fishing trawlers, merchant vessels, and small-scale cargo containers, launching assaults from fast motorized outriggers, or *bancas,* that are able to outrun any vessels that the ill-equipped Philippine navy can put to sea.[31] Typically, a ship will be threatened with an RPG or peppered with heavy machine gun fire and a payoff demanded. If this is not forthcoming, the vessel will be boarded, its cargo ransacked, the captain's safe stolen (often this will contain a large amount of cash to pay port fees and loading charges), and the crew killed.[32]

In addition to commercial carriers, the ASG has also periodically attacked passenger ferries that operate crossings in the Sulu and Celebes Seas. The monetary scale of these assaults is of a lower magnitude than that offered by cargo containers and fishing trawlers, and most ships are able to carry only a small number of paying customers, most of whom will not be particularly wealthy. But the ships themselves tend to offer a highly attractive target of opportunity given their lack of maneuverability, the frequency and regularity of inter-island sailings, and the near total absence of onboard security.[33]

Between 1996 and the end of September 2003, 811 actual and attempted acts of piracy were recorded in Southeast Asia, 11 percent of which took place in Philippine waters.[34] Although many of these incidents involved ships berthed at Manila port, a considerable proportion occurred in the vicinity of southern islands and inlets under the direct control of, or close to, Abu Sayyaf strongholds. It is this consistent

---

[31] Davis (2003b), p. 14.

[32] See, for instance, Virtual Information Center, "Primer: Piracy in Asia," October 31, 2003, pp. 19–20, http://www.vic-info.org/RegionsTop.nsf/45cb6498825bd61d0a256c 6800737df2/90b323f6d67ef5de0a256b9500807103?OpenDocument (as of March 22, 2006).

[33] Peter Chalk, "Threats to the Maritime Environment: Piracy and Terrorism," presentation given before the RAND Stakeholder Consultation Meeting, Ispar, Italy, October 28–30, 2002.

[34] See International Maritime Bureau (2003), p. 5. Generally speaking, only Indonesia has surpassed the Philippines in terms of the regional incidence of piracy.

correlation of attacks and geography that accounts for the ASG's current designation as one of the leading terrorist-piracy organizations in Southeast Asia.[35]

There are no reliable statistics as to how much money the ASG has actually made by engaging in maritime crime. However, most commentators believe it to be substantial, providing a largely self-generating source of income that is reflected in the group's ongoing pursuit of seaborne profiteering.[36]

Despite this active track record, there has as yet been no indication of direct ASG involvement in the most lucrative aspect of the piracy phenomenon, the outright hijacking of a targeted vessel for the purposes of repeat illegal trading. Known as phantom ships, these carriers are falsely documented under flags of convenience, generally from Honduras, Panama, and Liberia (all of which are notorious for their extremely lax registration requirements), and used to transport and then reroute the cargoes of unsuspecting commodity agents or brokers. However, there have been allegations that Abu Sayyaf members have worked in conjunction with phantom ship criminal syndicates, helping to hide hijacked vessels in secluded harbors under ASG control and to facilitate the discharge of diverted payloads to corrupt local officials and members of the armed forces.[37] Given the enormous profits that can be garnered from phantom ship frauds—the International Maritime Bureau estimates groups engaged in the practice can earn upward of US $50 million a year[38]—the possibility that this type of indirect involvement has indeed occurred cannot be discounted.

---

[35] See, for instance, Coast Guard Intelligence Assessment (2000), p. I-7.

[36] This perspective on the ASG was expressed to Chalk in various meetings and interviews in the Philippines, London (International Maritime Bureau), and Singapore between 2000 and 2003.

[37] Virtual Information Center, "Primer: Piracy in Asia," pp. 20–21.

[38] Personal correspondence between Chalk and Eric Ellen, IMB, London, January 1997. See also "Dead Men Tell No Tales," *The Economist,* December 18, 1999.

Kidnapping

Although the ASG has long engaged in kidnapping and extortion, under Janjalani's leadership such tactics were used exclusively as a means for raising funds for operational and logistical purposes. Since 1998, however, abductions have increasingly been aimed at generating money for its own sake. The practice has been encouraged by the general willingness of the victims' families to pay ransoms, as well as their reticence to involve the authorities or seek judicial redress, even in the event that the hostage takers are subsequently apprehended.[39] In one publicized case, two Hong Kong hostages were released for a "board and lodging fee" of 2 million Philippine pesos (P) (roughly $36,000) 106 days after their original capture.[40] At the time this was typical of most ransom demands, which according to the Philippine National Police generally ran between a minimum of P500,000 (roughly $9,000) and a maximum of P2 million.[41]

The scale of these incidents reached new heights in March 2000 when the ASG carried out a mass kidnapping of more than 50 elementary school children and teachers, including Catholic priest Rhoel Gallardo (who was later killed), from the village of Tumahubong on the island of Basilan.[42] The operation constituted the largest single abduction carried out by the group and has since been seen by several commentators as marking the turning point of Abu Sayyaf into a full-fledged kidnap-for-ransom business.[43]

---

[39] Chalk (2002), p. 202; Independent Insight Inc., "Kidnap-for-Ransom in the Philippines," Manila, November 12, 2001, p. 3.

[40] "Guerrillas Make a Killing Out of Abductions," *South China Morning Post,* December 28, 1998; "HK Hostages Released After 106-Day Ordeal," *South China Morning Post,* December 24, 1998.

[41] Chalk interview, Manila, June 1998. See also "Zambo Blast Cover Up for Weak ASG," *Manila Times,* January 5, 1999.

[42] See, for instance, "Abu Sayyaf Primer," Virtual Information Center, November 5, 2002, p. 12, http://www.vic-info.org/regionlist2002.htm; "Gunmen Take Foreigners Hostage in Malaysia," *The Washington Post,* March 25, 2000; "Philippine Military Begins Assault on Muslim Rebels," CNN Interactive Worldwide News, April 22, 2000.

[43] See, for instance, Lopez (2000); and Gunaratna (2001).

It was the following month, however, that the ASG gained international notoriety for engaging in criminally motivated abductions. On April 23, a faction led by Ghalib Andang (otherwise known as Commander Robot) carried out a lightening raid on a diving resort in Sipadan, Malaysia (Easter Island), capturing 21 hostages, including ten Malaysians, three Germans, two French nationals, two South Africans, two Finns, one Lebanese, and a Filipino. Initial ransom demands were cast in terms of provision of supplies and political stipulations (reversion to barter trading, curbs on foreign fishing, foreign mediation in the Mindanao dispute, release of prominent Islamist terrorists imprisoned in the United States) but quickly evolved into demands for money—$1 million for each of the Western tourists. Five months later, a Libyan-brokered deal was reached for the release of six of the captives, which the head of the Philippine armed forces, General Angelo Reyes, later confirmed netted the group over $16 million.[44]

The Sipadan operation proved to be a major boon as well as a prominent tactical watershed. The injection of money allowed the ASG to recruit impoverished local villagers who were reportedly offered "salaries" of P40,000 to P100,000 each; buy the loyalty of competing factions (intelligence sources claim that several million pesos were distributed for this purpose); and acquire the necessary weapons and logistical resources to sustain the group's activities over the short to medium term.[45] More to the point, it proved that "crime paid" both monetarily and in terms of institutional bargaining power, and ensured that kidnapping would remain the ASG's favored means of financial procurement.

---

[44] See, for instance, U.S. Department of State (2003b), pp. 101–102; Oxfam Small Arms Report, draft text supplied to author, 2001, p. 3; "Fears of the Hostage Takers," *The Economist*, August 26, 2000; "Libya Denies Ransom Offer for Hostages," *The Sacramento Bee*, August 13, 2000; and "Philippine Forces Continue All-Out Attack on Rebels," *The Washington Post*, September 17, 2000. According to Reyes, US $1 million was paid for the nine Western hostages and US $350,000 for each of the rest.

[45] Torres, "The Abu Sayyaf Ten Years After"; "A Clash of Civilisations," ASEAN Focus Group—Asian Analysis, Australian National University, May 2000, http://www.aseanfocus.com (as of March 23, 2006).

Reflecting this, in the 13 months following the Sipadan operation, no less than 102 people were abducted in various incidents across
the southern Philippines. The tally included French and German jour-
nalists, Malaysian resort workers, U.S. tourists, and Christian mis-
sionaries (one of whom was subsequently beheaded)—reportedly generating additional ransom payments of between $15 million and $20
million.[46]

Overall, the ASG is thought to account for roughly 20 percent
of all kidnappings that take place in the Philippines. However, if one
adds abductions perpetrated by ex-members of the police and security
forces, many of whom are alleged to retain close criminal ties to Abu
Sayyaf (and MILF), the total would rise to near 60 percent.[47] It was in
this context that the Minority Parliamentary House leader, Feliciano
Belmonte, famously referred to Ghalib Andang as the "Bill Gates of
the [Philippine] kidnapping industry."[48] (Andang was captured in
November 2003 after a gun battle in southern Jolo Island as he was
planning another abduction.)

Gunrunning

The third major form of criminal activity to which the ASG has been
connected is gunrunning. The southern Philippines has been awash
with weapons since the mid-1980s, emerging as one of the main sources

---

[46] "Abu Sayyaf Group," pp. 12–19; Independent Insight Inc., "Kidnap-for-Ransom in
the Philippines," p. 2; "Rebels Kidnap America; Philippines to Reconsider Ransoms," *The
Washington Post,* August 31, 2000; "A Hostage Crisis Confronts Estrada," *The Economist,*
May 6, 2000; and "Military Finds 2 Beheaded by Philippine Rebels," *The Washington Post,*
May 7, 2000. At the time of writing, the ASG held no hostages; those who were seized
between 2001 and 2002 either had been killed (generally by beheading) or had escaped from
their captors during military pursuit operations.

[47] Independent Insight Inc., "Kidnap-for-Ransom in the Philippines," p. 4. Thirty-five percent of abductions in the Philippines are carried out by drug groups (15 percent) and international syndicates (20 percent); 4 percent are perpetrated by ad hoc criminal groups (that
are organized due to a specific opportunity) or street gangs; only 1 percent carry demands of
a purely political nature.

[48] Lopez (2000).

for light arms in Southeast Asia.[49] Several factors account for the proliferation of munitions in the region, including (1) shortfalls in the disarmament, demobilization, and reintegration programs that followed the conclusion of the MNLF insurgency in 1996; (2) illicit transfers from corrupt members of the army and militiamen of the Civilian Armed Forces Geographic Units;[50] (3) diversion of arms from the U.S. Excess Defense Articles program in the Philippines;[51] and (4) local production both from the MILF and from skilled gunsmiths in Mindanao and northern Luzon. Prices on the black market reportedly range from US $660 for an M-16 assault rifle to US $37 for .38- and .45-caliber handguns.[52]

The ASG has effectively tapped the burgeoning stock of weaponry in Mindanao, both to augment its own supplies and to build up inventory that can be sold to other interested parties. The group has developed a particularly useful "business" in the latter regard, acting as an intermediary for the regional trafficking of Philippine-source weaponry. An established maritime tradition, combined with the lack of active coastal surveillance around Mindanao, as noted in the discussion of piracy, has ensured that Abu Sayyaf smugglers can move arms caches quickly with relatively little risk of interdiction. Members of the organization are also known to have built strong links with well-

---

[49] Philippine security officials conservatively estimate that between 75,000 and 100,000 weapons are loose throughout the southern Philippines, most of which are long arms as opposed to handguns.

[50] Between 1972 and 1986, a total of 8,000 army weapons, mainly Garand M-1 rifles, M-14s, and M-16s, went unaccounted for.

[51] Between 1992 and 1998—as part of its EDA program—the United States gave the Philippines 3,638 M-14s, an unspecified number of M-16s, 16,488 Colt M1911 pistols, and 116 A-1 automatic rifles. Many of these "offloaded" weapons subsequently found their way on to the black market as a result of leakage from the police and security forces. Oxfam Small Arms Report, pp. 5–6.

[52] Davis (2003a), pp. 32–37.

connected criminal and terrorist elements based in Malaysia, providing the group with the necessary points of contact through which to arrange and conclude regionwide, as opposed to purely local, deals.[53]

Most of the arms that are purchased for resale are trafficked over water, passing from bases in Zamboanga and Jolo, across the Sulu Sea to prearranged buyers and subcontractors in the Malaysian provinces of Sabah, Sarawak, and Kelantan. From here consignments are moved to key regional hubs in Cambodia (Sihanoukville), Thailand (Phuket, Ranong, Rayong), Bangladesh (Cox's Bazaar, Chittagong), and Singapore.[54] These same routes work in reverse, providing an effective two-way corridor that can be used for both the import and export of munitions.

The general level of ASG munitions trading activity has risen dramatically over the last four years as a result of the prolific ransom payments the group has received from its various kidnapping pursuits. According to local commentators, the unprecedented injection of cash triggered a major arms-buying spree across Mindanao, driving up prices for everything from mortars and "baby" M-16 assault weapons fitted with grenade launchers (M-203) to recoilless rifles, M-60, and even .50-caliber heavy machine guns.[55]

Flush with cash, the ASG has been able to pay top dollar for these armaments.[56] The cost is passed onto paying customers in the form of 50 percent markups, allowing the group to build up a modern and broad-ranging weapons inventory.[57] Demand for this base stock has been consistently strong, both because Philippine-source munitions

---

[53] Comments made during the Bureau of Intelligence and Research (INR) Workshop on "Radical Islam in Southeast Asia," Washington, D.C., October 31, 2003.

[54] Davis (2003a), pp. 30–32.

[55] Torres, "The Abu Sayyaf Ten Years After"; Lopez (2000); Oxfam Small Arms Report, p. 7.

[56] For example in 2001, the ASG was reportedly prepared to pay P48,00 for one M-16 rifle (the standard weapon of the security forces), nearly double the official listed price by the government (P25,000). The group was also offering P280,000 for an Ultimax light machine gun, which normally retails for around P93,000. Oxfam Small Arms Report, p. 7.

[57] Davis (2003a), p. 35.

are cheap in comparison to those coming from extraregional sources such as North Korea, China, and Pakistan (price inflation notwithstanding) and far more sophisticated than traditional supplies from Cambodia (most of which derive from surplus stocks left over after the Third Indochina War).

Rationale for Convergence with Organized Crime

As noted above, ASG involvement with organized crime primarily reflects the group's general organizational and ideological fragmentation since the death of Janjalani in 1998. Over the past five years, the group has steadily degenerated into a loosely based network of territorial "lost commands" concerned more with money than fundamentalist Islamist imperatives. Although the rhetoric of jihadism still infuses the group, it has been used largely to legitimate and cover up what is essentially a criminally based agenda.[58]

Exacerbating the ASG's general evolution into criminality have been two additional factors. First, the very success of the group's illicit endeavors, particularly kidnapping, not only demonstrated the financial worth of crime but also provided the necessary capital to offset unavoidable overhead operating costs (such as those associated with building up a viable weapons inventory).

Second, and no less important, ASG Islamist ranks have been steadily diluted by the importation of recruits who view the group less as a vehicle to achieve specific Islamic objectives than as a means of enrichment. Local bandits, laid-off agricultural and construction workers, and farmers suffering from poor crops simply gravitate into

---

[58] It should be noted that Khaddafy Janjalini—a leading ASG member and brother of the group's original founder—has been pushing to reintegrate the organization and return it to the pursuit of an explicit Islamist agenda. It is too soon, however, to tell if this attempt to regenerate the ASG as a "bona fide" jihadist force will be successful.

and out of the group as their own individual exigencies change.[59] Philippine intelligence sources estimate that the ASG's membership grew rapidly after the kidnappings in 2000 and 2002 as members of the local Moro community flocked to the group, lured by the promise of action and the huge ransom payments that had been coerced out of foreign government hands.[60] As one senior Philippine military commander remarked, the root causes of ASG can increasingly be summed up in two words: "thrills and joblessness."[61]

The group has used its wealth to purchase weapons, communication sets, and transportation vehicles. This has allowed it to repeatedly absorb, recover, and at times respond to government attacks that have been orchestrated under the auspices of Balikitan-02-I and Balikitan-03-II. Initiated in 2002 and renewed in 2003, these combined military exercises have involved Army, Marine, and Scout Ranger special force units and were designed to train the Philippine military to root out Abu Sayyaf cells in the southern Philippines. Philippine offensives (code named "Endgame") have been successful in Basilan and Zamboanga.[62] Nevertheless, the ASG's involvement in such terrorist attacks as the 2005 Valentine Day bombings in Manila reflect an organization that is not only very much alive, but is also capable of operating beyond the traditional Mindanao theater.[63]

---

[59] Comments made during the INR Workshop on "Radical Islam in Southeast Asia," Washington, D.C., October 31, 2003. Poverty is chronic in Mindanao, which remains the least developed of the Philippine provinces. According to the World Bank, a staggering 92 percent of the population lives below the official poverty line; in Jolo, the ASG's main center of strength, unemployment runs between 50 and 70 percent of the male population. See Davis (2003b), p. 18.

[60] Torres, "The Abu Sayyaf Ten Years After."

[61] Cited in Davis (2003b), p. 18.

[62] Davis (2003b), p. 17. At the time of writing, at least 300 ASG armed militants were thought to remain on Jolo, with between 100 and 160 scattered across Basilan and Zamboanga.

[63] Chalk interview, Philippine police, military, and intelligence officials, Manila, March 2005. See also Carlos Conde, "The Philippines: Bombs in Three Cities Kill 6," *The New York Times,* February 15, 2005; "Over 60 Hurt in Makati Explosion; GMA Inspects Site," ABS-CBN, February 16, 2005.

On a more general level, the reorientation from religious-separatist to material ambitions has effectively eliminated the option of a political accommodation. Indeed, if anything, one can expect to see the ASG deliberately fostering a climate of general instability in Mindanao to ensure the survival of what has proven to be an especially conducive environment for wider arms trafficking, kidnapping, and piracy. Over the longer term, there is also the risk that a criminalized ASG will emerge as a resource for foreign-based terror networks, notably al-Qaeda and its Southeast Asian affiliate, Jemaah Islamiyah (JI).[64] Such concerns should not be viewed as idle speculation. With the MILF keen to play down its own alleged support of transnational Islamic extremism in the context of ongoing peace negotiations with the Philippine government,[65] the ASG may well prove by default to be the favored conduit through which external radicals seek to extend the range and scope of their operations in Southeast Asia. Indeed, as recently as 2003, Philippine intelligence was claiming that JI and al-Qaeda terrorists had been working in conjunction with Abu Sayyaf members in the procurement, preparation, and distribution of explosive devices, including, cellular-detonated car bombs.[66]

Colombia: The Synergy of Drugs and Insurgency

Over the past decade, Colombia has confronted a metastasizing left-wing insurgency that has been sustained and further complicated by funds derived from an entrenched criminal economy. Three main players have been integral to this chronic situation: the FARC, the ELN,

---

[64] In 2003, Abu Sayyaf's chief explosives expert, Abdul Mukim Edris, escaped from prison with Fathur Rohman al-Ghozi, JI's principal operative in the southern Philippines and one of the network's most senior bomb-makers in Southeast Asia (al-Ghozi was killed by Philippine police three months later).

[65] At the time of writing, the MILF had announced its intention to pursue comprehensive peace talks with the Manila government aimed at consolidating a final settlement to the conflict by 2004.

[66] See, for instance, Davis (2003b), p. 18.

and illegal paramilitary self-defense forces, loosely organized under the umbrella of the United Self-Defense Forces of Colombia (AUC).

The FARC was established in 1964 as the military wing of the Moscow-line Colombian Communist Party under the leadership of Manuel Marulanda Vélez (alias Tirofijo or "Sureshot"). The group's long-term aim is the seizure of national power through a people's war, although its current public short-term agenda calls for land redistribution, disbanding of the military and the security forces, a crackdown on the AUC, and empowering the historically disenfranchised lower working and peasant classes.[67] The FARC has an estimated fighting force of 15,000 to 18,000 combatants who are organized into seven regional "bloques" (or blocs) and some 71 fronts (67 rural and four urban) that are deployed in a coordinated pattern across the country. The group also has some 10,000 militia members who help with logistics and intelligence gathering.[68] A lengthy process of peace negotiations between the Colombian government and the FARC—which involved the surrender to the FARC of an extensive demilitarized zone in south-central Colombia—collapsed at the beginning of 2002 after the FARC carried out a series of high-profile kidnappings and assassinations.

The Havana-line ELN was founded in 1964 by intellectuals from the University of Santander and is presently led by Nicolas Rodriguez (alias Gabino). Like the FARC, the group stresses economic and social reform and the general restructuring of the state security apparatus. However, it has also long contested oil drilling and production in northern Colombia and tends to emphasize an overall ideological agenda that mixes Cuban revolutionary theorizing with "liberation theology." The ELN is much smaller than the FARC, numbering 3,500–5,000 fighters

---

[67] For further details see FARC's Web site, http://www.farccep.org.

[68] Chalk interview, Bogotá, September 2001. See also Rabasa and Chalk (2001), pp. 23–29; International Crisis Group (2002), pp. 9–10.

and some 3,000 milicias, with most of its strength concentrated in the northeastern departments of Santander, Norte de Santander, the coastal department of Bolívar, and Antioquia.[69]

The bulk of Colombia's contemporary *autodefensas* (self-defense) groups, commonly known as paramilitary groups, emerged in reaction to the activities of the ELN and the FARC and found strong support in areas where the state was unable to effectively fulfill its local protection responsibilities.[70] Although the autodefensas were initially considered by many Colombians as a necessary evil in the containment of left-wing inspired insurgency and terror, they increasingly have been viewed as a significant domestic security threat. Despite allegations of collusion with the self-defense groups, the Colombian military maintains that it does not discriminate and treats actions against autodefensas that result in numerous casualties just as it does actions against any other illegal armed group. At the time of writing, the AUC leadership had declared a ceasefire and agreed to disarm in accordance with the so-called Justice and Peace Law that was passed by the Colombian congress in June 2005. The legislation provides for the demobilization and social reintegration of up to 20,000 fighters, but it also restricts the crimes for which paramilitaries can be prosecuted, most of which carry extremely light sentences that can be served on farms as opposed to prisons.[71]

---

[69] Chalk interview, Bogotá, September 2001. Rabasa and Chalk (2001), pp. 30–31; ICG (2002), p. 10. FARC and the ELN announced a tactical alliance in August 2003, the purpose of which was to coordinate strikes against the government of President Uribe. The union never materialized, however, and the groups have effectively remained as distinct entities.

[70] Whereas FARC and the ELN reject the right of the state to govern, the *autodefensas* question the ability of the state to govern.

[71] Not surprisingly, the law has been the subject of considerable controversy, with critics both in Colombia and the United States charging that it effectively shields senior paramilitary leaders from prosecution/extradition for serious crimes, including, notably, those associated with drug trafficking. See Juan Forero, "New Colombia Law Grants Concessions to Paramilitaries," *The New York Times,* June 23, 2005; and Juan Forero, "U.S. Threat Is a Blow to Colombia's Easy Terms for Death Squads," *The New York Times*, July 7, 2005.

The FARC, the ELN, and the AUC all appear on the U.S. State Department's list of designated foreign terrorist organizations.[72] All three have become intimately involved with criminal activities: the FARC and the AUC primarily support themselves through the drug trade; the FARC additionally engages in ancillary kidnappings for ransom (KFR) and extortion rackets, which are also a principal mainstay and specialty of the ELN.

The Drug Trade

Both the FARC and the AUC have established strong ties to the Colombian drug producers and traffickers, the world's largest suppliers of cocaine and the Western hemisphere's largest producers of opiates and such opiate-based derivatives as heroin.[73]

Although the FARC has been engaged in narco-related activities at least since 1982,[74] its involvement in the country's drug business has substantially increased over the past decade due to the increasingly dispersed nature of the illicit drug industry following the collapse of the Cali and Medellín cartels in the early 1990s. The group has developed particularly intensive coca and opiate growing and refining operations in the southeastern departments of Putumayo and Caquetá. Depending on the source, the FARC derives between US $300 million

---

[72] The FARC and the ELN were designated in 1997; the AUC in 2001. The placement of the latter on the list arguably reflects U.S. domestic politics and pressure by leading congressional members to justify the extension of military aid to Colombia despite its poor human rights record.

[73] In 2002, for instance, Colombia's coca yield was sufficient to produce an estimated 680 metric tons of pure cocaine, which represents some 80 percent of global illicit production. While Afghanistan continued to dominate the overall heroin trade, Colombia had effectively cornered the U.S. market, supplying the bulk of all refined opiates sold along America's eastern seaboard. For further details see Bureau for International Narcotics and Law Enforcement Affairs, International Narcotics Control Strategy Report, 2002, Washington, D.C.: United States Department of State, pp. II-3–II-5, IV-19–IV-26. See also "Coca Cultivation in Colombia, 2002," Office of National Drug Control Policy Press Statement, February 27, 2003, http://www.whitehousedrugpolicy.gov/NEWS/press03/022703.html.

[74] The policy of taxing the drug industry and mobilizing and recruiting people involved in the lower end of the drug business was laid out formally in the Conclusions of the FARC Seventh Conference in 1982. Before then, the FARC condemned drug trafficking as counterrevolutionary. See Rabasa and Chalk (2001), pp. 25–26.

and US $1 billion a year in income from criminal activities.[75] About half of that income is from the drug trade, the other half from extortion and kidnappings.[76]

The FARC controls and taxes the drug trade in its areas of influence by enforcing its role as the sole buyer and seller of coca or cocaine at various stages of production and transportation. The group has a precise schedule of fees, called *gramaje,* for protection and services to drug producers and smugglers. Table 7.1 shows the FARC fees in 1999.

According to Colombian officials, about half of the FARC's various fronts are linked to the narcotics trade. Some 11 fronts have a special command element called the "financial collective" that has the responsibility to manage the income from drug production and, to a lesser

Table 7.1
FARC Profits from Drug-Related Activity

Activity	Fee
Production of basic paste	$15.7/kilo
Chlorhydrate of cocaine	$52.6/kilo
Protection of laboratories	$5,263 each
Protection of coca fields	$52.6/hectare
Protection of poppy fields	$4,210/hectare
Security of landing strips	$2,631 each
Cocaine shipments	$10.5/kilo
River transportation	20% of shipment value
International drug flights	$5,263 each
Domestic drug flights	$2,631 each

SOURCE: Colombian Armed Forces briefing, March 2000.

---

[75] "Best estimates" of the income FARC derives from the drug trade generally fall in the range of US $200 million–$400 million. See Council on Foreign Relations and the Markle Foundation, Terrorism Q&A: FARC, ELN, AUC (2004), http://cfrterrorism.org/groups/farc_print.html (as of March 23, 2006).

[76] According to Colombian military figures, in 1998 the various illegal organizations (guerrillas and paramilitaries) derived 620 billion pesos ($551 million) from the drug traffic, 350 billion pesos ($311 million) from extortion, and 265.5 billion pesos ($236 million) from kidnappings (Rabasa and Chalk, 2001, p. 32). The Uribe government is currently engaged in an attempt to more accurately gauge the extent of the group's overall funding activities.

extent, trafficking (which remains a secondary as opposed to primary activity). The income is split between the "bloc" to which the front is attached and the FARC Secretariat. Like other large corporations, the FARC Secretariat employs accountants who rotate among the FARC fronts to verify the accounts.[77] However, Colombian military offensives in 2004 and 2005 may have disrupted the FARC Secretariat's ability to supervise and control the activities of the fronts.[78]

The FARC unit whose modus operandi was closest to that of a classic drug cartel is the 16th Front, based in the department of Vichada, under Tomás Medina Caracas, better known as "Negro Acacio." This individual does business with drug traffickers in the departments of Vichada, Guainía, Casanare, and Meta, in the eastern plains, and has exported cocaine to the United States through business associates in Brazil. According to Colombian authorities, the 16th Front derives an annual income of 144 billion pesos (US $128 million) from drug trafficking. The Colombian army has mounted several operations against the 16th Front. In February 2001, it captured the group's major Brazilian drug trafficking intermediary but has not succeeded in capturing Negro Acacio or shutting down the group's drug trafficking activities.[79]

In contrast to the FARC, the other major Colombian leftist rebel group, the ELN, has shown more reluctance to become involved in the illegal drug trade, probably because of its roots in Christian-Marxist "liberation theology." However, after the death of its long-time leader, *el cura* Pérez, a former Catholic priest, those who argue for a more

---

[77] Chalk interview, Colombian government, police and counternarcotic officials, Bogotá, September 2001. See also McDermott (2004b), pp. 29–31.

[78] Rabasa's discussion with senior Colombian military commander, Washington, D.C., August 2005.

[79] "Así funciona el 'cartel' montado por las FARC," *El País* (Cali), June 4, 2003, http://elpais-cali.terra.com.co/historico/jun042003/NALZ/A504N1.html (as of March 23, 2006); "Pruebas de EU Contra 'Acacio'" *El Espectador* (Bogotá), March 10, 2002. According to Colombian military sources, as of August 2005 Negro Acacio was at large and continued to be involved in large-scale drug trafficking. Rabasa interview with senior Colombian military commander, Washington, D.C., August 2005.

"pragmatic" approach to drugs gained ground within the organization. Nevertheless, the ELN's drug trafficking does not approach the levels of the FARC or AUC.[80]

The AUC—which is more a collection of *autodefensas* than a coherent organization—also finances itself by taxing the drug trade. Individual components of the AUC are believed to engage more directly in trafficking operations than does the FARC (which, as noted above, derives most of its narco-funds through taxation on production), working in close coordination with Mexican syndicates to move cocaine and opiates into the United States (see below). The extent of the income that the *autodefensas* derive from the narcotics trade is not known. However, in a televised interview in March 2000, Carlos Castaño, the AUC's national chief at the time, openly admitted that drug trafficking and taxation of peasants producing coca in Antioquia and Córdoba provided up to 70 percent of the financing for his forces.[81] (Castaño has since disappeared and is believed to have been murdered by rivals within the AUC.) A 2003 Colombian peace commission report claimed the AUC derived possibly as much as 80 percent of its revenue from the drug trade and that self-defense forces in general monopolize up to 40 percent of the country's entire narcotics industry.[82]

In conjunction with Mexican cartels, the AUC moves heroin and cocaine into the United States by several means. Considerable use is made of human couriers who smuggle shipments directly into the United States on commercial airlines at approximately one kilogram per trip (although individual batches of up to 20 kilograms have occasionally been intercepted). In most instances, drugs will be either secreted in clothing or hidden in specially designed luggage fitted with false bottoms.[83]

---

[80]   Alfredo Rangel Suarez, "Un campanazo de alerta: las lecciones de Putumayo," *El Tiempo* (Colombia), August 12, 2005, pp. 61–63.

[81]   "Colombian Death Squad Leader Reveals His Face," CNN Interactive World Wide News, February 3, 2000. See also Bruce M. Bagley, "The Evolution of Drug Trafficking in Colombia in the 1990s," unpublished paper provided to authors, February 2000, pp. 9–10.

[82]   McDermott (2003b), p. 7.

[83]   Bureau for International Narcotics and Law Enforcement Affairs (2003), p. IV-24.

Narcotics are also trafficked to intermediary distribution points in Mexico from South America, Haiti, the Dominican Republic, Puerto Rico, and Jamaica. Consignments will be loaded at sea, typically using "go-fast" transport boats that operate from secluded coastal areas located on Colombia's Caribbean coast and increasingly on the less-well-patrolled Pacific seaboard. They are then transported to American distributors either overland or via specially chartered flights or private yachts.[84]

Narcotics have been smuggled into major Pacific and Atlantic ports, such as Los Angeles, San Francisco, Boston and Baltimore, as camouflaged containerized bulk. However, there appears to be increasingly less reliance on this method of trafficking, which the U.S. Drug Enforcement Agency (DEA) believes reflects heightened maritime cargo inspections instituted under the framework of the Bush administration's Container Security Initiative.[85]

Recent peace overtures by the AUC formalized with the Peace and Justice Law in June 2005 have somewhat complicated the picture of the group's involvement in the Colombian drugs trade. The legislation requires the paramilitaries to renounce involvement in cocaine and heroin trafficking, but some critics charge it contains loopholes that will allow leading AUC "narco-kingpins" both to escape extradition and to retain their drug-related profits. According to Richard Lugar, the chairman of the Senate Foreign Relations Committee, the law will "leave intact the [paramilitaries'] mafia-like structures" by granting commanders the protection of "double jeopardy" while failing to require that they fully disclose knowledge of the AUC's operations

---

[84] Bureau for International Narcotics and Law Enforcement Affairs (2004), p. IV-24; Rabasa and Chalk (2001), pp. 13–14; "Drugs Flood in from Mexico," *The Washington Post,* November 29, 1999.

[85] Bureau for International Narcotics and Law Enforcement Affairs (2004), p. IV-24. For details on the Container Security Initiative, see U.S. Department of State press release, "Fact Sheet: Securing U.S. Ports," http://www.dhs.gov/dhspublic/interapp/press_release/press_release_0865.xml (as of March 23, 2006).

and finances.[86] Advocates of the law, however, defend the concessions as necessary in order to induce the *autodefensas* to lay down their arms and reintegrate themselves into society.[87]

Kidnappings for Ransom and Extortion

Virtually all KFR and extortion committed in Colombia are perpetrated by the FARC and the ELN.[88] According to Amnesty International, 2,200 kidnappings took place in the country during 2003, or roughly one every four hours.[89] Although figures for 2004 showed a sharp decline of roughly 58 percent, 1,250 cases were still recorded, 32 percent of which took the form of KFR incidents carried out by the FARC and ELN (compared to 9 percent attributed to paramilitaries).[90] Colombian government sources believe the two groups earn roughly

---

[86] See Juan Forero, "New Colombia Law Grants Concessions to Paramilitaries," *The New York Times,* June 23, 2005. Commanders will be given the opportunity to confess to drug-related charges in Colombia, which will prevent them from facing similar indictments in the United States. In addition, the law defines "paramilitarism" as a political crime, which under the country's constitution would safeguard AUC leaders from standing trial in foreign countries on related trafficking offences. Critics also maintain there is nothing in the legislation to ensure that commanders will, in fact, provide a full and honest confession of their criminal activities.

[87] See Alfredo Rangel's sophisticated argument on the requirements and limitations of a peace process with the autodefensas in the context of a continued conflict with the FARC. "Una ley instrumento de paz," *El Tiempo,* May 16, 2005.

[88] AUC's kidnappings are thought to constitute no more than 8–20 percent of all abductions that take place in the country, most of which are connected to the drug trade. In most cases, targets are families and relatives of traffickers who either have been arrested or are suspected of diverting or stealing drug shipments. In the first instance, hostages are held to ensure that detainees are not tempted to turn state's evidence and inform on former associates; in the second, to coerce compensation for the loss of the consignment in question. ICG (2002), p. 18; McDermott (2003a), p. 27.

[89] Fundación Seguridad & Democracia, "Balance de seguridad en Colombia, Año 2003."

[90] Amnesty International, Colombia Report for 2005, http://web.amnesty.org/report2005/col-summary-eng (as of March 23, 2006). See also "Kidnappings 'Halved' in Colombia," BBC News, July 22, 2004, http://news.bbc.co.uk/go/pr/fr/-/2/hi/americas/3916235.stm (as of March 23, 2006). According to the U.S. State Department, there were 185 kidnappings in Colombia during the first four months of 2005. See U.S. Department of State, Consular Information Sheet: Colombia, August 2005, http://travel.state.gov/travel/cis_pa_tw/cis/cis_1090.html (as of March 23, 2006).

US $230 million a year from these abductions, which has helped turn the nation into the KFR (and more generalized kidnapping) capital of the world.[91]

Traditionally, the bulk of FARC KFRs occurred in the agricultural crop and livestock production areas in the eastern part of the country. Most victims are cattle ranchers, farmers, and merchants. Beginning in the 1980s, however, the group started to expand the range and scope of its operations, increasingly focusing on wealthy and middle class residents of major cities such as Bogotá.[92] Although high-income members of the urban elite are still favored targets, improved security has limited the opportunities for carrying out such abductions. As a result, the FARC has once again begun to shift the tactical direction of its KFRs. They now routinely take the form of mass random seizures in rural or semi-rural areas—a practice that the police euphemistically refer to as *pesca milagrosa* (literally, miraculous fishing).[93]

ELN KFR activities have generally been more opportunistic in nature than those of the FARC and have largely not emphasized urban-based kidnappings. Most of the group's victims are abducted after being stopped at staged roadblocks, with the hijacking of school buses emerging as an especially favored tactic (largely because parents have been willing to pay quickly for the safe return of their children).[94] Although ransom demands are smaller than those demanded by the FARC, they still constitute an important source of income—roughly 60 percent of the ELN's total operating revenue.[95]

---

[91] For a comprehensive analysis of the country's kidnapping industry see Pax Christi (2001).

[92] Rabasa and Chalk (2001), p. 34.

[93] Chalk interview, Cali, September 2001. See also Mauricio Rubio, "Kidnapping and Armed Conflict in Colombia," paper presented before the International Peace Research Institute Workshop on Techniques of Violence in Civil War, Oslo, August 2004, p. 4.

[94] In 2002, 384 minors were kidnapped by the ELN; the release for most of them took days or weeks to negotiate rather than months.

[95] McDermott (2003a), pp. 26–27. Similar comments were made to RAND analyst Peter Chalk during interviews in Cali, September 2001.

The ELN and the FARC also engage in extensive extortion activity, which nets the two organizations an estimated US $300 million a year. The ELN, in particular, has moved to consolidate this form of criminality into its overall tactical agenda, viewing it as integral to its policy of influencing the oil industry in Colombia's northeast. Executives and high-ranking employees of petroleum companies have been consistently singled out for intimidation. At one point, the destruction of oil pipelines had become almost routine in the northern departments of the country, unless appropriate "revolutionary taxes" were paid.[96] This is no longer the case because U.S. training has dramatically improved the efficiency of pipeline protection.

More generally, the two groups have moved to coerce regular payments from wealthy individuals. The FARC's "Law 002" of 2001 provided that all persons or families with combined assets in excess of US $1.0 million were required to contribute a percentage of their net worth to support the group. Those who did not pay would be "detained," the FARC warned.[97]

Another form of extortion common to the FARC and the ELN has involved the intimidation of mayors, councilors, and other municipal leaders. The purpose has been to gain influence over local government structures in order to tap the financial resources made available as part of decentralization reforms carried out in the 1980s and 1990s. Both groups have been relatively successful in these endeavors, especially in rural towns, where they are now able to siphon payrolls, tax receipts, infrastructure development funds, and various other sources of income.[98]

Rationale for Convergence with Organized Crime

The principal factor accounting for the involvement of the FARC, the ELN, and the AUC in organized crime in the contemporary Colombian

---

[96] Rabasa and Chalk (2001), p. 31; Sweig, "What Kind of War for Colombia?" p. 123; International Crisis Group, "Colombia's Elusive Quest for Peace," p. 10.

[97] See "Ley 002, sobre la tributación," http://six.swix.ch/farcep/Leyes/ley002.html (as of March 24, 2006).

[98] Rabasa and Chalk (2001), p. 34.

context is their requirement for funds to pay their troops and to purchase weapons, ammunition, and other battle-related materiel. The need for these resources has risen exponentially over the last five years as a result of three main trends: (1) growing guerrilla-AUC conflict for control over the country's disputed drug-growing and resource-rich regions; (2) increased U.S. counternarcotics and counterinsurgency assistance to the Colombian military and police;[99] and (3) the heightened willingness of the state's security forces to crack down on militia self-defense activity. In effect, an escalating internal arms race has arisen, the dimensions of which can only be met by a sustained and highly costly procurement process. Crime presents the quickest and easiest way to meet these requirements.[100]

The FARC is a good example of these dynamics at work. In August 2000, the Colombian newsweekly, *Semana,* published the minutes of the group's Secretariat annual meeting, which included the following statement: "The acquisition of arms currently has permitted us a qualitative jump in our process of becoming the Ejercito del Pueblo [People's Army or FARC-EP]."[101] The assertion was important because it illustrates the strong psychological connection the FARC leadership has made between money, weapons, and power.[102]

This self-defined nexus was perhaps best underscored three months later when the group instructed its fronts to increase their various revenue-generating activities to approximately US $600 mil-

---

[99] The United States has provided well over US $3 billion in direct security assistance to Colombia since 2000 (aid currently totals more than $600 million a year), which makes the country the third largest recipient of U.S. foreign aid after Israel and Egypt. See McDermott (2005), p. 26; USIP (2004), p. 2; and Juan Forero, "New Colombia Law Grants Concessions to Paramilitaries," *The New York Times,* June 23, 2005. Initially this money could only be used to support counternarcotics operations. However, with terrorism now occupying a preeminent place in American foreign and security policy, the scope of U.S. aid has been extended to allow assistance for directed operations against the FARC, the ELN, and paramilitaries (all of which are designated as foreign terrorist organizations).

[100] For a comprehensive analysis of small arms trafficking in Colombia see Cragin and Hoffman (2003).

[101] "Los Planes de las FARC," *Semana,* August 7, 2000.

[102] Cragin and Hoffman (2003), p. 5.

lion.[103] The rationale behind the order was to ensure consistency in the receipt of arms shipments so that an effective response could be mounted against escalating AUC attacks as well as expected assaults by Colombian military forces reequipped by the United States. Because the FARC competes with the *autodefensas* and the security forces for military supremacy, it has logically sought to counter actual and latent challenges stemming from each group by procuring more weapons.[104]

Drug money has allowed both the FARC and the AUC to purchase a wide assortment of military-grade weaponry including, in the former case, alleged caches of surface-to-air missiles. The two organizations have also been able to augment the volume of their respective munitions stocks through bulk purchasing. Indeed, the FARC is believed to have been asking its international brokers and subcontractors to quote arms prices in singles and *thousands* from as early as 2000.[105] Just as noteworthy have been several interceptions of extremely large weapons consignments, including one shipment bound for the AUC that was seized in June 2000 and that reportedly contained 4,000 AK-47 rifles.[106]

Even the ELN, by far the smallest and weakest of the three main illegal organizations in Colombia, has been able to sustain a reasonably concerted war footing through the acquisition of weapons and explosives purchased with criminal proceeds. The group has repeatedly demonstrated its ability to blow up key infrastructure targets in the north of the country, attacking the strategically important Caño Limón

---

[103] "El Otro Plan Colombia," *Cambio,* March 20, 2000.

[104] See, for instance, Cragin and Hoffman (2003), pp. 40–41.

[105] "Gunrunner Sarkis Links Peruvian Army, SIN to Arms Trafficking," *La Republica* (Lima, Peru), September 21, 2000.

[106] "Traición en el Mercado Negro de Armas," *El Tiempo,* June 28, 2000.

Covenas oil pipeline in Arauca no less than 170 times in 2001.[107] In October 2003, it took responsibility for the downing of a U.S. State Department plane that was spraying cocaine crops with defoliants.[108]

Beyond considerations pertaining to weapons acquisitions, the FARC, the ELN, and the AUC no doubt have been attracted to the enormous profit potential that is available in Colombia. An entrenched criminal economy, weak state structures, and endemic civil conflict have provided an ideal environment for nonstate actors to engage in lucrative illicit activities that can be justified (and hidden) on the basis of left- or right-wing authoritarian populist rhetoric. The three groups have all benefited from the imposition of protection levies to pay for security against one another's attacks, and the FARC and the AUC have purportedly concluded agreements to ensure that their fighting does not unduly affect their drug business. According to one former paramilitary leader, Rodrigo Molano, "The self-defense forces do not necessarily fight the guerrillas. In many cases they only have a dis-suasive presence, respecting [established] territorial divides with the FARC."[109]

The latter aspect has encouraged many commentators to argue that the FARC, the ELN, and the AUC are approaching or may have already reached the critical point where political motivational drivers are balanced with, or even superseded by, the economic imperative to pursue designs of a purely commercial nature. Tamara Makarenko has observed this dynamic with respect to the FARC. Contending that cash flow has now become an objective in its own right, she portrays

---

[107] Caño Limón Covenas carries roughly 105,000 barrels of oil every day to ports on the Caribbean coast. Attacks on the pipeline cost the Colombian government an estimated US $430 million a year in lost oil revenues. See Sweig (2002), p. 135; "Once Again Colombia Mourns," *The Economist*, February 15, 2003.

[108] "Colombian Rebels Claim Responsibility for Downing U.S. Plane," Associated Press, October 3, 2003.

[109] Cited in McDermott (2003b), p. 8.

the group as one that has evolved (or devolved) into a quasi-insurgent entity that, while not fully abandoning its political agenda, is simultaneously interested in maximizing criminal profits.[110]

The growing involvement of the FARC, the ELN, and the AUC in organized crime carries significant implications for peace and stability in Colombia. The ability to acquire and maintain a sophisticated arms base has significantly heightened the potential violence threshold of the three groups. In the case of the FARC, it has also availed a general expansion of the group's operations beyond the rural theater to more urban-based settings, reflected in the wave of terrorist bombings that have taken place in major metropolitan centers since 2002.[111]

Finally, in common with the Abu Sayyaf Group in the southern Philippines, the nexus between crime, terrorism, and insurgency severely limits the opportunities for meaningful negotiation between state and nonstate actors. As noted above, the FARC, the ELN, and the AUC have all derived protection taxes from local populations in areas under their respective control. Moreover, the general chaos within Colombia that has been a by-product of the country's civil conflict has transformed the country's internal geopolitical landscape into a patchwork of dissident-controlled zones that have been used to support highly profitable drug growing and refining, kidnapping, and extortion activities. In short, each of the three groups has a strong financial incentive to continue the violence, which obviously has significant implications for the success of any eventual peace negotiation.

---

[110] Makarenko (2003), p. 11.

[111] Colombian intelligence sources believe FARC may have inserted as many as 10,000–15,000 agents in and around major cities such as Cali, Medellín, and Bogotá. They also allege the group has contracted with the Provisional Irish Republican Army (PIRA) to provide specific training in urban-based sabotage and terrorism. See Sweig (2002), p. 127; "Once Again, Colombia Mourns"; "Colombia's Peace Bid at Risk," *The Washington Post,* August 25, 2001.

Al-Qaeda and Hezbollah in Africa: The Conflict Diamonds Nexus

Even before the loss of their bases in Afghanistan, al-Qaeda leaders showed interest in the potential of sub-Saharan Africa for financial transactions as well as a source of strategic minerals. Al-Qaeda reportedly used sympathetic crime networks to convert funds into diamonds and gold, as well as in attempts to obtain nuclear, chemical, and biological material.[112] Al-Qaeda's interest in Africa also derives from the potential of the region's vast ungoverned territories for training and basing and the opportunities presented by conditions in the region to exploit religious friction and to support the expansion of Islamic radicalism.

The economic links between Islamic terrorism and organized crime in sub-Saharan Africa center on so-called conflict diamonds (also called "blood diamonds" or "terror diamonds").[113] The conflict diamond phenomenon was first noticed during the Angolan civil war, when National Union for the Total Independence of Angola (UNITA) leader Jonas Savimbi realized that the country's extensive diamond fields could finance his struggle against the ruling Marxist Popular Movement for the Liberation of Angola. UNITA capitalized on the smuggling routes that the movement had developed during the independence struggle in the 1970s. By 1993 Savimbi had in place one of the world's largest diamond trafficking networks, earning an estimated $4.1 billion between 1992 and 2000.[114] Subsequent international actions to restrict UNITA's diamond trade seem to have been

---

[112] Wannenburg (2003), pp. 77–90.

[113] The term *blood* or *conflict diamonds* refers generally to rough diamonds obtained by using or threatening to use coercion or military force, particularly in Africa. According to the European Commission, blood diamonds represent 2–4 percent of global diamond production: "Al-Qaeda linked to blood diamonds in Africa," Sapa-AFP, April 29, 2003.

[114] InvestigativeJournalists SouthAfrica.com. Discussion Forum, Blood Diamonds, February 2003, http://www.southafrica.com/forums/showthread.php?t=3478 (as of March 27, 2006); Cooper (2002).

relatively successful in limiting the supply of funds to the organization (from $700 million in 1996 to $100 million in 2002) and may even have contributed to its demise.[115]

This pattern—in which diamonds were used as war currency—has been replicated in other African conflicts, particularly in Sierra Leone, Liberia, and the Democratic Republic of the Congo.[116] The Revolutionary United Front of Sierra Leone, a murderous rebel force that has engaged in mass killing, looting, rape, and violence of the worst kind, supports itself largely through the extraction and sale of diamonds in the areas that it controls. In the eastern Congo, diamonds have been integral to the Congolese Rally for Democracy and the Movement for the Liberation of Congo insurgencies, and to the insurgencies' nexus with their external allies in Rwanda and Uganda.[117]

Although Central Africa does offer considerable strategic mineral assets for plundering, the area of greatest concern is the Parrot's Beak, a small wedge of land on Liberia's border with Guinea where rebel factions vie for blood diamonds.[118] Across the border in Sierra Leone, the government believes that illicit prospecting is rife, involving about three times the number of the 435 registered license holders. This is especially the case in the diamond-rich area of Kono, where the highest number of legal mining licenses has been distributed.[119]

The relationship between al-Qaeda and the terror diamond trade is a matter of some controversy. The *9/11 Commission Report* (July 2004) questioned whether al-Qaeda has been trafficking in "conflict" diamonds. The report noted, "We have seen no persuasive evidence that al Qaeda funded itself by trading in African conflict diamonds."[120]

---

[115] Cooper (2002).

[116] InvestigativeJournalists SouthAfrica.com.

[117] U.S. House of Representatives (2000a), p. 8.

[118] Greg Campbell, "Blood Diamonds," Amnesty Now, http://www.amnestyusa.org/amnestynow/diamonds.html (as of March 24, 2006).

[119] Rod MacJohnson, "'Blood Diamonds' Initiative a Mixed Success in War-Scarred Sierra Leone," Agence France-Presse, May 18, 2003, http://wwww.reliefweb.int/w/rwb.nsf/0/58053e67d50efe91c1256d2b0054b284?OpenDocument.

[120] National Commission on Terrorist Attacks Upon the United States (2004).

Nevertheless, there is a wealth of open-source information linking al-Qaeda to the illegal diamond trade in West Africa: the Sierra Leone Special Court (the war-crimes court investigating the conflict in Sierra Leone); the Belgian government's own investigation (this is important and relevant because Antwerp, Belgium, is the world's largest diamond market); the extensive investigative journalism of *The Washington Post*; and the most-in-depth report on this subject, that by Global Witness, a nongovernmental organization that has reported extensively on al-Qaeda's known or alleged "terror diamonds" connections.

The apparent discrepancy between the findings of the 9/11 Commission and those of the other sources noted above is due to the fact that each appears to have been asking different questions. The 9/11 Commission—and the FBI and CIA investigations on which the commission relied[121]—appeared to look at the question of whether al-Qaeda traded in diamonds to fund itself (as UNITA or other groups had in the past). In contrast, the other investigations looked at the question of whether al-Qaeda used diamonds and other precious minerals to hide and transfer funds. This would appear to be the reason why the 9/11 Commission (and other U.S. agencies) came up with a

---

[121] *The 9/11 Commission Report* cited a number of U.S. government reports only and did not appear to use—at least, by citation—any of the highly detailed open-source reports, such as those by Global Witness, cited in this report. The U.S. government reports cited by the commission (p. 499, footnote 129) included the FBI report, "Allegations of Al Qaeda Trafficking in Conflict Diamonds," July 18, 2003; CIA analytic report, "Terrorism: Assessing al-Qa'ida and Hizballah Ties to Conflict Diamonds," CTC 2002-40121CH, January 13, 2003; CIA analytic report, "Couriers, Hawaladars Key to Moving Al-Qa'ida Money," CTC 2003-40063CH, May 16, 2003; DOS cable, Brussels 05994, "WP Reporter Claims More Witnesses to 2001 Al-Qaida/Conflict Diamonds Link," December 12, 2002; DOS cable, Brussels 001054, terrorism and conflict diamonds, March 1, 2002; FBI situation reports and supporting documents from the Sierra Leone trip, February 2004.

negative response to their question, whereas the other investigations answered theirs in the affirmative. This distinction is extremely important because it ultimately shows two sides of a similar concern.[122]

Al-Qaeda is believed to have used diamonds (1) to develop anonymous, movable wealth prior to September 2001—perhaps expecting that known existing al-Qaeda assets would be frozen following the attacks—and (2) to launder funds from other sources, such as drug sales. Global Witness states that al-Qaeda uses diamonds for four principal reasons: to raise funds for its cells; to hide money targeted by financial sanctions; to launder the profits of criminal activity; and to convert cash into a commodity that holds its value and is easily transportable.[123] Most worryingly (see below), the Global Witness report also clearly outlines how al-Qaeda used both corrupt officials (such as Liberia's former president Charles Taylor) and the existing Hezbollah West African diamond-smuggling network to support its activities.

In 1999, Mohamed Hijazi, a longtime diamond miner and dealer in Sierra Leone, was appointed as RUF's agent "to negotiate with any person or company within or outside Sierra Leone for the prospecting, mining, buying & selling of diamonds."[124] Transcripts from court cases against al-Qaeda members contain evidence that the network has people with expertise in the diamond business in these areas, including those who previously were involved in the gemstone and diamond trade in Tanzania, which al-Qaeda has allegedly used to finance

---

[122] A recent trip (May 2005) to Sierra Leone by RAND researcher Kevin O'Brien to investigate this and other concerns regarding an al-Qaeda presence in West Africa further solidified this distinction and conclusion. In interviews with members of the U.S., UK, and other Western missions, the complexity of this question was notable: Although very few respondents believed that al-Qaeda had used Sierra Leone diamonds to fund its activities, most acknowledged that al-Qaeda operatives may have used such diamonds to provide readily transportable value, and that known al-Qaeda and Hezbollah operatives had been in Sierra Leone and Liberia during the period in question.

[123] Global Witness (2003), p. 28.

[124] "Lawmakers Back Bill Curbing 'Blood Diamonds,'" Reuters, June 24, 2001, http://webnetarts.com/socialjustice/diamonds.html (as of March 24, 2006).

operations.[125] The U.S. government made similar charges, linking the sale of tanzanite, a gemstone found only in Tanzania, to al-Qaeda financing.[126]

Al-Qaeda's use of precious gems is reported to have begun in 1993 when bin Laden was establishing his base in Sudan. To finance the organization, he allegedly bought and sold gems.[127] According to Lyman and Morrison, al-Qaeda subsequently took advantage of the Congolese civil war to extend its activities to the Congo. Al-Qaeda's illegal trade in gems has since spread to other countries in Africa, allegedly colluding with the governments of Burkina Faso and Liberia to buy diamonds mined by the RUF in Sierra Leone.[128] Both President Blaise Campaore of Burkina Faso and Libyan dictator Muammar Qadhafi are also mentioned in connection with both the Sierra Leonean and Liberian ends of these operations.[129] Although the RUF has denied having any links with al-Qaeda or selling diamonds to it, it has reportedly acknowledged that such sales could have taken place without its knowledge.[130]

In September 1998, following international efforts to freeze al-Qaeda and Taliban accounts after the August 1998 bombings of the U.S. embassies in Tanzania and Kenya, senior al-Qaeda financial officer Abdullah Ahmed Abdullah arrived in Monrovia, Liberia, to meet with Ibrahim Bah (an Afghan veteran from Senegal who went on to deal diamonds for Liberian president Taylor with the rebels in Sierra Leone) and talk with senior Liberian and RUF officials. At this time, Abdullah attempted a $100,000 arms-for-diamonds deal. Although the deal fell

---

[125] Douglas Farah, "Al Qaeda Cash Tied to Diamond Trade Sale of Gems from Sierra Leone Rebels Raised Millions, Sources Say," *The Washington Post,* November 2, 2001.

[126] "Africa Overview," U.S. Department of State (2002a).

[127] Lucy Jones, "Al-Qaeda 'Traded Blood Diamonds,'" BBC News Online, February 20, 2003, http://news.bbc.co.uk/1/hi/world/africa/2775763.stm.

[128] Lyman and Morrison (2004), pp. 83–84.

[129] Douglas Farah, "Report Says Africans Harbored Al Qaeda: Terror Assets Hidden In Gem-Buying Spree," *The Washington Post,* December 29, 2002, p. A01; Morrison (2001), pp. 15, 18, and 19.

[130] Dagne (2002), p. 21; Farah, "Al Qaeda Cash Tied to Diamond Trade Sale."

through, Abdullah maintained contact with the network he found there.[131] Fragments of correspondence alleged to be between Ayman al-Zawahiri and "Abu Mohammed al-Masri" (an alias used by Abdullah), found by *The Wall Street Journal* in a computer in Afghanistan, indicate that the subsequent diamond deals were controlled by al-Qaeda at the highest levels. Zawahiri is reported to have said that these deals will "transfer our activities to the stage of multinationals and [bring] joint profit."[132]

A joint investigation by European intelligence agencies,[133] reported in *The Washington Post* in December 2002, alleged that three men—Aziz Nassour, a Lebanese diamond merchant,[134] his cousin Samih Ossailly, and the aforementioned Bah—were the primary conduits linking al-Qaeda to the Liberian leadership and a company in Belgium that polished and sold conflict diamonds. In 2000, more than $14 million worth of diamonds were sold. Buyers' identities are known only to Bah and to a few others.[135] According to FBI sources quoted in the story, two al-Qaeda operatives implicated in the 1998 attacks, a Tanzanian called Ahmed Khalfan Ghailani and a Kenyan, Fazul Abdullah Mohammed, both on the FBI's wanted list, traveled between Liberia, Burkina Faso, and Sierra Leone and Afghanistan and Pakistan exchanging cash for diamonds. (Ghailani was arrested in Pakistan in

---

[131] Amelia Hill, "Terror in the East: Bin Laden's Dollars 20m African 'Blood Diamond' Deals," *Observer News,* October 20, 2002, p. 6.

[132] Farah, "Report Says Africans Harbored Al Qaeda."

[133] Much of the evidence comes from Western intelligence reports and from the trials of al-Qaeda suspects after the September 11 attacks and the 1998 bombings of U.S. embassies in East Africa. See Jones, "Al-Qaeda 'traded blood diamonds.'"

[134] Belgian intelligence also reported that Nassour and his family were implicated in the trade of diamonds with UNITA and are suspected of having links with the Amal Shi'ite militia and Lebanese leader Nahib Berri. The subnational groups that extend al-Qaeda's web of influence include Abu Sayyaf in the Phillipines, which controls territory and can levy taxes on citizens, and is known for counterfeiting (linked to the laundering of fake $100 bills in Hong Kong); the Albanian mafia (used as logistical support to the Balkan cells of al-Qaeda), which is linked to the Kosovo Liberation Army and is involved in heroin and cocaine trading; and Indian mafia figures. See Wannenburg (2003).

[135] Wannenburg (2003).

July 2004.) Bah is alleged to have begun using ASA Diam, a company associated with Ossailly and Nassour, in July 2000 to "front" diamonds secured in West Africa; ASA Diam's diamond trading subsequently took a sharp upward turn to over $14 million worth of diamond sales in 2000. In February 2001, Nassour and Bah met to discuss increasing these diamond purchases. Ghailani and Mohammed supervised the transaction. Judging from reports of diamond sales in both West Africa and Belgium in 2000, the pace of this activity had accelerated to such a point that, by August 2000, these operatives "appear to have cornered most of the Sierra Leonean and Liberian diamond markets." Local diamond merchants were hard-pressed to buy diamonds, and new buyers were paying a premium of between 15 and 30 percent.[136]

In January 2001, Nassour and Ossailly were trying to buy weapons—allegedly including SA-8 surface-to-air missiles and sophisticated rockets for BM-21 multiple rocket launchers—from the Nicaraguan army via an Israeli arms dealer based in Panama named Simon Yelnik. Other reports allege that al-Qaeda attempted to buy similar items via Bulgaria using precious gems. An intercepted email from the Israeli arms dealer to a Russian arms merchant, listing assault rifles, ammunition, ground-to-air missiles, and 200 rockets for multiple rocket launchers, said the consignment was for "our friends in Africa." The weapons were to be delivered to Liberia with an Ivorian end-user certificate. Nassour and Ossailly later acknowledged to Belgian officials that the transaction was discussed but never completed.[137]

In April 2001, however, when ASA Diam's purchasing in West Africa was at its height, it stopped reporting diamond sales in Antwerp.[138] Nassour and Ossailly were believed to have used couriers to exchange $300,000 for diamonds every week between December 2000 and September 2001.[139] In 2000, Ossailly and a Boston-based used car dealer, Ali Darwish, set up a safe house in Monrovia to funnel

---

[136] Farah, "Report Says Africans Harbored Al Qaeda"; Campbell, "Blood Diamonds."

[137] Farah, "Report Says Africans Harbored Al Qaeda"; "West African Leaders 'in al-Qaida Plot,'" *Guardian Unlimited*, December 30, 2002.

[138] Farah, "Report Says Africans Harbored Al Qaeda."

[139] Hill, "Terror in the East."

the wealth from the diamond fields to rebel organizations through-out the world;[140] Ghailani and Mohammed moved into the house in March 2001.[141] During the summer of 2001, Ghailani and Mohammed stayed in the compound of the president of Burkina Faso in the capital, Ouagadougou, before moving to Camp Gbatala, a military camp in Liberia near Taylor's private farm; for this, the Liberian president was allegedly paid US $1 million.[142]

By September 2001, al-Qaeda had laundered an estimated $20 million in diamonds, most of which were under United Nations sanctions aimed at preventing their use in fueling civil wars. Payment to al-Qaeda for the diamonds was made in cash or weapons.[143] According to David Crane, the chief prosecutor for the Special Court on Sierra

---

[140] According to sources, small packets of diamonds, often wrapped in rags or plastic sheets, are taken by senior RUF commanders across the porous Liberian border to Monrovia. There, at a safe house protected by the Liberian government, the diamonds are exchanged for brief-cases of cash brought by diamond dealers who fly several times a month from Belgium to Monrovia, where they are escorted by special state security through customs and immigration control. See Farah, "Al Qaeda Cash Tied to Diamond Trade Sale."

[141] According to the Belgian officials, couriers took weekly flights from Antwerp on the now-defunct Sabena airline to Abidjan. There, they hired light planes from Weswua Airlines to fly to Monrovia, Liberia, and then went on to meet rebel RUF commanders in Sierra Leone. Nassour, now living in Beirut, is being investigated concerning claims he conducted deals with al-Qaeda with his cousin Ossailly, who was arrested on weapons-related charges in June 2002 by Belgian officials. Nassour, Ossailly, and Bah all deny involvement with al-Qaeda. See Wannenburg (2003). Nassour told Global Witness that he met Liberian president Taylor in July 2001 to discuss setting up a mobile phone business and an airline company. Nassour claims he waited for four days for a meeting with Taylor before he gave up and left. An eyewitness maintains Nassour's visit was linked to problems that were threatening to destroy the arrangement. The source claims that Nassour arrived the day after a colleague fled with $500,000 of al-Qaeda money. The witness maintains Aziz Nassour, the Lebanese diamond merchant, met Taylor at Harpur port, where arms are delivered and timber illegally exported, and handed over US $200,000, apparently to ensure continuation of the smuggling trade. The alleged deal ended with the September 11 attacks two months later, although Global Witness is convinced al-Qaeda has continued its trade. Hill, "Terror in the East."

[142] The U.S. Defense Intelligence Agency allegedly monitored Ghailani and Mohammed in preparation for a Special Forces team in neighboring Guinea to snatch the two, but the mission was not carried out, because the team could not confirm the targets' identities, according to Douglas Farah ("Report Says Africans Harbored Al Qaeda").

[143] Jones, "Al-Qaeda 'Traded Blood Diamonds.'"

Leone established in January 2003 to try people accused of war crimes during that country's long civil war in the 1990s, al-Qaeda continued to operate in West Africa, principally to buy diamonds:

> They're all interconnected. They all work together. They know each other. It's a common plan, a scheme, to move diamonds as a commodity, to do whatever they need to trade it for cash, arms, or to launder money. . . . Diamonds fuel my conflict, and diamonds fuel the war on terrorism. Charles Taylor is harboring terrorists from the Middle East, including al Qaeda and Hezbollah, and has been for years . . . he is a player in the world of terror and what he does affects lives in the United States and Europe.[144]

In August 2004, a confidential Sierra Leone Special Court investigation was leaked to the South African press. The leaked report stated that "a series of witnesses place six top al-Qaeda fugitives in Africa buying up diamonds before the September 11 attacks." These figures "dealt directly with Liberia's former President Charles Taylor and other leaders and warlords in what was then a rogue West African nation from 1999 onwards," according to the accounts of witnesses interviewed by the Special Court. Its findings concluded that flight records and some "undisclosed evidence in Europe" appeared to support the accounts of pre–September 11 al-Qaeda diamond business in Liberia. The report further states that "al-Qaeda has been in West Africa since September 1998 and maintained a continuous presence in the area through 2002."[145]

U.S. government officials cited by the report stated that al-Qaeda proceeds from the diamond dealings were estimated to be $15 million. The al-Qaeda figures said to be involved in the network included

---

[144] Mike Blanchfield, "Al-Qaeda Funded by 'Blood Diamonds': Illicit Stones Traded to Pay for Terror Operations, UN Says," *The Ottawa Citizen,* Sunday Final Edition, February 9, 2003; Rod MacJohnson, "'Blood Diamonds' Initiative a Mixed Success in War-Scarred Sierra Leone," Agence France-Presse, May 18, 2003, http://www.reliefweb.int/w/rwb.nsf/0/58053e67d50efe91c1256d2b0054b284?OpenDocument (as of March 24, 2006).

[145] Much of the evidence comes from Western intelligence reports and from the trials of al-Qaeda suspects after the September 11, 2001, attacks and the 1998 bombings of U.S. embassies in East Africa. See Jones, "Al-Qaeda 'Traded Blood Diamonds.'"

Ghailani; Mohammed; Mohammed Atef (killed in Afghanistan in 2001); the Pakistani Aafia Siddiqui, al-Qaeda's only prominent female figure;[146] Kenyan Sheikh Ahmed Salim Swedan, wanted for the 1998 attacks in East Africa; and Abdullah Ahmed Abdullah. Abdullah was alleged by the report to have continued operating in Guinea into 2002, long after other reports had al-Qaeda operatives leaving West Africa. The report also cites Charles Taylor's extensive involvement with al-Qaeda in making arrangements for gems, weapons, and cash. Abdullah was later reported to have ordered Ghailani and Mohammed to do al-Qaeda's diamond buying "because they were of African descent and would not arouse any suspicion."[147]

Hezbollah and Africa

Lebanese Hezbollah was, in many ways, the precursor to al-Qaeda's activities in this area. Regardless of its Lebanese focus, Hezbollah is known to maintain a global network to support fundraising and operational and logistical requirements for its operations abroad. It is suspected that much of this is done in close cooperation with Iranian intelligence services. Similar to, and perhaps imported from, its operations in North and South America, Hezbollah raises and launders large amounts of money in Africa. It recruits and trains new operatives for both target selection and surveillance and operations, all with the aim of supporting its principal goals in the Middle East.

Hezbollah has also established numerous front companies in Africa, once again reflecting its practice elsewhere in the world. According to one source, many Hezbollah activists previously based in the tri-border region of South America relocated to Africa because of the "increased attention" on its activities there following the 1992 and 1994 bombings in Argentina. Other activists ended up in Europe,

---

[146] The presence of Siddiqui in Monrovia at this time, alongside Sheikh Ahmed Salim Swedan, an al-Qaeda leader on the FBI's Most Wanted Terrorist list, indicates just how important al-Qaeda's leadership considered the West African diamond operation. Glenn R. Simpson, "U.N. Ties al Qaeda Figure to Diamonds," *The Wall Street Journal,* June 28, 2004.

[147] Edward Harris, "Al-Qaeda in Africa," *The Mail and Guardian,* August 8, 2004, http://www.mg.co.za/Content/l3.asp?ao=120020 (as of March 24, 2006).

Asia, and less conspicuous parts of South America.[148] Some analysts hold the view—reportedly supported by Israeli intelligence—that, with the assistance of Tehran, Hezbollah has specifically been funneling religious students into Uganda and other African countries to recruit and train potential new operatives.[149] An example is Shafi Ibrahim, arrested by Ugandan authorities in late 2002 for being the leader of a cell of Ugandan Shi'ites believed to be working for both Hezbollah and Tehran.[150]

European, Israeli, and American intelligence sources have long known that Hezbollah has raised significant amounts of money in West Africa through the largely Shi'ite Muslim Lebanese communities in Sierra Leone, Ivory Coast, Burkina Faso, and Togo. There are an estimated 120,000 Lebanese in West Africa, mostly involved in import-export businesses.[151]

This fundraising is accomplished through a number of different means: First, Hezbollah has raised significant amounts of funds over the past 20 years through diamond sales from Sierra Leone, with Ibrahim Bah (noted above) suspected of brokering diamond deals through buyers connected to Hezbollah, assisted by sympathetic Lebanese businessmen across the region. As with al-Qaeda, the illegal diamond industry has provided Hezbollah with a means to raise and

---

[148] Matthew Levitt, "Hizbullah's African Activities Remain Undisrupted," *RUSI/Jane's Homeland Security and Resilience Monitor,* March 1, 2004, http://www.washingtoninstitute.org/media/levitt/levitt020404.htm.

[149] Levitt, "Hizbullah's African Activities Remain Undisrupted."

[150] He and his comrades in the theology school were taught to use small arms, produce explosive devices, collect preoperational intelligence, plan escape routes, and withstand interrogation techniques. The students were given fictitious covers, money, and means of communication, then "instructed to collect intelligence on Americans and Westerners present in Uganda and other countries." See Matthew Levitt, "Hizbullah: A Case Study of Global Reach," Conference on Post-Modern Terrorism: Trends, Scenarios, and Future Threats, International Policy Institute for Counter-Terrorism, Israel, September 8, 2003, http://www.washingtoninstitute.org/media/levitt/levitt090803.htm.

[151] "Hizbullah (Part I)," Intelligence and Terrorism Information Center, Center for Special Studies, June 2003, http://www.intelligence.org.il/eng/bu/hizbullah/Hizballah.htm; Levitt, "Hizbullah's African Activities Remain Undisrupted."

launder money.[152] Indeed, it has also been claimed that Hezbollah and other radical Islamic groups transferred millions of dollars made from Congolese diamond sales to their organizations.[153]

Second, Hezbollah raises large amounts of funds from the expatriate Lebanese community in West Africa, both through voluntary donations and by what one analyst refers to as "Mafia-style shakedowns." Across West Africa, Hezbollah is believed to raise the most funds in the Ivory Coast, followed closely by Senegal—these two have the highest concentrations of Hezbollah activity in Africa.[154] The importance of these networks to Hezbollah would appear to be so high that when, on December 25, 2003, Union Transport Africaines flight 141 to Beirut crashed on take-off in Benin with three key Africa-based Hezbollah activists on board, carrying (according to Arab press reports) $2 million in contributions raised from wealthy Lebanese in Africa, Hezbollah "immediately sent an envoy to Benin to console the sons of the Lebanese community"—indicating the value these networks hold for Hezbollah.[155] However, when such donations do not suffice, Hezbollah gangs attack the commercial properties of local Lebanese nationals who resist demands for solicitations.[156]

---

[152] Farah, "Al Qaeda Cash Tied to Diamond Trade Sale."

[153] "Africa Overview," U.S. Department of State (2002a).

[154] "Hezbollah: Profile of the Lebanese Shiite Terrorist Organization of Global Reach Sponsored by Iran and Supported by Syria (Part A)," Intelligence and Terrorism Information Center, Center for Special Studies, June 2003, http://www.intelligence.org.il/eng/bu/hizbullah/hezbollah.htm.

[155] Arab media reported that $2 million "represented the regular contributions the party receives from wealthy Lebanese nationals in Guinea, Sierra Leone, Liberia, Benin, and other African states," Hamid Ghiryafi, "Hizbullah Officials Carrying Donations Reportedly Killed in Lebanese Plane Crash," al-Siyasah (Kuwait), December 29, 2003; Miriam Karouny, "Benin Plane Crash Deaths Rise to 111," Reuters, December 26, 2003.

[156] Lansana Gberie, "War and Peace in Sierra Leone: Diamonds, Corruption and the Lebanese Connection," The Diamonds and Human Security Project—Partnership Africa Canada, International Peace Information Service, Network for Justice and Development, Occasional Paper #6, November 13, 2002, http://www.reliefweb.int/w/rwb.nsf/0/898ad5b9 f3f339a585256c7200799005?OpenDocument (as of March 26, 2006).

Hezbollah and Crime in North America

As the preceding discussion shows, Hezbollah's convergence with organized crime spans continents. The most important locus of Hezbollah's criminal activity is the Bekaa Valley, which has provided a continuous source of narcotics that Hezbollah has commercialized, despite international efforts to shut down opium cultivation there. With funding from Iran dwindling, Hezbollah is seeking to increase its drug trafficking niche by tapping new markets abroad.[157] This trend is now seen in North America.

Hezbollah in Canada

Hezbollah has used Canadian territory for ten years to recruit, launder money, raise funds, forge documents, and purchase military-related equipment for use in attacks on Israel. It has also built up a network of agents across the country. Mohammed Hussein al-Husseini, a Hezbollah member, told Canadian security officials that "Hezbollah has members in Montreal, Ottawa, Toronto—all of Canada."[158] One of these Canada-based agents, Fauzi Ayub, was arrested by Israeli authorities after being sent to the West Bank to engineer attacks against Israelis. Two others, wanted for terrorist acts committed elsewhere, were hiding out in Canada. One has since been charged in connection with the 1996 bombing in Saudi Arabia that killed 19 Americans.

Canadian police and intelligence reports show the group has been using Canada in recent years to buy materiel, forge travel documents, raise money, and steal luxury vehicles. In 1999 and 2000, Hezbollah sent detailed shopping lists to agents who were allegedly part of a network in Vancouver, Toronto, and Montreal to fill the orders and ship the equipment back to Lebanon in courier packages. Hundreds of thousands of dollars were moved through various Canadian banks, such as the Bank of Nova Scotia, to finance purchases for what the participants

---

[157] U.S. House of Representatives (2000b).

[158] Stephen Brown, "Canada—Terrorist Haven," *FrontPagemagazine.com*, December 9, 2002, http://www.frontpagemag.com/Articles/ReadArticle.asp?ID=5007 (as of March 27, 2006); Byman (2003).

referred to as the "resistance" and the "brave people." Canadian Hezbollah agents also discussed a scam they called a "miracle strike," which involved taking out life insurance policies on people and then having them killed in Lebanon.[159]

Two of the alleged Hezbollah Canadian agents, Lebanese immigrants identified as Mohammad Dbouk and his brother-in-law Amhaz, shopped at a "military supply warehouse and looked at some military supplies and instruments in Vancouver." Mr. Dbouk inquired at one company about buying "any equipment used to blow up rocks." The agents were cautious to protect the secrecy of their work, although apparently unaware that every phone call was being recorded by Canadian intelligence. "Amhaz expressed his concern about depositing large sums of money in the bank account and suggested that Dbouk give him smaller sums of money to avoid suspicion [by the banks]," the Canadian Security Intelligence Service wrote, "Dbouk advised Amhaz that he would give instructions that the money be transferred to Ali Bassal in Montreal, after which time Dbouk would fly/travel to Montreal to get the cash and return to B.C." Dbouk fled Canada and returned to Lebanon, but Amhaz still resides in Burnaby, British Columbia. He has denied any involvement with Hezbollah.[160]

The extent of Hezbollah operations in Canada first came to light in the 1990s, when Mohammed Hussein al-Husseini was arrested for deportation. He told the CSIS about a cross-Canada network and confessed that agents had spied on Canadians and reported on Canadian life and infrastructure. In two cases, alleged Hezbollah agents were found hiding out in Edmonton and Ottawa. One of them has been charged with taking part in the 1996 bombing attack in Saudi Arabia. "Hezbollah has members in Montreal, Ottawa, Toronto—all of Canada," al-Husseini told CSIS before he was deported in 1994. Hezbollah wants to collect information on Canada, on life in Canada and its infrastructure, "in case there's a problem with Canada." He

[159] Stewart Bell, "Hezbollah Uses Canada as Base: CSIS Agency Wiretaps Show Suspected Operatives Using Laundered Money to Buy Materiel," http://www.clhrf.com/documents/hezbollah.canada.htm (as of March 27, 2006).

[160] Bell, "Hezbollah Uses Canada as Base."

was reportedly referring to videotapes of Canadian landmarks sent to Hezbollah headquarters in Lebanon. The RCMP has also linked auto theft rings in Ontario and Quebec to Hezbollah, saying that a portion of the criminal proceeds were funneled to the group, and that luxury sport utility vehicles stolen in Canada were being driven by high-ranking Hezbollah leaders in Lebanon. The CSIS reports on Hezbollah's Canadian activities were made available recently to U.S. attorneys prosecuting accused operatives involved in a North Carolina cigarette smuggling ring.[161]

Another indication of how highly Hezbollah's leaders value their Canadian operation is that money raised from a Hezbollah cigarette-smuggling ring in North Carolina was sent to Canada. Mohammad Dbouk, the Hezbollah operative mentioned above, was sent from Lebanon to run the Vancouver cell. According to a U.S. Senate committee, Dbouk was so highly regarded by Hezbollah that his application to become a "martyr" was rejected five times. None of the members of Vancouver's Hezbollah cell has been charged in Canada. American attempts to extradite one cell member ended in frustration, prompting a couple of Senate hearing participants to remark that it's hard to extradite from Lebanon—and from Canada, too.[162]

The Hezbollah Criminal Nexus in the United States and Mexico

A new criminal nexus between Hezbollah and Mexican drug rings has emerged in Washington state (specifically the Olympic Peninsula), in central California, and in the American Midwest. Based on statements from informants and wiretaps, officials at the DEA said the Mexican cartels appear to have financial ties to Middle Eastern groups.[163] Bill Ruzzamenti, director of California's High Intensity Drug Trafficking Area (HIDTA) program, states, "We have a number of methamphetamine cases where we've made a direct connection between the

---

[161] Bell, "Hezbollah Uses Canada as Base"; Brown, "Canada—Terrorist Haven"; DEA/RCMP Joint Report, "Chemical Diversion and Synthetic Drug Manufacture," September 2001, http://www.rcmp-grc.gc.ca/crimint/chemical_e.htm (as of March 27, 2006).

[162] Brown, "Canada—Terrorist Haven."

[163] "Drug Money for Hezbollah?" Associated Press, September 1, 2002.

Hezbollah and Mexican cartels." [164] The DEA suspects that associates of the Lebanon-based Hezbollah have been smuggling large amounts of pseudoephedrine tablets in cars and trucks across the Canadian border for sale to the drug cartels in California. DEA and Cana-dian authorities arrested 65 people, including a number of Jordanian citizens, suspected of smuggling pseudoephedrine, a key ingredient of methamphetamine, bound for California.[165] The state narcotics bureau has come to suspect that the cartels are using profits from the resale of the pseudoephedrine to bankroll the sharp increase in marijuana cultivation on public land. Currently, there are three ongoing investigations concerning the involvement of Hezbollah-related activity with Mexican drug cartel activity in central California alone.[166]

The DEA says the trail starts in Canada and ends with Mexican drug cartels based in California. Cartel members travel to the Midwest to meet brokers, who smuggle cold tablets across the border. The cold tablets are then used in labs in Washington state. U.S. authorities determined that about one-third of foreign terrorist organizations are trafficking in narcotics on a large scale, providing insight into how two of the nation's most serious threats are connected.[167] In Southern California, the DEA San Diego Field Division and the California Border Alliance Group reported that Middle Eastern criminals (Iraqis, Jordanians, Yemenis, and Israelis) were distributing pseudoephedrine tablets in numerous U.S. urban centers.[168]

---

[164] Julie Cart, "Park's Pot Problem Explodes: Officials Say Mexican Cartels Linked to Mideast Terrorists Run the Operation," *Los Angeles Times,* May 14, 2003.

[165] Cart, "Park's Pot Problem Explodes."

[166] Karasik's interview with HIDTA official, December 2003.

[167] Josh Meyers, "Drug Trade Funding Terrorist Group Actions, U.S. Says," *Los Angeles Times,* July 31, 2002.

[168] U.S. Department of Justice (2000), p. 12.

The Middle Eastern Terrorist-Criminal Nexus in the Tri-Border Area of South America

The tri-border area, where Paraguay, Argentina, and Brazil meet, has long been a location of terrorist activity (see Figure 7.1). There are about 630,000 inhabitants in the region, some 25,000 of whom are of Syrian, Lebanese, and Palestinian descent. The Paraguayan city of Ciudad del Este and the Brazilian city of Foz do Iguaçu are separated only by the short *Puente de la Amistad* (Friendship Bridge). This is the area where the first immigrants from Syria, Lebanon, Jordan, Egypt, Iraq, and the Palestinian territories settled about 50 years ago.[169] In the 1980s, there was an additional influx of Lebanese migrants seeking to escape the Lebanese civil war.

The area is considered the most important center for financing Islamic terrorism outside the Middle East.[170] The permeable border between the three countries hosts one of the most active black markets in the world. The commercial district of Ciudad del Este, on the Paraguayan side of the Paraná River, is a mosaic of businesses owned mostly by merchants of Arab origin. The city is viewed by Argentine and Brazilian authorities as a regional hub where organized criminal enterprises, insurgent groups, and terrorist organizations enjoy safe haven and opportunities for strategic alliances. On the Brazilian side, in Foz do Iguaçu, two mosques are suspected of harboring radical activity.[171]

---

[169] "Middle East Terror Groups Find Sanctuary, Revenue in South America," The Jewish Institute for National Security Affairs (JINSA), January 15, 2004. Accessible online at http://www.jinsa.org/articles/articles.html/function/view/categoryid/1701/documentid/2331/history/3,2360,655,1701,2331 (as of March 27, 2006).

[170] Jose Meirelles Passos, "Tri-Border: U.S. Steps Up Investigation of the Muslim Community," *O Globo* (Rio de Janeiro), October 15, 2001.

[171] "Search Extends to Latin America," STRATFOR, September 19, 2001; Daly (2003); "Sources: Middle Eastern Terrorists Have South American Links," CNN, November 9, 2001; "Terrorist Sanctuary in South America? Tales from the 'Triple Border,'" *Pravda On-Line,* November 20, 2001.

Figure 7.1
Tri-Border Region, with Access to the River Plate

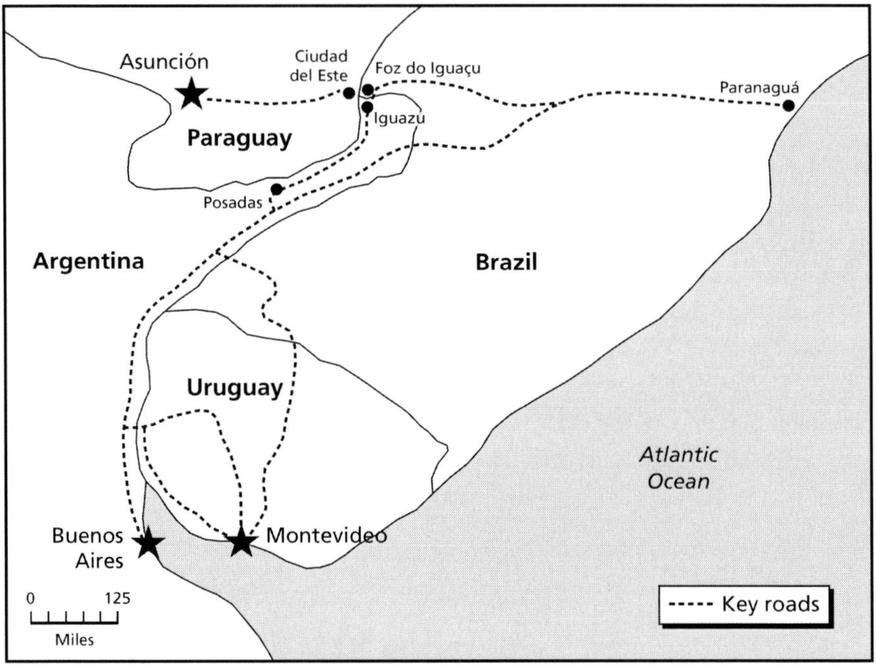

SOURCE: Col. William W. Mendel, "Paraguay's Ciudad del Este and the New Centers of Gravity," *Military Review*, March–April 2002.
RAND *MG430-1*

Middle Eastern terrorist organizations—primarily Lebanese Hezbollah, but also Hamas, and the Egyptian Islamic Jihad—have been detected in the tri-border area for at least a decade. These groups engage in black market operations, arms purchases, and planning for terrorist attacks on U.S., Israeli, and Jewish targets.[172] Argentina, home to the largest Jewish community in Latin America, about 300,000 strong, has taken the brunt of Islamic terrorism in the region. Hezbollah is suspected of carrying out the bombing of the Israeli embassy in Buenos

---

[172] In October 1998, a suspected Hezbollah member was arrested in front of the U.S. Embassy in Asunción, Paraguay, while surveying the facility in advance of a possible terrorist attack. "Search Extends to Latin America."

Aires in 1992, in which 29 persons died and 242 were injured, and the bombing of the Jewish Community Center in Buenos Aires on July 18, 1994, that killed 85 people and injured more than 200. The modus operandi of the terrorists was similar in both attacks. In both cases, car bombs were used while the buildings were undergoing repairs, and police officers on security details inexplicably disappeared before the bombings.[173]

According to a *New York Times* report of a secret deposition by a high-level defector from the Iranian intelligence service, who gave his name as Adbolghassem Mesbahi, the Iranian government organized the bombing and paid former Argentine President Carlos Menem US $10 million to say that there was no evidence of Iranian involvement. Menem's former chief of staff denied the allegations and suggested they were politically motivated.[174] The bombing remains unsolved in the Argentine judicial system. After a flurry of initial arrests, only one person was found to have a direct link to the bombing—a dealer in stolen motor vehicles accused of selling the white Renault used for the car bomb and refitting it for the bombing. There were allegations that local police and corrupt officials were involved in the bombing of the Jewish Community Center, as well as in the bombing of the Israeli embassy. Several senior policemen and a retired military officer were arrested as accessories in 1996 and 1997 but later released.[175]

According to a published report, Argentine State Intelligence Secretariat detected al-Qaeda operatives in the region following the

---

[173] "Search Extends to Latin America"; Daly (2003); "Sources: Middle Eastern Terrorists Have South American Links."

[174] "Iran Blew Up Jewish Center in Argentina, Defector Says," *The New York Times,* July 22, 2002. Mr. Mesbahi said that the money was paid from a $200 million Swiss account controlled by Iran's then president, Ali Akbar Hashemi Rafsanjani, and a son of the late Ayatollah Khomeini. According to the *New York Times* article, Argentine and German officials describe the defector as a senior operative who provided valuable information about Iranian terrorist operations in Europe and Asia through the mid-1990s. He defected to Germany in 1996, reportedly because he was upset at his agency's involvement in the killing of dissident intellectuals in Iran and abroad.

[175] Yael Shahar, "Investigation Plagued by Allegations of Cover-Ups," Institute for Counter-Terrorism, July 22, 2002.

bombings of the U.S. Embassies in Kenya and Tanzania. Al-Qaeda operatives reportedly did indoctrination and fundraising, provided cover for fugitives, and gave basic explosives training. According to intelligence officials, Khaled Sheikh Mohammad, al-Qaeda's reputed operations chief, visited Foz do Iguaçu in December 1995. Police data reportedly show that Mohammad entered Brazil via São Paulo from Pakistan on December 4 and left Rio de Janeiro for the Netherlands on December 25. (There was no warrant for Mohammad's arrest at the time of his visit to Brazil.) After the September 11 terrorist attacks, al-Qaeda and Hezbollah operatives apparently left Ciudad del Este and Foz do Iguaçu and moved to more-remote locations or back to the Middle East.[176]

In February 2003, Paraguayan security raided a store owned by Ali Khalil Mehri, a 32-year-old businessman of Lebanese descent. They recovered Hezbollah propaganda and documentation of money transfers to Canada, Chile, the United States, and Lebanon totaling more than $700,000. Also found were fundraising forms for the Middle East organization al-Shahid, which is dedicated to the "protection of families of martyrs and prisoners." Paraguayan prosecutors charged Mehri with selling millions of dollars of pirated software and channeling the proceeds to Hezbollah. Mehri, released on bail after his arrest, crossed into Brazil and then flew from São Paulo to Paris. Authorities now believe he is in Syria.[177]

There are also reports of an al-Qaeda presence in Uruguay and along the Uruguayan-Brazilian border. A leading Brazilian newspaper, *O Estado de São Paulo,* reported that Uruguay's intelligence services had shared information with the Brazilian government linking the mayor of Chui, a Brazilian town separated only by a street from the Uruguayan town of Chuy, to bin Laden (the mayor, Mohamad Kassem Jomaa, denied the allegations).[178]

---

[176] Daly (2003); "Police: Mohammed Visited Brazil in 1995," CNN São Paulo, March 9, 2003.

[177] "Middle East Terror Groups Find Sanctuary"; "Revenue in South America."

[178] "Search Extends to Latin America."

In April 2002, the Brazilian police arrested an Egyptian militant named Mohamed Ibrahim Soliman in Foz do Iguaçu at the behest of the Egyptian government. Soliman was accused of carrying out attacks in Egypt with Said Hasan al-Mohammed (or Said Hasan Mukhlis), a suspected member of the Egyptian terrorist organization al-Gama'a al-Islamiyya who was arrested in Chuy in 1999 trying to enter Uruguay from Brazil carrying a false Malaysian passport.[179] Two months before September 11, Argentine intelligence officials reported that they had arrested an Arab on smuggling charges and that the suspect had discussed upcoming terrorist attacks in the United States.[180]

In October 2002, the Argentine intelligence service issued a terrorist warning, noting that intelligence pointed to increased terrorist activity. According to intelligence sources in the Middle East, the effort was aimed at U.S. and Israeli targets and was being coordinated by Hezbollah terrorist mastermind Imad Mugniyeh.[181]

Smuggling, Black Market Activities, and Money Laundering Operations

Smuggling and black market activities are the principal source of income from Islamic extremists in the tri-border region. In 1987 the leader of a business association of commercial and industrial interests estimated that contraband accounted for two-thirds of Paraguay's foreign trade.[182] Paraguayan police estimate that about 70 percent of the 600,000 cars in Paraguay were purchased on the black market, with at least a portion of the profits likely going to terrorist groups. Recently, President González Macchi was exposed in the press as owning a stolen

---

[179] "Egyptian Militant Arrested in Southern Brazil," Reuters, April 16, 2002. Al-Mohammed was charged with having participated in the massacre of 58 foreign tourists and at least four Egyptians at the Egyptian temple of Luxor, in November 1997, the worst atrocity of the al-Gama'a al-Islamiyya campaign of terror in Egypt in the 1990s.

[180] Daly (2003).

[181] Mugniyeh masterminded the bombing of the U.S. Marine barracks and the French paratroopers headquarters in Beirut in 1983. He carried out several assassinations and attempted assassinations. He is believed to be living in Iran. See Gunaratna (2002), pp. 142, 147.

[182] "Paraguay: Crime," http://reference.allrefer.com/country-guide-study/paraguay/paraguay 121.html (as of March 27, 2006).

BMW and his wife a stolen Mercedes. Both cars had the same title document, which belonged to a Toyota.[183]

The smuggling and associated commercial activity also provide cover for money laundering operations. Argentine officials point to evidence of terrorist financial activity in the form of thousands of U.S. dollars stamped by Lebanese currency dealers from Lebanese currency exchange banks, tens of thousands of counterfeit dollars, and receipts from wire transfers made between the tri-border area and the Middle East.[184]

In 2002, the Hezbollah financial chief in Ciudad del Este, Sobhi Mahmoud Fayad, was convicted on charges of tax evasion. The Paraguayan authorities requested the extradition from Brazil of Hezbollah's reputed chief of operations in Latin America, Assad Ahmad Barakat, on similar charges. Barakat was the co-owner of one of Ciudad del Este's largest shopping malls, which intelligence sources believe he used as a front for fundraising and recruitment. He is suspected of being a major player in the bombing of the Israeli embassy and the Jewish Community Center in Buenos Aires. Barakat was caught and extradited to Paraguay in November 2003.[185] Two of his associates, Mazen Ali Saleh and Saleh Mahoud Fayoud, were arrested and charged with falsifying immigration documents and dealing in pirated compact discs.[186]

Drug Trafficking and Arms Smuggling

During the early 1980s, Paraguay emerged as a transit point in the international drug trade. Colombian and other international drug traffickers operate in Paraguay in association with corrupt military officers

---

[183] Mendel (2002), p. 52.

[184] "South America's 'Tri-Border' Back on Terrorism Radar," CNN, November 7, 2002.

[185] "Alleged Hizbullah Financier Extradited by Brazil to Paraguay," Naharnet, November 20, 2003, http://www.naharnet.com/domino/tn/Newsdesk.nsf/0/41BE05F953ABCE5542256 DE300318F15?OpenDocument&PRINT (as of March 27, 2006).

[186] "Sources: Middle Eastern Terrorists Have South American Link." Criminal charges were filed against the former Paraguayan Consul General in Miami, Carlos Weiss, for having issued 150 irregular visas, 18 to Arab citizens living in Ciudad del Este.

and politicians of the ruling Colorado Party. The U.S. Department of State estimates that Paraguay moves ten metric tons of cocaine annually to markets in Europe and the United States. Paraguay also produces some of the highest-grade marijuana in the continent and exports most of it to Brazil, which ranks as the largest market in Latin America for cocaine, heroine, marijuana, and boutique drugs such as Ecstasy.[187]

According to the Council on Foreign Relations, Hezbollah smuggles cocaine from South America to Europe and the Middle East.[188] On May 10, 2003, Paraguayan authorities arrested Hassan Abdallah Dayoub as he was preparing to ship an electric piano stuffed with more than five pounds of cocaine to Syria. Dayoub is a relative of Assad Barakat, the chief Hezbollah operative in South America. Dayoub was subsequently sentenced to five and a half years in prison for drug smuggling.[189]

A guns-for-cocaine connection between Paraguayan gunrunners and the FARC was uncovered and one FARC operative was arrested.[190] Jeffrey Goldberg, author of "In the Party of God," which appeared in *The New Yorker* in October 2002, spent three weeks in the tri-border area researching Hezbollah and its international funding and activities. He recounted crossing the borders of Argentina, Brazil, and Paraguay with extreme ease, and being offered an AK-47 rifle for $375. The price even included a hotel delivery. When he asked about acquiring explosives, he was told that was also possible.[191]

Rationale for Convergence with Organized Crime

Several factors account for the involvement of a Middle East terrorist organization in criminal activity in the tri-border area. First, there are demographic and geostrategic factors: the presence of a substantial Levantine community with links to their home countries, living in a

---

[187] "DEA boosts its role in Paraguay," *The Washington Times*, August 21, 2001.

[188] TerrorismAnswers.org (as of March 27, 2006).

[189] "Middle East Terror Groups Find Sanctuary."

[190] Cited in Mendel (2002), p. 54.

[191] Mendel (2002), p. 54.

remote and yet strategic area—on the Pan American Highway straddling the Argentine-Brazilian border. The area has fluvial communications by way of the Paraná River to the River Plate, Buenos Aires, and
Montevideo, as well as the Atlantic Ocean. Second, an existing criminal infrastructure exists (smuggling has been the economic mainstay
of this region since the establishment of independent states in the area).
Third, Paraguay's weak political institutions and investigative and law
enforcement capabilities, as well as pervasive official corruption, have
created the conditions for the unchecked growth of terrorist and criminal networks.[192] Fourth, and perhaps most important, Hezbollah and
other Middle East militant and terrorist organizations have established
a global presence. The last factor is likely to increase in importance
as the international pressure and denial of sanctuaries in traditional
host countries forces organizations like al-Qaeda to look for alternative
bases of operations.

---

[192] Transparency International lists Paraguay as 144 in its 2005 Corruption Perception
Index, with a score of 2.1 on a scale of 1 (most corrupt) to 10 (least corrupt), http://www.
transparency.org/cpi/2005/cpi2005.sources.en.html#cpi (as of March 27, 2006).

CHAPTER EIGHT

Conclusions and Recommendations

From a policy perspective, the first-order question is whether the trajectory of insurgent and terrorist groups outside the global jihadist movement will bring them closer to that movement. To answer this question, we examine what factors could affect this outcome and what the U.S. policy response should be. The second-order question is the level of threat these groups represent for U.S. regional interests, including the security of U.S. friends and allies, and what the U.S. policy response should be. Finally, we discuss how to harmonize U.S. policies to address these two questions.

With regard to convergence with al-Qaeda, the groups of greatest concern are, of course, the Islamist groups that share aspects of al-Qaeda's worldview. Of the groups examined, only two—Egypt's al-Wa'ad and the Iraqi insurgents—developed after bin Laden's 1998 fatwa against "Jews and Crusaders." The other groups were well established, active, and had articulated their own agendas prior to al-Qaeda's emergence in the international arena. Therefore, they can be assumed to be less receptive to al-Qaeda's ideology of global jihad than the groups that emerged since that time.

Among these groups, the majority interpret their jihad much more narrowly than groups affiliated or associated with al-Qaeda. Hezbollah's interests center on Lebanon and its immediate vicinity; Hamas is focused on the Palestinian issue; and the GIA on overthrowing the Algerian government. For the groups to which association with al-Qaeda might be operationally attractive, external and internal factors have held such tendencies in check. Hezbollah appears to be influenced by its ties to Syria and Iran as well as by its involvement in Lebanese politics. Al-Gama'a al-Islamiyya appears to be concerned about carving out some political space to operate in Egypt.

Even some of the non-Islamist groups could decide to cooperate with al-Qaeda or other Islamist groups for their own reasons. For example, many of these militant groups now maintain representatives in the criminal and black market world. This interconnectivity allows terrorists to acquire weapons as necessary, perhaps even to expand their capabilities. At this point, it is important to stress that some terrorist groups could shift their worldview, thus adopting an agenda similar to al-Qaeda's. Alternatively, others could simply capitalize on a perceived anti-U.S. trend, shifting the focus of their attacks toward U.S. targets to increase their potential by making alliances with more capable al-Qaeda–affiliated groups or simply to gain greater recognition.

A recent RAND study analyzed factors that caused terrorist groups to adjust their intentions (e.g., their ideology or worldview) and capabilities. The study isolated three key factors that cause terrorist groups to shift from their chosen paths: (1) counterattacks by security forces; (2) external support from states or other militant organizations; and (3) gain or loss of popular support.[1] To those, we could add a fourth: general shifts in the international security environment—such as that brought about by the U.S.-led global war on terrorism. Some extremist organizations, such as the MILF in the Philippines, have tried to distance themselves from al-Qaeda to reduce their exposure to the global war on terrorism.[2] Similarly, according to a well-informed Sri Lankan source, the global war on terrorism has reduced international tolerance of LTTE terrorism. There has been a crackdown on LTTE activities in the United Kingdom and Canada, and Thailand has become

---

[1] Cragin and Daly (2004).

[2] The issue of the MILF-JI relationship is contested. The MILF denies it and, as of August 2005, was cooperating with the Philippines military against the Abu Sayyaf Group (as it is obliged to do under the terms of the ceasefire between the MILF and the Manila government). Other authorities, however, such as Rohan Gunaratna and Zachary Abuza, believe that there is a continuing relationship between the MILF and JI. Rabasa's correspondence with Gunaratna and Abuza, September 2005.

more active in intercepting arms shipments to the group. These developments apparently influenced the LTTE's decision to enter into peace negotiations with the Sri Lankan government.[3]

A potentially dangerous shift can be seen in the emerging Hamas-Hezbollah nexus, as shown by the March 14, 2004, attack in the Israeli port of Ashdod. As discussed earlier, the significance of this attack was not the number of casualties but the demonstration of Hamas's ability to hit more strategic targets.[4]

This degree of aid and coordination is greater than anything prior in the Hamas-Hezbollah relationship. It demonstrates that Sunni and Shi'ite militants will work together, given a mutual enemy. Second, the pattern of behavior demonstrated by Hamas could be duplicated by other, nonaffiliated terrorists. That is, just as Hamas accepted linkage with Hezbollah, so other groups could accept guidance from al-Qaeda. Finally, a potential explanation for Hezbollah's behavior in this case is the need to sustain attention and support since Israel pulled out of southern Lebanon. Greater involvement in the Palestinian resistance could achieve this goal. It is possible, then, that Muslim anger at the U.S. presence in Iraq could provoke similar shifts in Hezbollah or other groups' agenda vis-à-vis the United States as these groups continue to vie for local recruits and support.

The bottom line is that most of the extremist groups discussed in this report—terrorists and insurgents alike—have a limited or localized political agenda, and this means that they are likely to accept political rules and social norms acceptable to a majority as opposed to al-Qaeda and its utopian vision of a restored global caliphate.

Several of the groups covered in the study have not welcomed the attention that al-Qaeda has brought to their various causes. This is particularly true of nonaffiliated organizations but also, arguably, of associated entities such as JI and elements of the MILF (both of which now seem to be debating the overall value of being linked to bin

---

[3] Discussion with retired international institution official, Washington, D.C., October 2004.

[4] Discussion with retired international institution official, Washington, D.C., October 2004, and Cragin interviews, Israeli counterterrorism experts, April 2004.

Laden's network in terms of availing their own respective objectives in Southeast Asia and Mindanao). In certain ways, this has acted as a useful brake on their militant actions and encouraged a greater disposition toward negotiation and compromise (to some extent illustrated by talks and ceasefires in former chronic terrorist theaters such as Sri Lanka and Colombia). The United States should seek to capitalize on these tensions and the movement that they have created, both as an adjunct to its general war on ideas against extremist ideologies, as well as in the context of more specific regional security efforts and assistance programs.

Nevertheless, beyond the question of convergence, it is important that we not dismiss groups as unthreatening just because they have not joined the global jihadist movement. Some represent deadly threats to the states that they seek to subvert; others, like Hezbollah, could suddenly emerge as global threats.

Implications for the U.S. Military and the U.S. Air Force

In the first volume, we discussed the use of air power as an option to attack terrorists in difficult or inhospitable terrain, as well as the use of air transport in counterterrorist or counterinsurgency operations in countries with widely dispersed populations and poor land transportation infrastructure. These considerations apply as well to many of the cases discussed in this volume. However, there is a difference: With the exception of the Iraqi insurgency, the United States is not—and as a general principle should not be—involved in direct military operations against these groups.

Therefore, the emphasis should be on strengthening the capabilities of friendly governments to confront insurgent and terrorist groups. U.S. Air Force Special Operations Forces (active duty, Reserve, and National Guard units)—at approximately 11,000 personnel, second only to Army SOF at 29,000—can be particular pertinent to the counterinsurgency and counterterrorism training role required by the new environment.[5]

The judgment in Part 1 of this study that these local wars have to be fought and won by local governments and security forces, with the United States in a supporting role, is even more valid in the case of those conflicts driven by local grievances and those in which the rebel movements enjoy significant support. By the same token, since some of these groups have limited political agendas, under the right circumstances they could become part of a negotiating process leading to a political solution of the conflict—a major difference from groups that are part of the global jihadist movement, which have to be destroyed or forced to leave the field.

To develop effective strategies against insurgent and terrorist groups, it is important to look at them in a broad context, even if they operate locally, because the migration of tactics, techniques, and procedures (TTPs) is creating a regionalization of violence—terrorists and insurgents and political opportunists. Many of these groups are learning what works best and adopting those best practices. These tactical models contribute to the proliferation of effective styles of unconventional warfare throughout different zones of conflict. Innovations include the use of IEDs by Hezbollah and their evolution into sophisticated weapons designed to interrupt supply lines. Hamas has been known to use ambulances as a cover for suicide bombers or logistical support. MANPADs and now suicide bombers with suicide vests first used by Palestinian groups against targets in Israel and the Palestinian territories are now used as mass casualty weapons by Chechens against Russian military aircraft.

The first implication for the U.S. military and the Air Force is a clear understanding that the TTPs used by all groups, whether they are

---

[5]   U.S. Air Force Special Operations Forces are made up of the following: (1) the active-duty 16th Special Operations Wing; (2) two Air Force Reserve units: the 919th Special Operations Wing and the 920th Rescue Wing; and (3) three Air National Guard units: the 106th Rescue Wing (New York Air National Guard), the 129th Rescue Wing (California Air National Guard), and the 193rd Special Operations Wing (Pennsylvania Air National Guard).

part of the global jihad or not, are beginning to mimic each other. This means that from a tactical standpoint U.S. military doctrine needs to anticipate the dissemination of those tactics across theaters in the war on terror.

The second implication is that, although the United States has a supporting role in opposing those groups in the "al-Qaeda universe," the potential role for the United States in countering extremist groups beyond al-Qaeda is even more indirect. The challenge for the U.S. military is to be prepared either to provide increased levels of support to key allies should they require it or to engage these extremist groups should they shift their attention toward the United States—while simultaneously avoiding direct involvement in these conflicts. This strategic challenge has particular relevance to the U.S. Air Force. Understanding the circumstances that might stimulate change in these extremist groups, for example, may require the allocation of intelligence, surveillance, and reconnaissance resources. It may also necessitate broad global readiness, incorporating regions such as Southeast Asia and Latin America, in addition to the Middle East, in the war on terrorism.

For the U.S. military and the U.S. Air Force in particular, tools for targeting terrorist groups can also be used in cooperation and coordination with host-state operations against terrorist, insurgent, and criminal groups. It is important to note that the criminal transport of narcotics, arms, illegal migrants, explosives, etc., occurs in hubs and spokes concurrent or co-located with terrorist groups—especially the FARC (at the crossroads of Colombia, Panama, Ecuador, Brazil, and Venezuela) and Maoists (in Nepal, for example, at the crossroads between Russia, China, and India; and in the Philippines and Peru). This argues for the "dual use" of U.S. security assistance for both counterterrorism and counternarcotics purposes. Older aircraft with high-tech intelligence-collection capabilities can be used against both terrorist havens and criminal nodes. In addition, air support for host country coast guard operations in and around waterways is a critical component of coastal and riverine surveillance and interdiction of smuggling routes used by terrorists and criminal networks.

Bibliography

Abu-Rabi, Ibrahim M., *Intellectual Origins of Islamic Resurgence in the Modern Arab World*, New York: State University of New York Press, 1996.

Abuza, Zachary, "The Moro Islamic Liberation Front (MILF) and Security in Southeast Asia," U.S. Institute of Peace, June 9, 2005, http://www.usip.org/fellows/reports/2005/0609_abuza.html.

————, "Balik-Terrorism: The Return of the Abu Sayyaf," Strategic Studies Institute (SSI), U.S. Army War College, September 2005, http://www.strategicstudiesinstitute.army.mil/pdffiles/PUB625.pdf.

Ahmed, Hisham, *From Religious Salvation to Political Transformation: The Rise of Hamas in Palestinian Society*, Jerusalem: PASSIA, April 1994.

Al-Gama'a al-Islamiyya (GAI)," *Jane's World Insurgency and Terrorism*, May 16, 2003.

"Al-Qaeda and the Zimbabwe Nexus," *Focus 34,* Helen Suzman Foundation, June 2004.

Athas, Iqbal, "Sri Lankan Narcotics Network Busted," *Jane's Intelligence Review,* January 1999.

Bedein, David, "Rabin's Hamas Compromise," *MidStream*, Vol. 39, 1999.

Berman, Paul, *A Tale of Two Utopias: The Political Journey of the Generation of 1968*, New York: W.W. Norton & Company, Inc., 1996.

Bickerton, Ian J., and Carla L. Klausner, *A Concise History of the Arab-Israeli Conflict*, New Jersey: Prentice Hall, 1995.

Black, A., *The History of Islamic Political Thought*, New York: Routledge, 2001.

Black, Ian, and Benny Morris, *Israel's Secret Wars*, New York: Grove Weidenfeld, 1991.

Bullion, Alan, *India, Sri Lanka and the Tamil Crisis, 1976–1994: An International Perspective*, London: Pinter, 1995.

Bureau for International Narcotics and Law Enforcement Affairs, *International Narcotics Control Strategy Report, 2002*, Washington, D.C.: United States Department of State, 2003.

———, *International Narcotics Control Strategy Report, 2003*, Washington, D.C.: United States Department of State, 2004.

Byman, Daniel, "Should Hezbollah Be Next?" *Foreign Affairs*, Vol. 82, No. 6, November/December 2003.

Byman, Daniel, Peter Chalk, Bruce Hoffman, William Rosenau, and David Brannan, *Trends in Outside Support for Insurgent Movements*, Santa Monica, Calif.: RAND Corporation, MR-1405-OTI, 2001.

Campbell, Tanner, and Rohan Gunaratna, "Maritime Terrorism, Piracy and Crime," in Rohan Gunaratna, ed., *Terrorism in the Asia-Pacific: Threat and Response*, Singapore: Eastern Universities Press, 2003, pp. 78–79.

Chalk, Peter, "The Davao Consensus: A Panacea for the Muslim Insurgency in Mindanao?" *Terrorism and Political Violence*, Vol. 9, No. 2, 1997.

———, "The Liberation Tigers of Tamil Eelam's (LTTE) International Organization and Operations: A Preliminary Analysis," Canadian Security Intelligence Service Commentary No. 77, March 17, 2000.

———, "Militant Islamic Extremism in the Southern Philippines," in Colin Rubenstein and Jason Isaacson eds., *Islam in Asia: Changing Political Realities*, New Brunswick, N. J.: Transaction Press, 2002.

Charbel, Ghassan, "The Khaled Mishaal Interview (2 of 7)," *Dar al-Hayat*, December 5, 2003.

CIA—*See* U.S. Central Intelligence Agency.

Clegg, Claude Andrew III, *An Original Man: The Life and Times of Elijah Muhammad*, New York: St. Martin's Press, 1997.

Coast Guard Intelligence Assessment, *Worldwide Maritime Threat Assessment 2000*, Washington, D.C.: U.S. Coast Guard, C-G-002-00, May 2000.

Cole, Juan, "The United States and Shi'ite Religious Factions in Post-Ba'thist Iraq," *Middle East Journal*, Vol. 57, No. 4, Autumn 2003.

Cooper, Neil, "The Business of War," *Ploughshares Monitor,* Vol. 23, No. 3, Autumn 2002, http://www.ploughshares.ca/libraries/monitor/mons02h.html (as of March 24, 2006).

Cragin, Kim, and Peter Chalk, *Terrorism and Development: Using Social and Economic Development Policies to Inhibit a Resurgence of Terrorism,* Santa Monica, Calif.: RAND Corporation, MR-1630-RC, 2003.

Cragin, Kim, and Sara Daly, *The Dynamic Terrorist Threat: An Assessment of Group Motivations and Capabilities in a Changing World,* Santa Monica, Calif.: RAND Corporation, MR-1782-AF, 2004.

Cragin, Kim, and Bruce Hoffman, *Arms Trafficking and Colombia,* Santa Monica, Calif.: RAND Corporation, MR-1468-DIA, 2003.

Cronin, Audrey Kurth, *Foreign Terrorist Organizations,* Washington, D.C.: Congressional Research Service Report for Congress, February 6, 2004.

Dagne, Ted, *Africa and the War on Terrorism,* Washington, D.C.: Congressional Research Service Report for Congress, January 17, 2002.

Daly, John C. K., "The Latin Connection," *Terrorism Monitor,* Volume 1, Issue 3, October 10, 2003, http://www.jamestown.org/publications_details.php?search=1&volume_id=391&issue_id=2877&article_id=23407 (as of March 27, 2006).

Davis, Anthony, "Tracking Tigers in Phuket," *Asiaweek,* June 16, 2000.

————, "Philippines Security Threatened by Small Arms Proliferation," *Jane's Intelligence Review,* August 2003a.

————, "Resilient Abu Sayyaf Resists Military Pressure," *Jane's Intelligence Review,* September 2003b.

————, "Thailand Cracks Down on Illicit Arms Trade," *Jane's Intelligence Review,* December 2003c.

Davis, Anthony, and Rahul Bedi, "Pressure from India Leads to Bhutan Insurgent Crackdown," *Jane's Intelligence Review,* February 2004, pp. 32–35.

Dawoud, Khaled, "Trying Times for Islamists," *Al-Ahram Weekly Online,* January 10–16, 2002.

De Silva, K. M., *Religion, Nationalism and the State in Modern Sri Lanka,* Tampa, Fla.: University of South Florida Press, 1986.

————, *The Traditional Homelands of the Tamils: Separatist Ideology in Sri Lanka: An Historical Appraisal*, Kandy, Sri Lanka: International Centre for Ethnic Studies, 1995.

————, *Sri Lanka: Ethnic Conflict, Management and Resolution*, Kandy, Sri Lanka: International Centre for Ethnic Studies, 1996.

Dixon, Bill, and Lisa-Marie Johns, "Gangs, Pagad & the State: Vigilantism and Revenge Violence in the Western Cape," *Violence and Transition* (Centre for the Study of Violence and Reconciliation, South Africa), Vol. 2, May 2001, http://www.csvr.org.za/papers/papvtp2.htm (as of March 16, 2006).

Drake, C.J.M., "The Role of Ideology in Terrorists' Target Selection," *Terrorism and Political Violence*, Vol. 10, No. 2, Summer 1998.

Emerson, Steven, "Meltdown," *The New Republic*, November 23, 1992.

————, *American Jihad: The Terrorists Living Among Us*, New York: Free Press, 2002.

Espejo, German, and Juan Carlos Garzon, "La Encrucijada del ELN," *Informe Especial*, Bogotá, Colombia: Fundacion Seguridad y Democracia, July 2005.

Furet, François, *The Passing of an Illusion: The Idea of Communism in the Twentieth Century*, trans. Deborah Furet, Chicago and London: The University of Chicago Press, 1999.

Global Witness, *For a Few Dollars More: How al Qaeda Moved into the Diamond Trade*, London: Global Witness Ltd., April 2003, http://www.globalwitness.org/reports/show.php/en.00041.html (as of March 24, 2006).

"Groupe Islamique Armee," *Jane's Intelligence Review*, July 30, 2003.

"Groupe Salafiste pour la Predication et le Combat (GSPC)," *Jane's Intelligence Review*, May 16, 2003.

Gunaratna, Rohan, *Indian Intervention in Sri Lanka: The Role of India's Intelligence Agencies*, Colombo, Sri Lanka: South Asian Network on Conflict Research, 1993a.

————, *War and Peace in Sri Lanka*, Colombo, Sri Lanka: Institute of Fundamental Studies, 1993b.

————, *Sri Lanka's Ethnic Crisis and National Security*, Colombo, Sri Lanka: South Asian Network on Conflict Research, 1998.

————, "The Evolution and Tactics of the Abu Sayyaf Group," *Jane's Intelligence Review*, July 2001.

————, *Inside Al Qaeda,* New York: Columbia University Press, 2002.

Gutierrez, Eric, and Saturnino Borras, Jr., *The Moro Conflict: Landlessness and Misdirected State Policies,* Washington, D.C.: East-West Center, Policy Studies, No. 8, 2004.

Hallaq, Wael B., trans., *Ibn Taymiyya Against the Greek Logicians*, Oxford: Clarendon, 1993.

Hellmann-Rajanayagam, Dagmar, *The Tamil Tigers: Armed Struggle for Identity*, Stuttgart, Germany: F. Steiner, 1994.

"Hizballah and Israelis Wage Electronic War in South Lebanon," *Jane's Intelligence Review*, February 1, 1995.

"Hizballah Lends Its Services to the Palestinian Intifada," *Jane's Intelligence Review*, November 1, 2001.

Hroub, Khaled, *Hamas*, Washington, D.C.: Institute for Palestine Studies, 2000.

"Hundreds Murdered in Widespread Algeria Attacks," International Policy Institute for Counterterrorism, January 6, 1998.

International Crisis Group (ICG), "Colombia's Elusive Quest for Peace," Latin America Report No. 1, March 26, 2002, http://www.crisisgroup.org/home/index.cfm?id=1538&l=1 (as of March 23, 2006).

International Institute for Strategic Studies (IISS), "Sri Lanka's Peace Process in Jeopardy," Strategic Comments 10/3 (April 2004).

International Maritime Bureau, *Piracy and Armed Robbery Against Ships, Report for the Period 1 January–30 September 2003*, London: International Chamber of Commerce, 1993.

"Interview with Mahmud Zahhar," *Journal of Palestine Studies*, Vol. 24, No. 3, Spring 1995.

Israel Defense Forces, IDF Spokespersons Unit, "Salah Shedhadeh—Portrait of a Hamas Leader," published online, November 10, 2002.

Israeli, Raphael, *Muslim Fundamentalism in Israel*, Exeter, UK: BPCC Wheatons Ltd, 1993.

Iyob, Ruth, "Shifting Terrain: Dissidence Versus Terrorism in Eritrea," *Terrorism in the Horn of Africa,* U.S. Institute of Peace Special Report No. 113, January 2004, www.usip.org/pubs/specialreports/sr113.html#eritrea (as of March 16, 2006).

Jabar, Faleh A., "The Worldly Roots of Religiosity in Post-Saddam Iraq," *Middle East Report,* No. 227, Summer 2003.

Jaber, Hala, *Hezbollah: Born with a Vengeance,* New York: Columbia University Press, 1997.

Jarbawi, Ali, and Roger Heacock, "The Deportations and the Palestinian-Israeli Negotiations," *Journal of Palestine Studies,* Vol. 22, No. 3, Spring 1993.

Jensen, Richard Bach, "The United States, International Policing, and the War Against Anarchist Terrorism, 1900–1914," *Terrorism and Political Violence,* Vol. 13, No. 1, Spring 2001, pp. 15–46.

Johnson, R. W., "Al-Qaeda and the Zimbabwe Nexus," *Focus 34,* Vol. 1, No. 4, June 2004.

Joshi, Charu, "The Body Trade," *The Far Eastern Economic Review,* October 26, 2000.

Joshi, Manoj, "On the Razor's Edge: The Liberation Tigers of Tamil Eelam," *Studies in Conflict and Terrorism,* Vol. 19, 1996.

Kalyvas, Stathis N., "Wanton and Senseless? The Logic of Massacres in Algeria," *Rationality and Society,* Vol. 11, No. 3, 1999.

Kattub, Doud, "Current Developments and the Peace Process," *Journal of Palestine Studies,* Vol. 22, No. 1, 1992.

Katzman, Kenneth, *Al Qaeda: Profile and Threat Assessment,* Washington, D.C.: Congressional Research Service, February 10, 2005, http://www.usembassy.it/pdf/other/RS22049.pdf.

Kepel, Gilles, *Jihad: The Trail of Political Islam,* London: I. B. Tauris, 2002. (Originally published as *Jihad: Expansion et Déclin de l'Islamisme* in 2000).

Knights, Michael, "Algerian Operations Compress Islamist Insurgency," *Jane's Intelligence Review,* November 18, 2003.

Little, David, *Sri Lanka: The Invention of Enmity,* Washington, D.C.: United States Institute of Peace Series on Religion, Nationalism and Intolerance, 1994.

Logan, Sam, "Guns, Cocaine: One Market out of Control," International Relations and Security Network (ISN) Security Watch, Swiss Federal Institute of Technology (ETH Zurich), February 28, 2006, http://www.isn.ethz.ch/news/sw/details.cfm?ID=14921 (as of April 24, 2006).

Lopez, Antonio, "For the Love of Money," *Asiaweek,* Vol. 26, No. 5, 2000.

Lyman, Princeton N., and J. Stephen Morrison, "The Terrorist Threat In Africa, *Foreign Affairs,* January/February 2004, pp. 83–84.

Makarenko, Tamara, "A Model of Terrorist-Criminal Relations," *Jane's Intelligence Review,* August 2003.

Manogaran, Chelvadurai, *Ethnic Conflict and Reconciliation in Sri Lanka,* Honolulu: University of Hawaii Press, 1987.

Marks, Thomas A., *Maoist Insurgency Since Vietnam,* London: Frank Cass, 1996.

———, *Insurgency in Nepal,* Carlisle, Pa.: Strategic Studies Institute, December 2003.

McDermott, Jeremy, "Kidnapping Increases in Latin America," *Jane's Intelligence Review,* June 2003a.

———, "Colombia Pursues Paramilitary Peace Deal," *Jane's Intelligence Review,* October 2003b.

———, "The Shining Path Glimmers Again," *Jane's Intelligence Review,* January 2004a, pp. 22–26.

———, "FARC and the Paramilitaries Take Over Colombia's Drugs Trade," *Jane's Intelligence Review,* July 2004b, pp. 29–31.

———, "Colombian Insurgency Escalates as Guerrillas Go Back on Offensive," *Jane's Intelligence Review,* July 2005, p. 26.

Mendel, William W., "Paraguay's Ciudad del Este and the New Centers of Gravity," *Military Review,* March–April 2002.

Merari, Ariel, and Yosefa Braunstein, "Shi'ite Terrorism: Operational Capabilities and the Suicide Factor," *Terrorism, Violence and Insurgency Journal,* Vol. 5, No. 2, Fall 1984.

Miller, Martin A., "The Intellectual Origins of Modern Terrorism in Europe," in Martha Crenshaw (ed.), *Terrorism in Context,* University Park, Pa.: Pennsylvania State University Press, 2001, pp. 41–58.

Miro, Ramon J., *Organized Crime and Terrorist Activity in Mexico, 1999–2002,* Washington, D.C.: Library of Congress Federal Research Division, February 2003.

Mishal, Shaul, and Reuben Aharoni, *Speaking Stones: Communiqués from the Intifada Underground,* New York: Syracuse University Press, June 2004.

Mishal, Shaul, and Avraham Sela, *The Palestinian Hamas,* New York: Columbia University Press, 2000.

Misra, S. S., *Ethnic Conflict and the Security Crisis in Sri Lanka,* Delhi: Kalinga Publications, 1995.

Morrison, J. Stephen, "Prepared Statement of J. Stephen Morrison," United States House of Representatives, Hearing Before the Subcommittee on Africa of the Committee on International Relations on Africa and the War on Global Terrorism, One Hundred Seventh Congress, November 15, 2001.

Nakash, Yitzhak, *The Shi'is of Iraq,* Princeton, N.J.: Princeton University Press, 2003.

National Commission on Terrorist Attacks Upon the United States, *The 9/11 Commission Report: Final Report of the National Commission on Terrorist Attacks Upon the United States,* Washington, D.C.: U.S. Government Printing Office, 2004.

Pax Christi, *The Kidnap Industry in Colombia,* The Hague: Pax Christi–Nederlands, November 2001.

Paz, Reuven, "The Heritage of the Sunni Militant Groups*: An Islamic Internacionale?*" International Policy Institute for Counter-Terrorism, January 4, 2000, http://www.ict.org.il/spotlight/comment.cfm?id=379 (as of March 10, 2006).

Perez-Agote, Alfonso, "The Future of Basque Identity," in William A. Douglass et al., eds., *Basque Politics and Nationalism on the Eve of the Millennium,* Reno and Las Vegas: University of Nevada Press, 1999.

Pugh, Michael, "Piracy and Armed Robbery at Sea," *Low Intensity Conflict and Law Enforcement,* Vol. 2, No. 1, 1993.

Rabasa, Angel, Cheryl Benard, Peter Chalk, C. Christine Fair, Theodore W. Karasik, Rollie Lal, Ian O. Lesser, and David E. Thaler, *The Muslim World After 9/11,* Santa Monica, Calif.: RAND Corporation, MG-246-AF, 2004.

Rabasa, Angel, and Peter Chalk, *Colombian Labyrinth: The Synergy of Drugs and Insurgency and Its Implications for Regional Stability*, Santa Monica, Calif.: RAND Corporation, MR-1339-AF, 2001.

Ramati, Yohanan, "Islamic Fundamentalism Gaining," *Midstream*, Vol. 39, No. 2, 1993.

Rangel Suárez, Alfredo, *Colombia: Guerra en el fin de siglo*, Bogotá: Tercer Mundo, 1998.

Redmond, Robert, "Phantom Ships in the Far East," INTERSEC, Vol. 6, No. 5, May 1996.

Reeve, Simon, *The New Jackals: Ramzi Yousef, Osama Bin Laden and the Future of Terrorism*, Boston: Northeastern University Press, 1999.

Ridolfo, Kathleen, "A Survey of Armed Groups in Iraq," *RFE/RL Iraq Report*, June 4, 2004.

Rood, Steven, *Forging Sustainable Peace in Mindanao: The Role of Civil Society*, Washington, D.C.: East-West Center, Policy Studies, No. 17, 2005.

Rotberg, Robert, ed., *Creating Peace in Sri Lanka: Civil War and Reconciliation*, Washington, D.C.: Brookings Institution, 1999.

Rupesinghe, Kumar, ed., *Negotiating Peace in Sri Lanka: Efforts, Failures and Lessons*, London: International Alert, 1998.

Saad-Ghorayeb, Amal, *Hizbu'llah: Politics and Religion*, London: Pluto Press, 2002.

Saikal, Amin, "Reflections on Autonomy: the PNA and Hamas Must Find a Way to Work Together," *Middle East Insight*, Vol. 11, No. 1, November–December 1994, pp. 28–30.

Santos, Soliman M., "Peace Negotiations Between the Philippine Government and the Moro Islamic Liberation Front: Causes and Prescriptions," Washington, D.C.: East-West Center Washington Working Papers, January 2005.

Schwartz, Stephen, "Jihadists in Iraq: An Unwelcome Saudi Export," *SOURCE*, Vol. 9, No. 20, February 2, 2004.

Singh, Depinder, *The IPKF in Sri Lanka*, New Delhi: Trishul Publications, 2001.

Sisty, Leo, and Maud Beelman, "Arrested Italian Cell Sheds Light on Bin Laden's European Network," *An Investigative Report of the Centre for Public Integrity*, October 3, 2001.

Sobelman, Daniel, "Hizbullah Lends Its Services to the Palestinian Intifada," *Jane's Intelligence Review*, November 1, 2001.

Soueid, Mahmoud, "Islamic Unity and Political Change: Interview with Sheikh Mohammad Husayn Fadlallah," *Journal of Palestine Studies*, Vol. 25, No. 1, Autumn 1995.

Spencer, David, "FARC's Innovative Artillery," *Jane's Intelligence Review*, Vol. 11, No. 12.

Strauss, Mark, "Anti-Globalism's Jewish Problem," *Foreign Policy*, November/December 2003.

Suryanarayan, V., ed., *Sri Lankan Crisis and India's Response*, Delhi: Patriot Publishers, 1991.

Sweig, Julia E., "What Kind of War for Colombia?" *Foreign Affairs*, Vol. 81, No. 5, September/October, 2002.

Takeyh, Ray, "Islam in Algeria: A Struggle Between Hope and Agony," *Middle East Policy*, Vol. 10, No. 2, Summer 2003.

Thomas, Raju, "Secessionist Movements in South Asia," *Survival*, Vol. 36, No. 2, 1994.

Turner, Mark, "Terrorism and Secession in the Southern Philippines: The Rise of the Abu Sayyaf," *Contemporary Southeast Asia*, Vol. 17, No. 1, June 1995.

Ulph, Stephen, "Al-Zawahiri Takes Hamas to Task," *Terrorism Focus*, The Jamestown Foundation, Vol. 3, No. 9, March 7, 2006.

United Nations Development Programme, "Emergencies Unit for Ethiopia," *Horn of Africa Monthly Review*, September–October 1998, http://www.sas.upenn.edu/African_Studies/eue_web/hoa0998.htm (as of March 16, 2006).

United States Institute of Peace (USIP), *Civil Society Under Siege*, Washington, D.C.: USIP Special Report 114, February 2004, http://www.usip.org/pubs/specialreports/sr114.html (as of March 24, 2006).

U.S. Central Intelligence Agency (CIA), *World Factbook 2004*, "South Africa," http://www.cia.gov/cia/publications/factbook/geos/sf.html (as of March 16, 2006).